GROWTH RECURRING

Growth Recurring

ECONOMIC CHANGE IN WORLD HISTORY

E. L. Jones

CLARENDON PRESS · OXFORD
1988

Oxford University Press, Walton Street, Oxford OX2 6DP
Oxford New York Toronto
Delhi Bombay Calcutta Madras Karachi
Petaling Jaya Singapore Hong Kong Tokyo
Nairobi Dar es Salaam Cape Town
Melbourne Auckland
and associated companies in
Beirut Berlin Ibadan Nicosia

Oxford is a trade mark of Oxford University Press

Published in the United States
by Oxford University Press, New York

British Library Cataloguing in Publication Data
Jones, E.L. (Eric Lionel)
Growth recurring: economic change in
world history.
1. Economic development   2. Economic policy
I. Title
339.5   HD87
ISBN 0-19-828300-8

Library of Congress Cataloging-in-Publication Data
Jones, E.L. (Eric Lionel)
Growth recurring.
Bibliography: p.
Includes index.
1. Economic development—History.   2. Economic
history. I. Title.
HD78.J65   1988   330.9   87-24825
ISBN 0-19-828300-8

Set by Downdell Ltd, Abingdon, Oxon
Printed and bound in Great Britain by
Biddles Ltd, Guildford and King's Lynn

TO SYLVIA

Acknowledgements

Colleagues and students at several institutions in three continents have listened to me and commented helpfully on the ideas for this book as they evolved. Without giving virtual staff and student lists I can only pick those closest to me for thanks. In addition, a pleasant consequence of authorship has been that stimulating people from several countries have written to me about *The European Miracle*, and given me new ideas. I thank these people collectively.

During the gestation and writing of *Growth Recurring* I have been to the United States three times. I was Visiting Professor and Irving Fisher Research Professor in Economics at Yale University for a semester in 1982 and have especially to thank Bill Parker, David Weir, T. N. Srinivasan, John Beggs (now of the ANU), and my teaching assistant Adrienne Cheasty (now of the IMF), as well as the entering graduate class in Economics— most of all Dale Ballou, who by clinging so hard to the conventional view of the industrial revolution made me think much harder about my opinion that it has been blown up out of proportion. Two of the Professors Emeriti also influenced my thinking. One was Lloyd Reynolds, then writing *Economic Growth in the Third World, 1850–1980*. The other was Ray Goldsmith, who had been Sombart's student—think of it!—and whose wife had been assistant to Max Weber's wife.

In April 1985 I was invited to an NEH Conference at Michigan State University on the Survey Course in History, which gave me a chance to try out my ideas. The proceedings of the Conference have since been edited by Josef Konvitz, under the modest title, *What Americans Should Know*. On the way to Michigan State I passed through Stanford and stayed with Nathan Rosenberg, and through Evanston, staying with John Hughes. No visit to the States is complete without seeing the 'Greater Chicagoland' economic historians, particularly my old Northwestern colleagues Hughes and Joel Mokyr, and Lou Cain from Loyola; neither is it complete without contacting Stan Engerman at Rochester. At his house one Thanksgiving, Stan convinced me that I ought to write two separate books, one mainly on *intensive* growth, the other mainly on *extensive* growth. This is the former.

For 1985–6 I was a Member of the School of Social Science, Institute for Advanced Study, Princeton. Who dare one leave out among the stars in that heaven? I am going to be ruthless and mention my gratitude only to Albert Hirschman and John Elliott on the permanent faculty, Kaushik Basu and Ekkehart Schlicht among my fellow Members, and Susan Cotts Watkins, who returned to the School in summer 1986. Yet I talked endlessly, too, and with profit to many others in Social Science and many Members of the School of Historical Studies, notably as far as the present work is concerned to the classical historians Glen Bowersock, Ann Ellis Hanson, and Jenny Roberts. The list really cannot end there: Tom Allsen of Trenton State College, a Mongol specialist, and many members of Princeton University (the Institute is a separate body) were immensely kind and helpful, notably Arthur Waldron, Jim Geiss, and Denis Twitchett of East Asian Studies, Charles Issawi and Bernard Lewis of Middle Eastern Studies, Jane Menken of the Office of Population Research, and Lawrence Stone of the Davis Center. This book was mostly drafted in Princeton.

In England I have to thank Michael Havinden, Dean of Social Studies at the University of Exeter; Barry Turner, former Dean; the staff of the Department of Economic History; and a number of colleagues elsewhere in the university. I have had several profitable spells as Visiting Professor of Economic History at Exeter; in January 1985 I was the Invitation Lecturer in the Faculty of Social Studies, and the lectures gave me the chance to air an early version of the theme of this book. There have been pleasant side-trips in England to various friends, notably Patrick Dillon of Bulmershe College, Reading, and Colin Tubbs of the Nature Conservancy Council, both of them ecological historians, and Tom Arkell, demographic historian at the University of Warwick.

At La Trobe, John Anderson, my other colleagues in the Comparative Economic History Group, and a succession of our honours students have had to hear it all as it developed; as have those two comparativists, Colin White (*Russia and America: The Roots of Economic Divergence*) and Claudio Veliz

(*The Centralist Tradition of Latin America*); as has my student and, colleague Geoff Raby, now of the Australian Embassy in Peking; and my Chinese graduate students Deng Gang, Shen Gensheng, Sung Hsien-yi, and Zhou Linong, together with Tom Fisher, who supervised them jointly with me. Tom Fisher hosted a splendid Qing Economic History Workshop, which brought from overseas relevant scholars such as Susan Naquin and Pierre-Étienne Will.

Also at the Australian corner of the triangle I need to thank my friends Michael Tarrant of the Australian Counter-Disaster College and Peter Turner of Sale Technical School for their invariably stimulating company. Who but Pete Turner would have in a hut in the Victorian bush a bevy of electronics magazines, a model of the Great Western Railway, an original Chartist magazine, and a copy of Chapman's *Tractat om Skepps-Byggeriet* (*Treatise on Shipbuilding*) of 1768? The collection in the Borchardt Library at La Trobe University is perhaps not as unusual, but it is a good one for my purposes and the staff remain, as always, exceptionally helpful. My secretary Lorraine Chai has been amazingly patient and efficient in the face of my stumbling prose and many changes of draft.

My own family I thank for much specific help: Deborah as a geographer, Christopher for teaching a 'techno-peasant' to operate the word processor, and my wife Sylvia for simultaneously debating Linguistics with me and doing an embarrassing share of the domestic chores. That she also put up with the expense and loss of family time which Australian academic authors and takers of sabbaticals suffer, struggled with the incompetent bureaucracies that bedevil academic travel, continued school-teaching, and found time to study at La Trobe and Princeton heaps coals of fire on my head. Not least, she was the one who coped with the Byzantine complexities of trying to find books for me in the Firestone Library at Princeton.

It seems strange to leave thanks to one's wife until the end, but that is the convention, and the book is dedicated to her.

Contents

Introduction

The day that I was born was H. G. Wells's seventieth birthday. He celebrated by releasing a book called *The Anatomy of Frustration*. Perhaps it is this coincidence which has prompted me to investigate history's greatest frustration, defeat of the tendency towards economic growth. However, I also take up the theme of the recurrence of growth and this is really what the book celebrates.

Economic history may be thought of as a struggle between a propensity for growth and one for rent-seeking, that is, for someone improving his or her position, or a group bettering its position, at the expense of the general welfare. Ordinarily we believe that growth won only once, in the 'industrial revolution' (when I use the phrase in future, please assume the quotation marks). Yet although growth may have triumphed very seldom, it did win a few times. The underlying tendency for growth has been hidden by the apparent economic stagnation of most of history, but it was nevertheless there, so basic and restless a trait that it may have been selected for in the evolution of our species. Whenever conditions permitted, that is, when rent-seeking was somehow curbed, growth manifested itself. Occasionally it rose to full stature. This implies a more mutable history and requires a more mutable conception of the struggle against poverty than is usual. It necessitates a new explanation of the process of growth.

For particular emphasis I shall compare the growth achieved in Japan and Europe with the frustrated growth in the major societies of mainland Eurasia. The appropriate timespan is what Europeanists call the 'long early modern period'. Some of the mainland societies had earlier shown great promise, above all Sung China, which, by any reasonable definition, experienced a remarkable economic flowering. Yet in early modern times, when the peripheral areas of western Europe and Japan were beginning to change dramatically, mainland Asia ceased to keep up.

The signal fact is that while growth was checked most of the time it was not checked quite every time. There was plenty of constructive economic and technological activity in remote times and many places. A new explanation of growth will have to lie outside the conventional explanations that depend on tracing it to the one Western industrial revolution. Other outstanding cases, Sung China and Tokugawa Japan, are important to the thesis precisely because they were independent of Europe's rise and thus challenge the formulation of growth as a unique process. A 'theory' of growth dealing with only a single instance is a contradiction in terms. A theory has to be generalized from a number of instances; only then can it be extended to the next case. It cannot be deduced from one example and used among other things as the explanation of that example.

The histories of the Sung and Tokugawa cases become of such logical importance that we have to take them into account. They are deserts as far as aggregate statistics are concerned, yet surrounded by the bristling thorns of specialist descriptive scholarship. To penetrate more than a fraction of even their secondary literatures one would need a knowledge of several languages notoriously difficult for Westerners to learn. Yet understanding the ebb and flow of their economies is indispensable to grasping the nature of the growth process, and we cannot exclude some consideration of them, if only from sources in English.

There are other places with some claim to have experienced real growth at early periods, the Abbasid Caliphate for one, and plenty of hopefuls, such as the Roman Empire, where pressures for change were evidently dissipated by negative forces. I have glanced at these only in passing. Their record is hard to be certain about, given the relative lack of interest in economic history on the part of the appropriate specialists. But we should be aware of them as well as of the less doubtful specimens of early growth on the one hand and the major contemporaneous examples of frustrated growth on the other: the Ottoman empire in Turkey and the Near East, the Mughal empire in India, and the Ming and Manchu empires in China. In these economies, despite some continued expansion in size, the promise of further growth capable of raising average per capita incomes was stifled.

With this reading we break from a version of the pre-modern past as made up of meaningless political cycles relieved only by the arrival of the industrial revolution, to one that admits a degree of fluctuation in economically relevant variables. History has more structure. Outsiders come up and pass the vast, ancient, physically productive economies of mainland Asia. The dark horses, Europe and Japan, were 'ecotone' states since they lay between the core cultures of Eurasia and the seeming nothingness beyond the margins of the landmass. Both attained the relevant, because generalizable, goal of rising per capita GNP before either went on to industrialize. If a mechanized industrial sector be seen as the finishing post, Europe won the race. Yet recent scholarship shows that Japan independently achieved rising per capita real incomes, whatever she later borrowed from Europe. Meanwhile, mainland Asia tended to mark time, to resurge again only in the past two or three decades, in which recent period Japan has gone on to surpass the West.

Japan's present riches would make her a more appropriate end-point for courses in economic history than the European or American industrializations towards which so much teaching aims. Other faster-growing Asian economies might be even more appropriate, were any static goal a proper one. But history keeps moving on and we ought to try to explain general processes of change, rather than contenting ourselves with describing sequences leading to the shape of particular economies, dominant at this period or that. The reshaping of economic distributions during the 1970s and 1980s, the new importance of the Pacific rim, should indeed help us to view in a less Europocentric way not merely the present but the past that helps to explain it.

The wisdom of writing economic history as if its main point were the industrial ascent of the British and other Western economies fell into doubt the minute we adopted the absurd labelling of Japan as 'Western', let alone that of Taiwan, South Korea, Singapore, and Hong Kong. Further, the days of seeing economic history as a climb to industrialization, and in the form of the old staple industries at that, ought to have passed once it became apparent that as far as employment goes many Western countries have been *deindustrializing* since 1950. They have externalized some of their industry and industrial employment; even though their own manufacturing output is still growing, they import quantities of industrial goods from Japan and elsewhere. In terms of employment, their own industrial sectors are following agriculture; their share of the total workforce is shrinking to a few per cent of the whole. The Western economies today are often referred to as 'post-industrial'. They *are* still growing, but more slowly than before, less through manufacturing than services, and more slowly than the revitalized parts of the Sinitic world, whose ancient energy has long been ignored.

If economic growth, industrialization, and the history of European cultures seem inextricable, this is because of the towering but nevertheless passing associations of the Western industrial revolution. As these things slowly separate out on the modern world-scene we are given the opportunity to rewrite their individual stories. The past was more complicated, more shadowy, but perhaps more compelling and less improbable than one in which all decisive change was portrayed as beginning (and ending) in English forge and mill. A pointer to the need for revising our approach may be that there has never been an entirely satisfactory answer to that old examination chestnut, 'what were the causes of the industrial revolution?' Other peoples in other parts of the world shared in the experience of growth and did so early and at wide intervals, whether or not they were frustrated on given occasions.

We are looking at a world in which growth rates and certainly technical and organizational changes have been very variable, requiring subtler if less categorical explanations, involving a gentle but considerable rearrangement of the conventional wisdom. The message may be harder to get across than a clarion call to overthrow the textbooks entirely, but the textbooks are right that prolonged high rates of growth are not to be found until the Europe of the eighteenth or nineteenth centuries, where growth did indeed take the form of industrialization. The standard accounts only become misleading when they depict European industrialization as the sole beginning and sole vehicle of growth.

Historian friends were dismayed at the scope of my previous book *The European Miracle*, which discussed developments over several centuries and two continents. Others confused the difficulty of the exercise with questioning whether there is a need for work on this scale (but where does it leave the study of history if for some unexplained reason shorter segments can never be knitted together?). I was pointedly told about the question asked by a specialist in one sort of history in one country in one century, when he heard that a colleague was writing a history of the world: 'what will he do for an encore?'

John McPhee tells us in *Basin and Range* about the geologist, prominent in establishing the theory of continental drift, who was once asked a similar question, what was he planning for an encore. He answered that he did not know, 'but possibly the most exciting thing to do next would be to prove the theory wrong.' *Growth Recurring* is a doubling back too, but more from the implications of the title of *The European Miracle* than from its account of Europe's performance. The aim there was to explore the reasons for Europe's unique achievement of development leading to industrialization. Many countries have since followed the European ones in reaching growth through industrialization. But only Europe converted an original growth into industrialization without a prior model, and I still see that as history's greatest consummation of a general materialistic urge.

On the other hand, I no longer see it as miraculous in the sense of 'the natural law of a unique event'. The more profound transition is the conversion of whatever precedes income growth (I think expansion and not simple stagnation, but more on this later) into growth in the sense of rising average per capita real incomes. Europe was not unique in achieving growth of that kind. For a number of important analytical purposes industrialization and growth have to be separated; growth has to be subdivided into two kinds; development is something different again; capitalism, which is a much more slippery term, has to be kept apart too. If we use these terms as synonyms we shall not be able to see that processes which happened to run together in the modern history of Europe are in reality distinct and had beginnings in various places at different times.

If I may be insistent about this for a moment, running the terms together may mean a muddle for anything except a quick sketch of European and American economic history during a tremendous, but transient, phase of two industrial centuries. The argument that growth proper repeatedly started up in the past and came to fruition more than once requires us to find a non-local (meaning not only Western) explanation, and one that is not limited to the eighteenth century. This book is a search for such an explanation. Its theme is more generalizable than any study of the fortunes of a single continent at a single period could be. Admittedly only the reshaping of world economic distributions during the last decade or so, previously mentioned, has enabled us to see what a realistic model might look like. Until now, Europe and its history could overshadow everything else. As a title *The European Miracle* was just a little too seductive.

My own encore thus seemed likely to be a bit bothersome. I confess that I took a long time trying to write what would have been another descriptive early modern economic history. The prospect of a different strategy came back to me when I stumbled over answering a question in an Honours class at La Trobe University. Years before, in 1975, I had given seminars entitled 'Growth as the Normal Condition' at Northwestern University and the Yale University Growth Center, but had let slide the notion that pressure for growth was there all the time. The dead weight of growthless history seemed to make it a hard case to argue. What brought it back so forcefully was the difficulty of providing a respectable answer to a question about Japan which could assimilate the Tokugawa Japanese experience to standard Western accounts of the origin of growth-as-industrialization.

I began to ponder whether I had been right to hunt for special positive features that may have enabled Europe to become the first continent to achieve sustained growth. The trap seemed to lie in assuming that because Europe is different, the difference must tell us about the inception of growth *in general* and not just about its timing, shape, and scale in the European case. The Islamicist Marshall Hodgson had made a similar point, but his writings did not come my way until later. History is written by the victors. Europe was preternaturally successful in the industrial sphere, and as a result European historians have constructed a stage for world history where a youngish actor in a stove-pipe hat struts at the front, and older actors from elsewhere are banished to the wings.

It proves to be more fruitful to insist on asking why there were many tentative moves in the direction of growth—as one looks, they reveal themselves—yet few cases of successful development arising from them. This may seem to require searching each satisfactory case for the positive factors impelling its advance. Given the poor results of that approach in the case of the British industrial revolution, the fact that it has left us with a list of 'causes' but no means of deciding among them, it may be best to come at the problem from the other direction. That implies asking why, when *intensive* growth did emerge, it was typically diverted back into *extensive* growth: in short, what were the negative forces. Only after identifying these can we usefully go on to enquire what eventually removed them.

Trying to do this has meant reshaping much of what I thought I knew and learning many new things. The form the book takes is as follows. The first chapter examines the conventional onset of growth in the British industrial revolution. The older and even now widespread view of this, however hedged around it may be, is centred on the sudden introduction of machinery during the third quarter of the eighteenth century. Research during the last decade has shown conclusively that industrialization began earlier than was usually thought, took much longer to build up and to affect more than a handful of industries, and was not initiated solely in Britain. But even modern, quantitative research offers surprisingly little in the way of an explanation of the start of the process. Most accounts still begin in the eighteenth century, because they depend on available statistical series and on the lingering conventions of the discipline. This chapter reviews opinion on British industrialization, stressing more of a long, slow climb than the older and in many ways still standard literature.

Readers who are already aware that change was gradual even in the British case, should skip Chapter 1 and start with Chapter 2, in which an alternative to the great discontinuity or industrialization approach is sketched. From here up to the end of Chapter 10 the argument about the nature of economic change in world history is unfolded: from a hypothesis about ever-present impulses for growth and evidence of early moves in that direction, through a discussion of explanations of the suppression of early prospects, to the separate recurrences of growth elsewhere in Tokugawa Japan and early modern Europe.

Chapter 2 urges that in all or most large societies the impulse for growth was apparent all along, but had to be unchained and allowed to come to fruition. Chapter 3 discusses many examples of technical innovation in early societies, and Chapter 4 gives a sketch of the 'economic revolution' in Sung China as an instance where conditions successfully produced rising average per capita GNP.

What chained up growth elsewhere and what suppressed it after the Sung? With Chapter 5 we start to discuss the main possibilities. This chapter concentrates on 'obstacles to growth' in mainland Asian societies where early changes had suggested that growth was not impossible (as indeed the case of the Sung demonstrates). These so-called obstacles took the form of unhelpful values and institutions, especially religious values, the guilds, and the Indian caste system. Chapter 6 discusses the impact of invasions from the central Asian steppes by the Mongols and their successors; the invasions captured the largest societies in the world. Chapter 7 introduces the idea that for systematic reasons institutions in the conquered societies may have behaved defensively, become conservative, and reduced the chances of recovery. Chapter 8 considers the role of pre-modern governments in grasping too many re-sources or offering too little in the way of economic manage-ment.

The circumstances which frustrated the prospects of mainland Asia and the Middle East during what was in European terms the early modern period are often un-thinkingly taken as indicating permanent backwardness. At that time the two areas at either end of Eurasia were slowly but surely emerging into a prominence relative to mainland Asia which their own earlier technical and cultural achievements would not lead us to expect.

With Chapter 9 we thus turn to the emergence of real growth in the Japanese economy from the sixteenth to the nineteenth centuries. Japanese growth was independent of Europe's—the borrowings of technology from the West after the Meiji Restoration of 1868 merely fuelled a flame that was already flickering and gave it a modern industrial hue. Growth in the economy of Europe before factory or machine industrialization is described in similar gradualist terms in Chapter 10.

Chapter 11 surveys and summarizes the argument and clarifies a number of positions taken on particular issues and debates.

How It All Really Began

ONE

A Know-all's Guide to the Industrial Revolution

The great mysteries of other fields, the searches for the origin of the universe or of life, seem to have a parallel in economic history.[1] This is the quest to understand the beginnings of *intensive* growth—a rise in average per capita real incomes. The assumption is that economic historians, too, should be looking for a unique transformation; that we have already found it; and that it was the British industrial revolution. In reality there were many moves towards growth, and one or two successful ones, but they have been overpowered by the subsequent victory of industrialization. A parallel is the way in which the history of Mithraism and the other oriental mystery religions of the Roman empire has been masked by the success of Christianity.

An operational definition of the term 'industrial revolution' is still lacking. It is the emperor's clothing of economic history. Defences of the term appeal to little more than pragmatism. Works on the concept continue to appear as though it may be taken for granted, nowadays needing only a protective belt of statistics. Yet many of the series of macro-statistics are without demonstrated foundation in primary documents and have been constructed only from 1700 or 1750, arbitrarily abolishing earlier change. The subject needs more digging in the archives, with the results elevated to the macro-economic level by the raised sample method. The relevant subject is economic history, not a macro-economic analysis that assumes modern data; what is required is traditional scholarship on a wholly untraditional scale.

Even that approach must founder while the central defini-tion remains vague. What would be clearer? The question is not crucial to this book, where the focus is on growth and development rather than industrialism or capitalism, nevertheless it is worth noting that Joel Mokyr suggested a useful approach in a 1976 paper.[2] His idea is that the industrial revolution represented a phase during which the economy 'grew up' as a result of advances in manufacturing techniques powerful enough to raise the productivity of whole industries. These industries made up a modern sector of the economy which achieved increasing returns and expanded faster than the traditional sector, ultimately at its expense, although traditional manufacturing was itself not exempt from change and went on expanding for some time.

The eighteenth- and nineteenth-century economy of Britain may thus be seen as a changing mixture of old and new. What changed were rates of productivity growth, those of the activities in the modern core eventually coming to dominate and raise the average rate for the whole economy in a way that had no precedent. (Yet 'eventually' was quite late: the modern sector employed fewer than 20 per cent of all workers as late as 1841.) There is no claim in Mokyr's scheme for a single, sudden chronological break. The two sectors pulled apart and their relative sizes altered as time went on; no one is going to be so foolish as to pretend that nothing momentous was happening in Georgian and Victorian Britain.

Actually assigning an industry to the new or the old sector is another matter. This depends on classifying productivity rates. These are seldom really computable, especially for early periods, and what we are left with is a method of conceptualizing a process of industrialization which we are unlikely to be able to measure properly. The scheme is not intended to apply to economic growth in general. For that we need to distinguish our terms. Someone once said of religion (or was it economics?) that it is a perfectly logical system founded on a preposterous assumption. Industrial revolution studies rest on the assumption that the histories of industrialism and economic growth are the same thing. 'A failure to recognize the difference between economic growth in the aggregate and industrialization has confused much of the history of Britain from 1750 to 1850.'[3]

Industrialization was a symptom, not a cause. The principle has been expressed most directly by Gerald Gunderson, although he was writing about the American case.[4] Gunderson begins by attacking the take-off model of W. W. Rostow, which dominated economic history during the 1960s and into the 1970s.[5] The take-off idea assumed that growth is modern, occurring during the 200 years since the British industrial revolution, which allegedly began it. In this perspective, growth is viewed as a process of increasing capital formation and the founding of new industries, created by higher rates of saving and dramatic technical innovation.

Gunderson counters this by pointing out that while rising industrial productivity did contribute massively to growth, it cannot be a defining characteristic. Industrialization was simply one way of supplying goods for which rising incomes were offering a market. Technical innovation may be a sufficient but is not a necessary condition of growth. Real incomes can also rise through squeezing more output from known methods and existing resources. It is a secondary matter where one's pay cheque or even the national income comes from, whether from farming or trade or services or industry, since one's first concern is surely the degree of command over goods and services it gives. Consumption is the end of all production and not all production is industrial.

Already by 1800, Gunderson points out, incomes in the United States were higher than those in Britain. If industrialization were the sole cause of rising incomes, we would have to conclude that America was the earlier country to industrialize. She was not. Even before the phase of factory and machine industry, the rates of growth of per capita output in the United States were almost as fast as they became during that phase: 1.2 per cent per annum from 1800 to 1835, 1.3 per cent per annum from 1835 to 1860. The economy had built in an accelerating rate of growth before industrialization, as a result of widening markets stemming in turn from improvements in transport. Industrialization, Gunderson concludes, was partly the *result* of prior growth.

Distinguishing in this way between industrialization and growth opens the way to a reduced emphasis on the British industrial revolution. The attempt is likely to bring the weight of specialist tradition down on one's head. Non-specialists presumably continue to use the term because they find it convenient and assume that the specialists can justify it. They may even suspect the motives of anyone who wants to remove the shine from such a golden oldie. In his *Advice to a Young Scientist*, Sir Peter Medawar declares:

No form of words is more characteristic of the Knowall than the following; 'Of course, there is really no such thing as *x*; what most people call *x* is really *y*.' In this context, *x* can be almost anything people believe in, such as the Renaissance, the Romantic revival or the Industrial Revolution; *y* is usually something declared to be stirring for the first time in the bosoms of the proletariat.[6]

Don't worry, Medawar tells his young scientist, the two greatest Knowalls he has ever met were both economists.

The root of the industrial revolution is usually held to be an eighteenth-century change in the relative prices of labour and capital, leading plausibly enough to substitutions of capital (embodied in new machines) for hand labour. Yet the descriptions that follow are commonly worded not in economic but in physical terms: animate sources of energy are replaced by inanimate sources, above and beyond all else by the steam engine, while organic sources of raw material are replaced by inorganic ones, especially wood by coal. Further structural changes follow automatically, such as shifts of organization from household to factory and of population from countryside to town. Despite a wealth of detail the scope is uncontrollably wide, relationships among variables are seldom tightly specified, and although the chief effect of a cloudburst of innovation should have been a steep fall in the real price of manufactures, even this is usually assumed rather than charted.

An expansion in the output of old handicraft techniques took place both before and during the so-called machine age. When this involved the adoption of better hand tools owned by individual workers it is not easily captured by studying firms or industries through conventional sources, for improvement in these humbler methods was of long standing. In the vital operation of spinning, the distaff had been replaced during the Middle Ages by the 'great wheel', and this in turn during early modern times by various types of hand spinning-wheel.[7] Spinning-wheels, yarn-winding devices, and fulling mills, three 'very capital improvements' in the woollen industry as Adam Smith reported them, had all come in since as early as the late Middle Ages.

Smith also pointed out that a watch movement that had cost £20 in the mid-seventeenth century was 95 per cent cheaper by 1776, and better made too. This was the result of better industrial and workshop organization rather than any striking advance in equipment, and it indicates a cumulative progress in methods of production that can seem slow only by later standards, that required no infusions of high science, and that showed no signs of diminishing returns.

History, then, did not debouch from static technique onto the novel machines of the eighteenth-century Lancashire cotton industry. The spindle or distaff, which had originally replaced spinning on a simple stick, had been in use for three and a half thousand years, but was changing in Europe in the Middle Ages. The spinning-wheel that succeeded it had probably been invented in India between AD 500 and 1000, to be borrowed a few centuries later by the Europeans (after they had borrowed the whole notion of producing cotton from the Islamic world in the twelfth century). We notice, then, that European technology was already in an unusual state of forward motion by the medieval period, judged by relevant historical standards, that is, what had happened previously. By the eighteenth century, best-practice diffusions had come a long way and still had a lot of scope.[8]

The role of steam has been dethroned by Dolores Greenberg in a survey of the accumulating studies that now permit a more exact estimate of an importance once taken for granted.[9] Water-power remained immensely significant, having before the industrial revolution period already permitted the mechanization of the fulling of wool, the spinning of silk, and several stages in the production of linen. There was no significant break in this innovative tradition between the Middle Ages and the setting up of cotton factories in the eighteenth century: 'no really sharp breaks . . .', declares the historian of the water-wheel, Terry Reynolds, 'only a series of rather modest, incremental shifts'.[10]

A study of the Kentdale district in Westmorland shows a climb in the number of industrial water-mills from 18 to 36 between the 1650–1750 and 1750–1850 periods.[11] The area contained only three or four steam-engines before the 1850s. This was not the industrially trivial district its remoteness may suggest. In horsepower per inhabitant it was not overtaken by Birmingham until the mid-nineteenth century. The harnessing of water-power for industrial purposes had been going on in Kentdale since the thirteenth century: 'it was clearly industrial growth which produced the steam-engine and the railway, not the steam-engine and the railway which made possible industrial growth', claims the investigator, anticipating Gunderson.

A more general paper on industrial motive-power by Musson extends these and related perspectives.[12] During the first half of the nineteenth century the 'steam revolution' was confined mainly to cotton. Only a small minority of the labour force worked in factories tending steam-driven machinery. Much of the available steam-power was used outside manufac-turing, in draining mines or turning the grindstones of flour mills. Canals were not at all quickly abandoned in face of the competition from steam trains. At sea, sail remained pre-eminent until late into the second half of the nineteenth century.

According to Musson, if the total industrial steam-horsepower in 1850 is set at 100, some calculations would make it only 326 as late as 1870, but it had jumped to 3,217 by the first Census of Production in 1907. In Greenberg's summary, 'reliance on tra-ditional power for much of the nineteenth century is one of the most outstanding, if one of the most neglected characteristics of the industrializing process in Britain and in the United States. . . . Increased output, rather than increases in steam utilization, is the benchmark of the Industrial Revolution until 1850.'[13]

Equally, the switch to new materials has now lost its classical sharpness of definition. F. T. Evans refers to the 'iron and steel propaganda of the Industrial Revolution' and shows instead that native-grown and imported timber were not in short supply and did not fall out of favour.[14] Wood continued to be employed in an endless list of products. As late as 1850 less than 10 per cent of the shipping tonnage built in Britain was made of iron. As a clincher, Evans refutes Nikolaus Pevsner, who had claimed that among the outstanding features of Paxton's Crystal Palace, built for the Great Exhibition of 1851, were ' "the absence of any other materials, and an ingenious system of prefabrication for the iron and glass parts" '.[15] Not so, says Evans: Paxton's longest arches, the 72-feet span transept arches, were made of laminated Memel fir. There were 205 *miles* of wooden sash-bars and 34 *miles* of wooden guttering in this ostensibly iron and glass conservatory.

The prolonged and overlapping technical, economic, and business developments revealed in these more recent studies are harder to grasp than the version in which modernity swept all before it. Much was in flux before 1750, yet few aspects of economic life were thoroughly altered by 1850. The new picture of change is sepia, more plausible than black-and-white, but harder to hold in the mind. The old story was fruitful in that it inspired so many industrial and regional studies, but while these may have amended the basic framework in detail, they seldom challenged its outline. The technicist interpretation has nevertheless been fading ever since the publication of Deane and Cole, *British Economic Growth*, in 1962, which generated a great deal of excitement at the time and much refinement since.[16] Despite this, the old interpretation remains a dead horse that is not altogether willing to lie down.

Research which took industrial breakthrough as gospel was above all the province of scholars in northern and midland England. They looked on economic history almost as prologue to the urban industrialism of their region, embodied outstandingly in the staple industries reported by the Census of Production of 1907. The hidden agenda of industrial revolution studies in the hands of a master like my own teacher, David Chambers of Nottingham, celebrated north midland society as it was celebrated in the novels of D. H. Lawrence, in one of which Chambers himself had a walk-on part as a small boy.

There was love here, an effort to understand a landscape cosy for all its griminess, or as a southern Englishman like myself would say, grimy for all its cosiness. Only the vestiges of that world now survive. The dark satanic mills are museums of technology or warehouses for Japanese motorcycles. A self-conscious search for that yester-year's scene and its particular social ills is less compelling than it was. Where I would urge that studying it single-mindedly obscures the true early history of world growth, Malcolm Falkus has urged that it likewise distracts us from the more recent origins of much that is important in the British economic scene today.[17] Histories that concentrate on cotton and steam, canals and railways, seldom get the second wind they need to account for plastics, electronics, hypermarkets, or the Common Market. They stand suspended as studies of the middle phase of a transition from cottage industry to the micro-chip assembly room, endlessly scanning the eighteenth century for embryonic limbs that swelled into the great industries of 1907 but which have shrivelled away in turn.[18]

The view that growth began decisively in an eighteenth-century British take-off or turning-point falls short in many ways. In a backward economy held in a low-level equilibrium trap the possibility nevertheless would have existed of a sudden start. Incomes would be low and so would savings and investment, but a growth spurt might be induced, say by a government plan. In these circumstances induced growth might be 'analytically distinct and statistically recordable', as Donald Whitehead said of it.[19] Nevertheless it would be arbitrary in the British case to mark off a phase of growth from a prior phase of preconditioning, because growth was spontaneous there, not the result of state intervention. Whitehead was unable to identify in Britain sudden forces that might have brought a turning-point into being, or any sign in the British evidence that a shift of that kind actually occurred. Studies which claim to concentrate on the release of pent-up forces for growth would not of course be the same thing, since we would then have to explain the genesis of the earlier growth that supposedly became pent up.

Just how far back British real incomes began to rise continuously may be uncertain, but for a long time there had been progressive change in what might be called the Mokyrian variables. The allusion is to a remark made by Joel Mokyr about the gap emerging between Europe (not merely Britain) and the remainder of the world before 1750, to the effect that, 'the disparity in income may have been a relatively recent phenomenon, the disparity in a host of other economic variables was not'.[20] Mokyr mentions sources of energy, transport, education, public health, a higher capital-to-labour ratio, advancing technology, and probably some improvement in economic management by European governments. If we assess these tendencies only backwards, base-weighted in the nineteenth or twentieth centuries, they may seem unimpressive.

But the early distinctions, however fine, need to be given their due. With the base-weighting earlier, say in the Middle Ages, the mass of this subsequently and slowly rising complex of production and consumption indicators seems anything but trivial.

A picture of gradual change is highlighted by a last point, that conventional measures too glibly assume that the study of economic growth ought to be about the private manufacture of goods for private consumption. Calculations of real wages tend to capture that aspect, especially for historical periods. They are indexes of money incomes divided by the price of some market basket of goods. Public goods have a habit of vanishing in the course of this exercise. Yet if private manufacturing were undergoing change before the customary age of industry, the provision of public goods was even more clearly affected.

During the early modern period production was increasingly privatized. It was taken out of guild control or extricated from the sway of communal farming. At the same time, much of what may very broadly be termed welfare was being collectivized. Governmental and civic provision of elementary services was rising, and since by definition no one can be excluded from using a public good, this meant that real incomes rose. This especially benefited the poor for whom public goods constituted a bigger share of consumption than for others. Income growth, *intensive* growth, is not all about the historical equivalents of tight jeans and colour—or off-colour—videos. When we take into account the consumption trends for all goods and services we find once again a less dramatic history than we were taught, a longer, flatter hill. A different kind of geomorphology is needed to explain it.

The decaying research programme centred on the industrial revolution concept offers in itself only more of what it has always induced, more industrial studies, more regional studies, such is the attraction of the follow-my-leader approach in academic work. As Sidney Pollard observed in 1984, 'progress has indeed been limited', and he asks: 'who among us can be certain that we have done all that could be expected of us in questioning our tradition, in using our widening opportunities for historical investigation, and in adding to the store of historical insights that we have inherited?'[21] Yet if we put together the findings of recent research we find after all that a very non-standard history has emerged piecemeal, without much fundamental rethinking of concepts.

The rate of growth of the output of books and articles on industrialization may have slowed down in the late 1970s, but it seems to have picked up again and taken a more analytically economic, less technicist, form. The freshest insights have come from outside the British tradition or have been written by authors heavily influenced by overseas scholarship, mainly American. Examples include work by one of the editors and several contributors to Floud and McCloskey (eds.), *Economic History of Britain since 1700*; Mokyr's definitive introduction to *The Economics of the Industrial Revolution*; Crafts's several reassessments of the statistical record of growth; Greenberg's review of energy history; contributions by Roehl, O'Brien and Keyder, Crafts, and Schon on the comparative economic performance of Britain and the Continent; and Harley's work on the slow pace of output growth.[22]

Harley's separate indexes of industrial production and demand coincide with one another far more than either agrees with the chronologies outlined in previous works. The result is to show that growth was much slower between 1770 and 1815 than had been supposed, and that by 1770 the industrial sector was already almost twice as large as once thought. Together with estimates by Crafts, this implies that per capita incomes and total productivity accelerated steadily and in a fairly balanced way across the economy from a much earlier period than had been believed. It is consistent with the further development of an already vigorous commercial, agricultural, and 'proto-industrial' economy.

The other prong of what has been a powerful forked attack on the conventional wisdom comes from the Roehl, Crafts, and O'Brien and Keyder work on the comparative economic performance of Britain and France during the eighteenth century. The French economy was once derided or ignored while one got on with the serious task of describing the British scene. Now it is argued that the French economy performed almost as well as the British, until the cotton and iron inventions late in the eighteenth century.

One might half-seriously suggest that this ecumenism reflects the adjustment of British academics to the reality of the Common Market, the abandonment (still incomplete)[23] of the vision that it is the Continent which is isolated by fog in the Channel. Britain and the continental countries were probably responding separately to similar stimuli. Lennart Schon has pointed out that continental Europe was not pressed into mechanizing by price competition from British goods. His argument is that had new technologies set up severe price competition, traditional methods would not have survived even within Britain. Markets were too fragmented for competition to be that close. On the Continent the old methods of some regions were even more protected by the poor integration of markets, fortunately for them because not only northern Britain but a number of mainland European regions were rapidly adopting newer methods.

Earlier writers, such as Rostow, and Blum, Cameron, and Barnes, claimed that had an industrial revolution not come in Britain, it would still have come in the not-too-distant future somewhere in western Europe or the United States.[24] This counter-factual may be untestable, but it does extrapolate trends that can be observed in these other areas. The vigour of several regional economies in mainland Europe is attested, for example, by Max Barkhausen's study of the evolution of mining and metallurgy in the Rhineland and southern Low Countries.[25] That evolution stretched from the Middle Ages just like the use of water-power for milling in Kentdale. To take another example, the silk industry in Italy was carried out in four- and six-storey mills as early as the sixteenth century. Water-power was used, the architecture of industrial northern England was anticipated, and John Lombe stole away from here to Derby the secrets of manufacturing silk. One last example: the Wood Museum at Kew contains an exhibit of an eighteenth-century lathe from Saxony on which flat wooden Noah's Ark animals were mass-produced. This owed nothing to Britain; it sprang from deeper European wells of creativity. Some may wish to shrug off toy-making as trivial, but the methods of mass-production were highly generalizable, as the 'American System' soon showed. Mainland European developments were not all borrowings, though some studies of the diffusion of British devices set out to create that impression, and even where they were, only well-prepared societies could have hoped to import inventions as quickly as they did.

Work that has been going on since the late 1960s on the industrialization, or proto-industrialization, of parts of the countryside in Europe as well as in Britain, right from medieval times, reinforces this broader view. Rural domestic industry amounted to a dispersed factory system already in place and highly specialized by product and process. It was becoming denser in many regions of most countries. With rural people moving part of their labour, or at any rate part of their labour time, from farming into handicrafts, a hidden shift in occupational structure was already occurring. Studies which count only full-time operatives miss the scope of this.

A great deal of interregional trade had to be set up to feed the increasingly specialized workers in these industries and distribute their products. One or two recent criticisms do bring into question the direct link between proto-industry and the factory, though even there Mokyr's demonstration that low-wage proto-industrial regions were the most rapidly industrialized has not been falsified. [26] It seems unlikely after all that proto-industrialization was simply a dead end. Too much financing was generated, too much trade put in train, too many resources mobilized, too many skills imparted, for it not to have had an effect favourable to the rise of factory production.

Altogether the work of the past decade or two has suggested a gradual growth in output and real incomes right through the early modern period, not only in Britain but also in several parts of the Continent. The case is building up for assigning to the seventeenth century the formation of patterns once thought to have begun only in the late eighteenth or nineteenth centuries, reserving for the Victorian era big changes in scale but not so many in principle. A few years ago Peter Burke perceptively queried the choice of the nineteenth century for the start of a new phase in European urbanization. [27] He noted that differences in degree between the civic organization of early modern and Victorian cities had been treated as though they were differences in kind, and that some admittedly unimpressive features of small early modern cities had been passed off as indicating the limited quality of early urbanization instead of being merely incidental to small size. More recently, Jan de Vries has shown that the cities of Europe can be understood only as a system, one that formed during the seventeenth rather than the nineteenth century, with the industrial city as a much less conspicuous outgrowth than was supposed.[28] De Vries also confirms that industry was extensively ruralized during the seventeenth century, thus helping to create an undue impression of industrial expansion when industry re-located in the cities after the eighteenth century.

Ann Kussmaul has demonstrated from the unexpected evidence of the seasonality of marriages that specialization emerged in English agriculture during the seventeenth rather than the eighteenth century, which is a beautiful generalization of existing regional studies.[29] Thus North American scholars of a generation for whom quantitative techniques are second nature are beginning to invade the economic history of early modern Europe. This will reinforce the diminished relative importance of Britain and of the eighteenth century. That importance will not vanish, of course, but it is ceasing to dominate our understanding of the shape and processes of growth.

The quantitative work of Crafts shows that growth was slower between 1780 and 1831 than the earlier literature claims. There was indeed an acceleration during the last two decades of the eighteenth century, and the output of cotton and iron did increase quite fast, but neither these things nor the growth of exports bulked large enough to determine the national trend. Between 1760 and 1820 living standards altered little. Population growth was pressing closely on the growth of productivity and absorbed most of the eighteenth-century increase in the investment ratio. This meant that much of the change was economic expansion using existing techniques, rather than a shift to new methods that instantly and automatically produced a great rise in productivity or average income.

Truly high rates of productivity growth awaited the nineteenth century.[30] Donald McCloskey has pointed out that one may well admire their pace in modernized sectors of the economy between 1780 and 1860, but notice at the same time just how much output was still produced by sectors remaining unaffected by steam and iron.[31] The ratio of the average growth rates in the old and new sectors was 1:1.3. Had the rate of growth in the traditional sector determined the national growth rate outside agriculture, per capita national income would still have been rising agreeably. It would have doubled between 1780 and 1860. That is a measure of the degree to which economic change was an extension of what had gone before. The contribution of the sector that was modernizing rapidly was to create 27 per cent more income per head in 1860 than would otherwise have been achieved. 27 per cent is substantially less than the rhetorical accounts would lead one to expect. Was it impressive or not? Work in this subject almost never specifies in advance what level it would accept as significant.

Here, in any case, the quantifiers run into a check. Reviewers of the influential textbook edited by Roderick Floud and Donald McCloskey have noted the embarrassment.[32] Growth is measured more precisely than before, but no convincing explanation of it is offered even in those self-consciously cliometric pages, to which the present writer himself contributed. In the neo-classical models underlying modern research, industrialization remains mainly a function of technical change. This in turn is largely unaccounted for, the models tell us little about it, their authors allude only to an increased but essentially mysterious responsiveness to alterations in factor costs. They do not capture the reasons *why* European society became so inspired to innovate, although that is how they express the problem when they mention it. They are right to prefer the gentle contours of recent scholarship, where growth is cut down to size. But sharp peak or smooth swelling, the morphology has still to be explained, and in this respect the new work is scarcely more satisfactory than the old.

Once upon a time it seemed we had a definite event to learn about. Growth began with, growth was, an industrial revolution in late eighteenth-century Britain. Now we know quite securely that the event was really a process, smaller, far less British, infinitely less abrupt, part of a continuum, taking much more time to run. We are still not sure what the explanation of such a process ought to look like. Perhaps it has absorbed the profession's energies to establish a new descriptive history in the face of previous historiographic expectations. Perhaps those of a quantifying bent have little taste for seemingly intractable issues. We all recall decisive events more easily than slowly unfolding plots, patterns sooner than shades of grey, jingles better than poems. But if the history of growth really was an expanding universe instead of a big bang, gradualism is going to be what we are obliged to explain.

TWO

Economic Growth as Virgin Birth

Like the White Queen, economic historians have managed to believe several impossible things before breakfast. One of these is that they can hold take-off and gradualism in their minds at the same time. This is carrying things too far. It involves on the one hand believing that the modern world economy originated by 'taking-off' in eighteenth-century Britain. Every schoolchild knows that, since almost any syllabus in economic history begins at this point. But on the other hand it means accepting an incompatible proposition, that economic and technical change was an evolutionary saga, starting far back in pre-history, involving cultures totally removed from the British, and not so much 'taking-off' as accumulating. Every schoolchild knows this too, if he or she has watched one of the television series on the rise of our species.

Trying to bisect the whole of human economic experience in the Britain of 1750 while remaining conscious of the remote antiquity of change is like simultaneously accepting both the 'big bang' theory and the theory of an expanding universe, or the views of the creationists as well as those of Charles Darwin. Such an anomaly in thinking ought to suggest that something is amiss. We should find a way of rejecting at least one of the theories or a better way of blending them.

An economy as complicated as that of Georgian Britain could not have sprung suddenly out of stagnation, like Pallas Athene from the head of Zeus. Yet the current edition of a widely used textbook is still talking about economic stagnation lasting in Britain into the eighteenth century.[1] That may be convenient for teaching courses on industrialization or the modern economy which are prepared to dismiss everything more than a couple of centuries old as not 'relevant'. Yet change was already hoary with age by that time. The conviction that it began abruptly always reminds me of a mix-up in the births column of an Oxfordshire newspaper: 'suddenly, at the age of eighty-four'.

The opinion that we need not bother with early developments has been strongly expressed by Denison.[2] Referring to the high proportion of the growth of output even in the developed countries that has been secured only within the last few decades, he disputes that we should bother with earlier times. The temptation is to retort, 'what use is a baby?' Leaving out the first few steps is fatal and facile. Once output per head is on the rise the task of explaining why it goes on is comparatively routine, given the ample statistics of modern periods. The challenge is to understand how a rise ever got started. 'The real problem', as an eminent theorist puts it, 'is not to catalog the characteristics of economies that have already become differentiated, but rather to account for the emergence of differentiation in the first place.'[3]

The puzzle concerns the transition from *extensive* to *intensive* growth. The terms are from Lloyd Reynolds, after Kuznets.[4] *Extensive* growth occurs when total output and population are both increasing, but at approximately the same rate, so that there is no secular rise in output per head. Something like this state of affairs characterized the world economy, on average, over thousands of years, although our attention is drawn away from its rich implications by our understandably greater concern with income growth.[5] In the *very* long term, economic capacity and total output (but not output per head) were constantly on the rise. The known increase of the human population, slow though it was, guarantees this, at least on the reasonable assumption that incomes were at first so low that they cannot have fallen much and still supported life, so that the total must have grown.

This 'static expansion' was enough gradually to remould economic society. A car rolling down an incline is moving even before the engine is switched on. Stagnation, or since there may have been cycles, stagnation on average, was restricted to the dimension of per capita income. Other variables grew in size. A glacially-slow but inexorable expansion, rather than complete stagnation, was therefore the background from which emerged economic growth as we normally think of it, that is, *intensive* growth. In other words there has almost always been growth of a sort; the deeper issue is, how did expansionary growth change to income growth?

Intensive growth (which is meant when I refer just to 'growth' or 'economic growth') occurs when average real income per head is rising. In practice, population has usually gone on rising as well, faster than before. The definition must include at least population stability. Simon Kuznets always noted that population must not fall or we find ourselves in the apparently unacceptable position of treating the Black Death as a great engine of growth. After all, the survivors found themselves commanding many more resources and had higher incomes than before. Usually, too, *intensive* growth involves structural change, when part of the occupied population shifts from primary production into the secondary (manufacturing) or tertiary (service) sectors. We should probably expect structural change in any phase of *intensive* growth sustained and robust enough to have made a historical mark. To that extent *intensive* growth embraces economic development, this usually being taken to imply institutional, structural, or distributional change in addition to rising incomes. Another way of expressing *intensive* growth is as rising per capita GNP (gross national product). Rising life expectancies can also sometimes be detected, so that *intensive* growth may occasionally have been more agreeable and have come close to raising what is called NEW, net economic welfare.

There is a sense in which this definition of *intensive* growth can be trivialized. It would be possible to have had Pareto-optimal *intensive* growth, when the real income of at least one person went up and no one else's income fell. The arithmetic average of income would undeniably have risen, to a resounding chorus of yawns. To escape this very formal dilemma, we ought to specify just how much growth it is going to take to get us excited. Differing degrees of growth will turn on different people, as with intensities of other sorts of pleasure. Unfortunately, economic statistics from the distant past are very, very poor, or they are simply not available at the macro- or whole society level, so that we cannot go in for real measurement. This is no field for the strict cliometrician, who thus misses working on some fascinating periods (which are illuminating precisely because they differ from industrial economies) or doing much comparative work—at least until cliometricians start compiling more of their own statistical series from primary resources. But that is no excuse for avoiding cliometric methods of debate, which require us to state how much *intensive* growth is enough to interest us.

Given that we cannot measure growth in the ways that economists nowadays expect, and despite firmly believing that there were other cases where true growth did take place, I shall stick to cases where descriptions of economic change are overwhelmingly positive. Historical judgement is unavoidably involved, and for that reason I take the consensus of appropriate specialist opinion as the basis. This means restricting cases of *intensive* growth to the outstanding ones where the tendency is conspicuous even to scholars whose central interest does not happen to be the economy. The most persuasive examples are where large fractions of the population are reported to have been using new methods and consuming more than ever before, where change continued for more than a century, and where it altered the structure of the economy so that a noticeable proportion of the workforce moved out of agriculture into more productive occupations.

The vital question, then, is how did a world of static expansion give way to one of *intensive* growth. When and where did this happen? Did it begin with some accidental upturn in real incomes which was held onto, such as the perverse result of the Black Death? Must we assume it happened only once? The answer to the last question at any rate is 'no'. History is to be thought of as repeated, tentative efforts of *intensive* growth to bubble up through the stately rising dough of *extensive* growth.

To write comparative history we need agreed terms. We need to stick closely to the definitions of growth just outlined, and to steer clear of terms which divert or restrict the debate to particular times and particular, more limited, phenomena which may seen to be synonyms for growth but really are not. Industrialization should be avoided for the reason mentioned in the first chapter, it was a symptom not a cause. Kuznets's term 'Modern Economic Growth' (MEG) is, as its name implies, of limited rather than general application and is also less objective and more judgemental than the claims for it admit. Capitalism is also to be avoided. Definitions of capitalism are misty where not merely rhetorical and lie, like beauty, too much in the eye of the beholder. Although the forms of ownership to which the term directs attention are important for many purposes, they are not a priori relevant to the question whether or not an economy achieved *intensive* growth. After all, the modern socialist countries have economies that grow; 'capitalism' is not *sine qua non*.

We have already noted that the world saw many hesitant approaches to *intensive* growth and more than one that reached it. Looking for a single 'great discontinuity' is therefore beside the point. This is one reason why Max Weber's otherwise plausible approach to world economic history does not do. Finding the key to history, as he did, in the emergence of a Protestant ethic has the merit of broadening the approach beyond Britain and its 'industrial revolution', but still retains the assumption that the topic to be discussed, taken by Weber to be the rise of capitalism, occurred spontaneously only in Europe.

The central difficulty is not in any of the severe 'internal' problems of the Weber thesis—specifying it operationally, making some accommodation to the record of growth in the Roman Catholic states of Europe, or grappling with the possibility that Protestantism was less the source of change than a result of development and turmoil. The difficulty is that the thesis seeks to explain a capitalism peculiar to Europe but cannot explain a growth that was not limited to this part of the world.

Just as the search for the 'causes of the industrial revolution' in one or other deviant sector of the British economy is forlorn, so is a geographically broader search that still assumes all relevant change to have been European or at any rate Western. Attempts to rescue the Weber thesis by stretching it to include Japan are equally unpromising. We are asked to believe that as the result of some giant historical fluke, Shintoism was an aberrant Calvinism, just as other scholars have sought to find the source of Japanese development in an accidental parallel between Japanese and European feudalism. Leaving aside the evidential difficulties, and the desirability in any case of dropping an empty term like feudalism, there is something uneasy about pretending that any successful eastern economy must secretly have been 'Western'. Furthermore, the 'Protestant ethic' explanation cannot be extended to Sung China and any other case that turns up.

No purely European process can explain enough. Even the North and Thomas thesis, which is attractive for its breadth and its cold dismissal of the industrial revolution as an epiphenomenon of earlier changes in property rights, suffers because it cannot be generalized beyond Europe.[6] The argument depends on the expected results of a change in factor proportions. As the medieval European population built up, the advantage supposedly shifted to those who could establish title to the now-scarce resource, land, which was increasingly privatized. The shift is supposed to have happened in a Europe where the population density had reached only 8 per km^2 by AD 1300. Since China had reached a density of 10 per km^2 by 200 BC, and the density in India in AD 1300 was over 21 per km^2, we are bound to ask why they did not undergo the same evolution of property rights.

'The current preoccupation of Western scholars with American and European—largely northwestern European— economic history can only seem provincial,' writes Richard Easterlin, 'for the striking feature about these areas is the fundamental similarity in their experience.'[7] The title of Easterlin's paper raises the real issue, not why did one or other part of the West develop, but 'why isn't the whole world developed?'

We need to find a way round the puzzle set by Crafts in a paper which asked, 'Why England First?'[8] Relying on revisionist scholarship which puts French economic perform- ance in a favourable light, he argues that England only beat France to the industrial revolution by chance. The process was a stochastic one. This, however, explicitly depends on a narrow rather than a broad view of industrialization and the technical changes at the heart of it, and it is doubtful whether Crafts would hold to such indeterminacy over a wider sweep of history. The gulf in preparedness between, say, Switzerland and what is now Zaire would have been so vast that they could not have had the same chance of industrializing. Nevertheless the question brings to mind the macro-historian's favourite poser, 'why Europe rather than China?' If *intensive* growth was no more than a once-only race between two great rivals, was the result also indeterminate?

The dilemma becomes less pressing if we rehearse pre-modern history in the changeable light thrown on it by modern scholarship:

1. For at the very least 3,000 years the trend of world population has been upwards. For some purposes it is legitimate to focus on the fluctuations, yet none of these ever produced more than a century or so of stagnation or mild decline at a time. By modern standards rates of population growth were very low, but they *were* positive. Assuming, as we have done, a start at an average real income little above subsistence, so that there was no room for much downward flexibility, the trend of population becomes a measure of the trend of income. Total population may be taken as a lower-bound proxy for total output and total income. Pre-modern history thus has a trend as well as fluctuations. The systematic experience was *extensive* growth, that is, rising total output and total (but not average) income, measured by the inching up of total population in the *very* long term.

2. Within the not-so-static expansion implied by *extensive* growth there is a record of continual technical change and many cases known to history of keen entrepreneurship. This is evident in the archaeological and documentary evidence. The monumental debris that most impresses us from remote periods gives a misleading impression. It denotes the private megalomania of pharaohs and other rulers masquerading as public works. To that extent tourism distorts our sense of history, since the ground-swell of change is virtually invisible to travellers who visit the spectacular monuments. Evidence of investment and technical change in agriculture, much the largest sector of any early economy, is far harder to see, but however slow it was by the febrile standards of the twentieth century there was a good deal of it.

3. There was indeed a recurring tendency for growth to overtake the increase of population. Vulgar Malthusianism may make us think that history was a perpetual outstripping of average income by population growth, but a little reflection will show that history was a perpetual race between the two. Even Malthus assumed there was a tendency towards output

growth as well as population growth. He may have been convinced that rising numbers must win, but he was not right
about every case.

The cases where Malthus was wrong were of course few.
Identifiable *intensive* growth was always rare. Many possible
episodes are made problematical because students of early
periods seldom provide even an order-of-magnitude framework
for their work. We are obliged to make what we can of indirect
indicators. The term 'identifiable' *intensive* growth is used for
that reason; we would undoubtedly find more cases if we had
better evidence, or looked at some of the available evidence
more closely. After all, windfall gains from good harvests or
conquests must sometimes have raised average per capita
GNP, though admittedly the effect could not be guaranteed to
last or to be accompanied by development in the form of
structural change. But sometimes things did work out right and
there was growth as a result.

Modern scholarship therefore reveals economic history to
have been much more than a single contest between Europe
and China in which, for all her early glories, China supposedly
never achieved the *intensive* growth that came only once, in 'the'
industrial revolution. We are not limited to watching one race-
meeting or a race only run once, and as a result we have some
prospect of identifying the systematic forces that produce
growth.

It is particularly instructive to consider the case of Sung
China (tenth to thirteenth centuries AD). There are no grounds
for ignoring it simply because it was a long time ago, is
unfamiliar to most Westerners, and was brought to a sorry
close. What is pertinent is not how strange the social forms may
now seem, but whether the episode satisfied the criteria of
intensive growth. As it happens, China under the Sung, and
probably under the preceding late Tang, dynasty underwent a
transformation that included many 'industrial revolution'
features. There was enormous monetization and industrialization, presupposing structural change on a scale usually associated with modern growth, and reflected in the swelling of Sung
cities. There was a string of innovations in ceramics, movable
type, gunpowder and firearms, pound locks, sternpost rudders,
paddle-wheels, water-powered spinning-wheels, and more.

The technical innovations of the Sung period make our claims for the primacy of things British ring hollow. Teaching about eighteenth-century innovations as the *first* is rather parochial: the *first* Iron Bridge for example. The elegant 1779 specimen at Coalbrookdale was made of cast iron, certainly, but it was mortised and pegged as if it were made of wood. The Chinese had hundreds of iron-chain suspension bridges up to a thousand years earlier, and they were quite capable of carrying traffic. They are also known to have inspired eighteenth-century Western engineers.

Large increases in productivity are inherent in all these Chinese innovations. It is unlikely that they failed to bring about rising per capita income, and in more than the trivial sense of a rising statistical average. A real majority of people must have shared in the gains under the Sung, whether or not continued population growth forced down the average return under later dynasties. One has only to consider the extent of structural change and read descriptions of the size of the mercantile and other urban classes to see that. This was a phase of true growth, which we will discuss in more detail in the next chapter.

The history of Tokugawa Japan is at least as impressive. A historiographic revolution over the past fifteen or so years has swept away the old conception of its economy imprisoned helplessly within a decaying 'feudal' system. Entrepreneurial vitality, rising productivity, urbanization, and modernization have been demonstrated to a fault. The latest scholarly opinion is that, taking appropriate criteria, which means considering evidence of rising life expectancies alongside regular indices of material consumption, by 1850 the standard of living was higher than in Britain.[9]

The previously reigning interpretation of Japanese economic history insisted that nothing of note happened before the Meiji Restoration of 1868, from which date the country embraced Western methods, achieving industrialization and economic growth from a standing start. Earlier scholars had not taken this line: Elizabethan England was Sir George Sansom's analogy for Tokugawa Japan. Opinions like his were later set aside. The literature came to concern itself with a somewhat ahistorical listing of those Japanese national characteristics which may have promoted rapid growth. More attention to how a 'decaying feudalism' could have managed such a smart about-face might have inspired a closer look at how far it really was from 'decaying' and 'feudal'.

Historians still often fashion Meiji economic growth in a distinctly Western mould. The phrase 'the Britain of the East' turns up as a title. Japanese industrialization seems to prompt a search for parallels with aspects of Western history. It is as if by some bizarre accident Japan, and Japan alone among non-Western countries, had chanced to hit on the magic of the West. We have already mentioned the supposed parallels in religion and feudalism. The former seems an ethnocentric attempt to find Calvinist virtues in Confucian-Shintoism. A version of this is R. N. Bellah's claim that Japanese religion extols diligence and frugality, on which he comments, 'that such an ethic is profoundly favorable to economic rationalization was the major part of Weber's study of Protestantism and we must say that it seems similarly favorable in Japan'.[10] It may have been. Whether it originated growth is another matter.

A second parallel has been sought and found in the feudal system. Great ingenuity has been devoted to establishing a correspondence between the Japanese and European versions of 'feudalism', which is, however, an arbitrary codification of some Western medieval tendencies that even specialists now tell us should be abandoned as a working tool.[11] The parallel, then, is with something that scarcely existed in a useful or operational sense even in the West. Were the effort successful, and if it could be shown in addition that a 'feudal' past necessarily accounts for later economic growth, Japan would have had to mimic Britain or Western Europe along the length of a very complicated chain of experiences: nowhere else, not even the China from which Japan's culture descended, had managed that. It could only have been a very recherché accident that the exact social form of the force driving one economy, set on an archipelago off eastern Eurasia, was the same one that had driven another, located far away at the western end. This accident moreover is always portrayed as an accident for Japan, enabled thereby to duplicate Europe and thus to become the first non-Western country capable of copying Western growth. The whole awkward argument is necessitated by the belief that Japan's growth must have been derivative. We will look more closely at the evidence about this in a later chapter.

As to European economic change, various versions of its nature and timing exist. One great debate in the Marxist tradition deals with 'the Transition' from feudalism to capitalism, with capitalism seen as the goal and as a necessary condition for industrialization and growth. Non-Marxist economic history cavalierly sweeps aside all that, assumes a 'great discontinuity', and proceeds to find it in the industrial revolution. A small but impressive number of authors do however sidestep both debates and imply a gentler ascent that depends on no social convulsion at all. They have made surprisingly little impact on either school. Nevertheless, Cipolla, Kuznets, Landes, and Maddison have all independently offered estimates of a slow rise in average per capita GNP for Europe as a whole from as early as AD 1000.[12] They do not say much about the causes, but their interpretation does tend to coincide with the strand of scholarship in the general history books which finds a major upturn in European economic life in the tenth century.

At that period Viking, Magyar, and Moorish attacks ceased, the population went up, and agricultural output started to rise. The precise connections among these events are unclear, but what our authorities are saying is that from this time on there was always a positive rate of growth, however low. By definition it kept ahead of the population growth thereafter evident in European history. A turbulent political and economic setting does not prevent growth from occurring, does not destroy it when in motion, yet holds it to a permanently low rate. Growth like this asks too much of the usual models. It happens too gradually and over too long a span. Very low growth rates would have been vulnerable to shocks and setbacks. What could have produced such a slow-moving, robust equilibrium for so long in such an unstable environment? Surely the answer has to be a gradual lifting of restrictions on a tendency for growth that was already present, not some hypothesized breakthrough or take-off.

The question arises at this point whether Europe can be treated as a single economic system. Different levels of development across the continent are obvious at any date we care to choose. There was always a big divide between eastern and western Europe. Even so, a European culture was definable. There was greater similarity within Europe than between any part of it and places outside. There was plenty of exchange among the constituent regions. The location of the most advanced region, or country, varied from time to time, but this was change only within a system which continually levelled up and can for our purposes be treated as a unity.[13]

Tackling each country in Europe separately would not give us the same chance of coming up with an explanation of growth. The emergent nation-states were too alike in fundamentals, and too good at imitating one another, too affected by the same stimuli, for that particular comparative approach to be adequate. It cannot give a comprehensive view of the circumstances under which growth may emerge. A broader comparison is needed, because, as Marshall Hodgson wrote, 'one cannot simply look at the combination of conditions that happened to occur in western Europe, and assert that only this could have led to any sort of major acceleration of productivity and innovation'.[14]

Hodgson was convinced that the major Eurasian civilizations had advanced together, each building a similar stock of knowledge and productive techniques. That was his impression of the *very* long term. His strategic position as an Islamicist enabled him to spot that there had been a common evolution (which we might call *extensive* growth) across the great societies, a trend underlying the turning of dynastic cycles. He thus saw economic history as a slow, linked, forward drift, not a jolt out of ageless stagnation. Advanced societies had replaced archaic societies and there was more to come.[15] In the early modern period Europe merely happened to run ahead of its peers. The expansion of Europe's industrial sector, when it came, was however on so grand a scale that it seemed even to Hodgson to dwarf all previous history. If we accept this formulation we are embracing *ex post* history with a vengeance, and allowing industrialism to obscure the evidence of earlier changes which we would perceive if we looked at the periods we are interested in more appropriately, that is, *ex ante*. Western uniqueness is easy to credit if the Sung are forgotten; or if

Tokugawa growth is forgotten simply because, after Meiji, Western *industrialism* did clasp Japan (or was it the other way round?).

Despite resistance on the part of some historians, a good general explanation is inherently preferable to an explanation of a single instance. We should accordingly look to see what unites the three cases we have now mentioned. At first sight the appropriate method would be to try to isolate a common denominator among forces that may appear to have pushed these economies into growth. But isolating such a variable in the case of the industrial revolution has not been successful and we need not expect to succeed where the data are even less precise.

Fortunately the assumption that we need to find a positive factor at all is redundant. We do not know that one existed. To hypothesize its existence violates the principle of Occam's Razor; it introduces an unnecessary complication, a phlogiston of the economy. There was an exchange between C. E. M. Joad and a theologian in which the latter taunted Joad that a philosopher is like a blind man in a dark room looking for a black cat. Joad retorted that the theologian is all those things too—looking for a black cat that is not there. A propulsive force may be another such cat.

Instead of thinking of growth as an aberration, let us try thinking of it as the norm. Consider how many individuals in every population of any size have managed to demonstrate, through all the gaps in the record, that they did want to better their lot. Entrepreneurial tendencies seem to have been widespread and so does a delight in technical tinkering, however much some societies may have disparaged and repressed these things (especially among women). Once we take the position that initiative was widespread, yet only occasionally produced a whole growing economy, our interest ought to shift from hypothetical push forces to whatever forces blocked growth, or (more identifiably) reversed it when it did begin to sprout. We shall look for these in the histories of China, India, and the Middle East. The final item on the agenda will be to investigate the circumstances in which, in the successful cases, the repressive or suppressive forces were eroded or cancelled themselves out.

This takes a universalist (not a universal) attitude to humanity's talents, furthered by a postulate which is long-term and probabilistic. What it says is that motives, talent, and energy of kinds likely to facilitate economic growth are widespread. It does not say that everyone has them or that all societies express them equally, repression apart. Few historians ever state explicitly what their assumptions are in this regard, but one can find more directness in the social sciences. For instance, the sociologist Michael Mann writes: 'I make two assumptions which I will in no way justify here: that mankind is restless and greedy for more of the good things of life, and that essentially this is a quest for greater material rewards.'[16]

The economist G. L. S. Shackle states that: 'my own assumption is that mankind's originative powers are limitless in the number and diversity of what they can bring into being in thought, and that this work of imagination is an uncaused cause, that its productions can be in some respects *ex nihilo*.'[17] Like Shackle I take it that this is demonstrated by the artistic, intellectual, commercial, and technical achievements of an uncountable number of people across the earth throughout recorded history. That it was not only men is also sufficiently obvious. There is a submerged part of women's history here, as a study of the large contribution by wives and sisters to creative acts has shown.[18] History has tended to give husbands and brothers the credit.

A sense of restless curiosity is a mark of the species as a whole. To convert this into something practical was often desperately hard, but it took only a small proportion of individuals to do so. The history of ideas shows that new methods have often expanded by diffusion, but that time and time again new ideas have come up too, or old ones have been rediscovered, by people of all sorts, conditions, localities, and eras. The implications are profound. As the world historian W. H. McNeill observes, 'the assumption of uniformity in the range of human behavior has more to recommend it than any assertion of systematic differences between civilized and uncivilized, rational and non-rational, Western and non-Western modes of conduct'.[19]

Nevertheless, we do not have to accept a so-called neoclassical maximizing postulate. (Many of the ideas criticized as 'neoclassical' are not purely neoclassical at all but are common to more than one school of economic thought.) There is no need to believe that everyone has been a profit maximizer, or eager for scientific speculation or technical experiment, or shared any absolutely universal attribute, not even the curiosity that was so common. All we need is to respect that these were frequent enough to add up to a widespread tendency to strive.

Hence many people will try, *ceteris paribus*, to reduce their poverty. Some will actively endeavour to get rich. They will truck and barter. They will develop skills in making tools and gadgets. At its least elevated, humanity will appear in the guise of greedy tinkerers, but certain people will transcend that grubby and useful role. They are the ones who will try to understand the phenomena of nature. A few of these will go on to convert their knowledge into new ways of scientific thought, and others to convert that science into practice. This is an undertone heard throughout history, not the creation of one society in one age alone.

The position is not particularly stringent. It does not urge the existence of a timeless capitalist rationality, checked only by the state, along lines that have been critized as 'apologia for capitalism'.[20] The postulated behaviour is more plastic than this. To avoid facile labelling as an apologist for anything, of the kind arising from what a Hungarian described to me as 'hermeneutical suspicion', I am adopting only the relatively weak version of human behaviour outlined. Too many disputes in this subject proceed by *non sequitur*. As Hume said, 'should' statements cannot be derived from 'is' statements, and it is tendentious to imply that the holder of any given view about what *happened* in history necessarily holds a particular view as to whether or not this was the result of what would be *desirable* policy today.

Judgement on what really did impede the growth tendency can be reserved until later chapters, including on whether or not it was the action or inaction of governments (meaning not 'the' state in the abstract, but particular governments that actually existed). For the moment we need only refer once more to the contrary general principle, rent-seeking, a problem essentially of institutionalized free-riding. The check lies somewhere here. Perhaps we should however agree with Godelier at his most severe when he writes about general principles that, 'when we state that this principle is a universal one we merely record a fact which, as such, *explains nothing* about the multiple content of human activity or the reasons for the rise and fall, in the course of history, of various economic and social systems'.[21] Neither growth propensity nor rent-seeking has enough content to tell us exactly how particular passages of history turned out; but once we envisage history as the record of economies constantly dashed by the one against the rock of the other, we do have an organizing device.

The growth principle attributes economic purpose to some in any large population, at whatever date, of whatever creed, ethnicity, or colour, and of both genders. It does not assert an equality of behaviours across these categories (though the differences observed may be the effect of differential upbringing and constraints), merely that all conditions of humanity are represented in the canons of invention and, more to the point, innovation. I would add, too, that so are people of any age (I am getting older). Half the one hundred top American scientists picked out by *Science Digest* in 1985 were over 40 years old.

A powerful objection to the universalism implied here might perhaps be read into Adda Bozeman's immensely knowledgeable *The Future of Law in a Multicultural World*.[22] Her primary interest is rather different, but one may take note of the dust-jacket claim that 'this brilliant book should have a sobering effect on anyone who is trapped in the cage of assuming that universalized rhetoric implies universalized conduct'. Bozeman's interpretation is that Europeans alone escaped, by virtue of Greek thought, from the restrictions which came to bind initially progressive non-Western societies. Beyond the Western world, philosophies came to dominate which emphasized there is nothing new under the sun. Under them there was seemingly no chance of 'rational' behaviour. Perhaps the quick rejoinder is that material growth is a baser goal, easier to agree about than more symbolic and other-worldly matters, and is in practice compatible with a range of abstract philosophies just as it is with a range of modern political programmes.

Effective behaviour certainly varied from society to society and period to period. The position here is that the varying weight of negative forces pressing down on the initiative and ingenuity of the individual has more to do with these differences than differences in positive effort. Different societies have encouraged or discouraged innovation in very diverse ways. Obviously not everyone had even remotely the same chance of self-expression. Most people in history have had very little such opportunity. I heard the entertainer, Sammy Davis Jr., asked what his (golf) handicap was, and he replied, 'I'm a one-eyed black Jew!' One can only weep for humanity's tendency to waste talent, for the ruthless historical conditioning of human potential. Yet raw talent *is* widely distributed, as is shown by the fact that its light has broken through in enough places to make illumination always seem possible.

Our restricted maximizing principle may seem to reduce people to puppets of want and therefore be inadequate for coping with the confused richness of historical action. Part of the answer to such a charge would be that it is precisely that part of action which is driven by want, or by the avoidance of want, that we intend to discuss. Even so, the approach may still seem to deposit finer variables like culture far enough outside the count to invite the sort of attack on 'economism' recently launched by Clifford Geertz.[23] If so, some clarification is needed. It may be useful to decide what are the minimum conditions needed for an economy to operate, to gauge just how simple our assumptions may be made and still have reason on their side. Are economies largely self-generating, self-referring systems, or are they intelligible only as part of cultures—or in even more advanced vein than that of the cultural anthropologist, are they intelligible only semiotically as reflections of systems of symbols underlying the cultures themselves?

Economism, as Geertz stigmatizes it, comes in two forms. First there is the structuralist, Marxian, mode-of-production version, and second there is the neoclassical version. From the standpoint of a cultural anthropologist these are brothers under the skin. Class analysis and market analysis both seem to shut cultural (and other) considerations out in the cold. Their unifying principle, Geertz states with irony, is that, 'deep down, culture is shallow; society runs on the energies of want'.[24] In the Marxian conspiracy theory of human action, culture is translated as obfuscating ideology. Neoclassicists reportedly shrug it off as collective illusion. Either dismissal could seem to be implicit in my assumption of a driving propensity for material advance.

The conflict is however not so stark. Economies and cultures interact. Assertions that one is paramount, the other its creature, are not to be made lightly. The choice between studying the one or studying the other is not a matter of personal taste or intellectual tradition. Since the two strands influence one another, the choice must depend on reasoned hypotheses about their relative stability over whatever period has been selected for analysis.[25] Does the economy mould itself more to the requirements of the culture, or does culture adjust more to the imperatives of the market? Which reacts more and modifies the other? Advocates of culturism or cultural explanations of history and anthropology are nowadays inclined to take the strong position that culture is what drives the system, modifying economic action and itself remaining relatively immune to modification by the economy. (This may have its origins in a natural reaction against the imperialism of economics, both Marxian and neoclassical. Economists tend rather glibly to take the view that economic considerations come first.) Although cultural preferences do demonstrably affect the intensity and shape the face of economic action, I see no reason to grant them priority. This amounts to arguing that at the fundamental level want and desire do drive, or do drive enough to make this a good starting-point, that culture is vital for form but does not replace substance.

The question of logical priority has been raised in more pertinent form by Alexander Field.[26] His argument is that for an economy to operate at least two prerequisites must be met. These are the existence of rules, since it is not clear that the market can generate and enforce the rules needed for its own functioning, and the existence of language, without which no exchange can presumably take place. But one could push this reasoning back and back, to a rule which states only that rules will be formed—and a rule of that generality would have no operational significance. If we choose to start with the economy we are entitled to explain economic action in its own terms and not obliged to start with the prior, exogenous formation of a set of rules.

Language, too, is not indispensable. The occurrence of 'silent trade' shows this, where merchants left goods on foreign beaches to be selected by unknown natives, to be paid for in local goods set out in return. The English, discovering Tahiti in 1767, found the Tahitians ' "appeared cheerful and talkt a great dale but non of us could understand them, but to pleas them we all seemd merry . . ." '.[27] Further, ' "we made all the friendly signs that we could think of, and showed them several trinkets . . . we made signs to them, to bring of Hogs, Fowls and fruit . . . the method we took to make them Understand what we wanted was this, some of the men Grunted and Cryd lyke a Hogg then pointed to the shore. . . ." ' It worked, but a language of hand-waving and imitated animal noises (which in any case would hardly describe the fruit) is language only by courtesy.

Many languages—pidgins, which by definition have no native speakers—have been manufactured on the ground, to fill the needs of new trading circumstances like the one above. Language is immensely useful but scarcely indispensable, and as part of culture it is in any case susceptible to manipulation at the hands of economic behaviour. There is therefore nothing awry with relegating cultural variables in historical or anthropological analysis, unless they can be shown in the cases under review to manipulate economic activity more than the reverse. Decorate it though they may, cultural features are not likely to *prevent* effort driven by want.

Culture's role is more certain in forming preferences than in creating or blocking the impulse to acquire. McPherson's criticism of the treatment of want formation by economists attacks what he portrays as the mean-spirited conception of *Homo economicus* where preferences are taken as given.[28] They are, he says, culturally moulded. Agreed, an ironclad assumption of taste as a 'given' may be a lapse, but the matter we are concerned with is the impulse to acquire more of *something* material, the exact cultural origin or decorative form of which is secondary. Like R. M. Adams in his review of ancient trade, I see no absolute distinction between ancient and modern behaviour in this respect, only differences in the constraints on action, some of which may perhaps be cultural.[29] Adams notes that anthropologists and others have too much deprecated the extent of entrepreneurial behaviour in ancient society. Trade, as he says, has been a recurrent agent of change.

Want and greed are mediated by many things, notably politics. In the pre-modern world, as now, politics meant rent-seeking or pie-slicing behaviour, the carving up of what had already been produced by force, or by the threat of force however cleverly concealed in institutional arrangements. We have already characterized economic history as a tug of war between growth propensity and rent-seeking. Another useful way of looking at it is to look at the way these propensities have switched economies between *extensive* growth and *intensive* growth. Thinking in terms of switches implies that, when *intensive* growth did appear, energies were being redirected or intensified rather than conjured up out of nothing, which is consistent with the emergence of these episodes out of an already-expanding matrix of *extensive* growth. Switching-in takes place when the growth propensity overwhelms the rent-seeking propensity, switching-out when the reverse occurs. Political variables accordingly play a large part in events. This is not quite a war between economics and politics, but between economics and the wrong sort of politics. Cultural variables, comparatively speaking, act out a subsidiary role by filtering economic forces into the costume of the time and place.

The potential for growth as we have crudely described it looks at first sight like unexpressed demand in an economic model. For practical purposes, if it is unexpressed it does not exist. If it is expressed, then it must exist. What independent measure can there be of an unexpressed potential? The answer is that it is hard to find one. But the reason for this is not that the argument short-circuits itself—that we can only detect potential when it has expressed itself. The reason is that historical records of the existence of the relevant type of human capital, people with innovative drive, are usually hard to find. Yet as we approach the present the potential begins to manifest itself, at least in the proxy form of a class of educated, literate people. For example, such individuals were present in

eighteenth-century Scotland and Sweden in numbers quite out
of proportion to the initial limited achievement of rising living
standards there.[30]

One should not altogether equate education or literacy with
a drive for wealth. Nevertheless there is a correlation between
the two, the link probably being that education teaches not
only the subject at hand but the more general concept that new
skills may be formally learned. It is not to be doubted that the
resource represented by educated Scots and Swedes reflected a
genuine propensity for growth which had something to do with
the ability of their countries to catch up with western Europe's
leaders, as well as with the performances of the countries to
which so many of them emigrated. Identifiable talent, then, is
one measure of potential. Another may be the number of titles
of books published. As long as the books address practical
matters, this quantifies part of the stock of knowledge. The
accumulation of titles can definitely be measured, as with
agricultural works in early modern England or the equivalent
Nong Shu treatises in China beginning much earlier than that.
Another measure, though of more limited application, may be
the number of patents registered.

Inducement models, like this one with its ready assumption
that talent will out, are said to be easy to construct but flawed
because they assume a response. Demand for an invention does
not guarantee its discovery, let alone its adoption. If a response
were automatic, everywhere might have been developed,
always. The model is however protected by its *ceteris paribus*
clause. This directs us to investigate just what it was that
violated the condition of 'other things being equal'. We need
an alternative history. The result may be only a gestalt: do you
see the white picture or the black one, the forces for growth or
those against it? The value of the approach will lie in its
generality, whether it can link together and illuminate more
episodes of growth than the hypothesis of a novel push force has
managed to do.

A particular doubt may arise about the expression of this
responsiveness because of what we have been told by the
'substantivist' school, which asserts the uniqueness of cultures
and the lack of price-responsive markets in the pre-modern
world. These opinions are associated among social scientists

with the work of Karl Polanyi and among ancient historians with the writings of Moses Finley. There are misconceptions here about the limits to 'rational' economic behaviour both in the ancient world and in non-European cultures.[31] Dampened growth is not itself evidence that behavioural impulses among the ancients were 'irrational' and thereby different from those of modern people, or that price-forming markets did not exist (though factor markets were very much more limited). This has been amply demonstrated by critics of Polanyi and Finley, such as Gunderson and Frederiksen. Even Roman senators can be shown not to have been so devoid of commercial sense that they tried to maximize only status instead of income. What was different about the ancient world was the weight of the depressants on *intensive* growth, pushing energies back down into *extensive* growth. Finley's 'status-based model is not wholly false', Frederiksen somewhat savagely concludes, 'but it is not a substitute for economic history'.[32]

As Max Weber wrote, 'the notion that our rationalistic and capitalistic age is characterized by a stronger economic interest than other periods is childish; the moving spirits of modern capitalism are not possessed of a stronger economic impulse than, for example, an oriental trader'.[33] For Weber the issue was how a general impulse was rationalized into 'capitalism' rather than intermittently unchained in more ordinary, less ideological, forms of economic energy. Our concern here, however, is with 'ordinary' *intensive* growth and that has never been the sole prerogative of capitalist societies.

Overcoming the Primal Forces

THREE

Intimations of Ancient Growth

The assertion predominates that economic growth could never have happened outside Europe, and not there until relatively recent centuries. Caglar Keyder, for example, dismisses the 'false claim that the periphery could have made it'.[1] He insists that the Asian Mode of Production forbade all hope of endogenous change. In India, although a few nationalist historians would have it otherwise, there was, according to Tapan Raychaudhuri, 'no distant announcement of industrial revolution'.[2] Most ancient historians likewise insist that there was a total lack of promise in the classical world. The occasional scholar who raises the possibility of early growth runs the risk of derision.

In a review of Finley's *The Ancient World*, M. W. Frederiksen protests that 'Finley even suggests that western capitalism ought to have appeared in the ancient world, and therefore our problem is to identify the value-system that prevented it appearing. That is to take the doctrine of economic man very seriously indeed.'[3] The doctrine certainly does deserve to be taken seriously. Because something does not appear to have happened does not mean that it could not happen. Contrary to Frederiksen, this proposition need not amount to rolling all history into one in a way that disarms enquiry. What it does is indicate the need to enquire closely into the nature of the constraints on change. Although Finley's particular assumption that these must have lain in the ancient system of values is open to dispute, this enquiry will be one of our tasks.

As influential an economist as Keynes took a dim view of the contribution, not to mention the economic prospects, of most historical periods. He thought that there had been no progress in living standards until the sixteenth or seventeenth centuries AD, merely a few oscillations. 'Almost everything which really matters and which the world possessed at the commencement of the modern age,' he stated, 'was already known to man at the dawn of history.'[4] The same domesticated crops and stock, major implements like the plough and wheel and ships' sails, textiles, leather, bricks, pottery, several metals including iron, and banking, statecraft, mathematics, astronomy, and religion, all these things had been invented in some unknowably ancient time, in the Garden of Eden maybe. Once invented, seemingly, that was that. It is as if humanity were unable to improve its technical or intellectual equipment from the Fall until three or four centuries ago.

Keynes's list of completed innovations is a formidable one which raises more problems than it solves. How would we set about explaining, firstly, his postulated early (and non-European) phase of remarkable fertility? How would we account for the interminable age in which he thought nothing of note was added to the stock of science, technology, or human institutions? How would we explain the thunderous breaking of the log-jam in sixteenth-century Europe?

Keynes himself offered no systematic explanation of any of the phase transitions or of the forces that supposedly inhibited change during his vast middle period. Looking for those forces would be pointless because the chronology is utterly misleading, though we may note one attempt to give historical structure to the long empty span. Gerhard Lenski claims that the rate of technical change did fall between the third millenium BC and the industrial revolution.[5] This is misleading too, but it does have the merit of being couched in terms of changing rates of change rather than denying all change. Furthermore, Lenski does advance a plausible reason—that the more elaborate aristocratic empires first founded in the Middle East during the third millenium BC taxed away the crucial investment surplus from the populace for consumption by the rulers.

Keynes implicitly looked on technical change as necessary and sufficient for growth. Technical change in the civilian sector is certainly likely to raise total income, and so produce *extensive* growth, but it is neither necessary for *intensive* growth (which may be obtained by better organization) nor sufficient (the gains may be offset by other factors, such as population growth). The nexus between technology and economic growth is not particularly strong. If the new economic history has taught us anything it is that no individual invention, not the railway, not steam, ever transforms a whole economy. Our concern here with early evidence of technical innovation has a less ambitious purpose: to demonstrate that a pressure for growth did constantly rumble in the corners of history and prehistory.

The prolonged period of inaction protrayed by Keynes is a polar view of technological history. This type of analysis envisages 'the lands of "perpetual dawn" in the East, whose societies, after an initial outburst of creativity, had remained motionless and frozen for millenia'. That was how it was put by Sinai in a book on modernization published in 1964, a year when Western confidence still ran high. No Asian society had produced its own Renaissance, Reformation, or Enlightenment, none, he declared, had 'ever known what spring is . . .'.[6]

Others see a rather shorter gap during which the Asian and Middle Eastern cultures remained slumbering until, like some resentful Rip van Winkle, they were prodded into life by an upstart Europe. 'Asian economies had virtually stagnated from 500 B.C. to 1500 A.D.,' declares Raymond Crotty, 'but Europe during that period had emerged from a barbaric wilderness and in 1500 A.D. was poised to make its capitalist culture dominant world-wide.'[7] A much less extreme version was presented by Lacoste in 1966. He observed that 'in spite of past wealth and prestige such [non-Western] countries remained relatively static, and, after a series of often painful convulsions, they appear to have entered a phase of slumber towards the end of the Middle Ages'.[8] With some reservations about how deep the slumber really was, this describes the history with which we are concerned, in which economic and technical leadership has repeatedly changed and is not correctly described in those formulations which treat all significant development as waiting on modern centuries and the rise of Europe.

To adopt such a position seems to rob European history of its genuine achievement, as must, so Perry Anderson has claimed, the Marxist insistence that Feudalism existed everywhere in the world. After all, he insists, only in Europe did industrial capitalism emerge, and to proclaim a uniform sequence in history denies this a unique origin. 'All privilege to Western development is thereby held to disappear, in the multiform process of a world history secretly single from the start.'[9] The distinction we make is that, whereas 'industrial capitalism' may have been the European contribution, *intensive* growth was not restricted to Europe.

There is a wealth of evidence of early technical invention. There was even some innovation. We need to consider this precisely because it does not usually seem to have stimulated growth. What were the conditions that could repeatedly bring invention (and some innovation) into being, yet prevent society from capitalizing on it?

During the latter part of the supposed stagnation in the East, the great technology transfers of the Arab Agricultural Revolution brought Indian crops as far west as Spain, repeated diffusions of earlier and earlier ripening strains of rice took place in China and Japan, and the Columbian Exchange meant that New World crops fed into the farming systems of China, Africa, and Europe. All were massive examples of change. Episodes like these, superimposed on slower diffusions, involved many different hearths of invention or discovery. They can be matched in the record of industrial methods. This should not surprise us because technical creativity was playful, not necessarily deliberate, 'more like love than purpose' as the metallurgist and historian of science, C. S. Smith, concludes.[10] 'Discovery is art, not logic,' says Smith, 'Nearly everyone believes, falsely, that technology is applied science', but the spark of technique comes from aesthetics, at any rate in the history and prehistory of casting metals. In short, for many people it is fun and there were always people tempted by fun. This makes technical invention, even innovation, a much more likely general tendency than if it had relied on revealed demand, special investments, or ordered science.

There are innumerable instances of technical change, many of multiple discovery. New archaeological finds are constantly elaborating the record of ingenuity. To take a few examples almost at random, copper was smelted before 4000 BC, its use radiating from the Near East and south-eastern Europe, and was probably discovered independently in China or South-East Asia, in sub-Saharan Africa before the Christian era, in North

America before 3000 BC, and again independently in Peru in AD 800.[11] In the classical world, methods of producing wine, glass, olive oil, pottery, and iron were all improved and slowly diffused after 450 BC. Roman villas were heated by hypocausts. Roman Gaul had a mechanical reaper pushed, not pulled, by horses. Plenty of Roman arches, some carrying aqueducts, survive in good condition today. In north-western Europe even the so-called barbarians of the period found better ways to make barrels, trousers, shirts, stockings, laced boots, and the fibulae which were the precursors of safety-pins. New products such as soft soap and wagons were invented.[12] Technologically slow-moving by our standards the world may have been, but it was not static.

At the risk of implying, wrongly, that economic growth depended on technical advance, we must consider closely why invention and innovation were slow. That the classical world, for example, really lacked operating markets and therefore missed out on competition was not the case and change at some rate is therefore to be anticipated. That ancient society was not 'capitalist' is, so to speak, a red herring. Even those substantivists who wish to argue that institutions and goals were fundamentally different in the pre-modern world concede that by the fifth or fourth century BC there was both national and international trade, a shrinking farm sector, and expanding industries with some competing factories (manufactories) producing for export. Altogether this was an economy with many of the features subsequently found in late medieval Europe. 'As far as I am concerned,' to quote the ranking economic historian of Rome, Rostovtzeff, 'the difference between the economic life of this period and that of the modern world is only quantitative, not qualitative.'[13]

Nevertheless, one cannot escape from the fact that by the standards of the developed world in recent centuries, technical and economic change were agonizingly slow. The many and various reasons for this which have been put forward by classical historians are nicely collected and reviewed by John Oleson at the end of his own study of hydraulic devices, under the subheading, 'Reassessing Classical Technology'.[14] His essay is more comprehensive than any available for the later pre-modern Asian empires with which we will be more specifically concerned and is therefore a better place to raise the general issues. We will however leave aside Oleson's section entitled 'The Potential for an Industrial Revolution in Antiquity', since the direct entry to the world of steel, steam-engines, and petrol engines to which he refers would have been complete fantasy. The possibility of growth based on actual technical changes cannot however be ignored on that account.

Before examining the explanations which Oleson has assembled, we should note that his secondary sources are seldom explicitly comparative in approach. When they do make comparisons these tend to be with medieval Europe or the industrial revolution, as if no other phases and no non-Western society could be illuminating. His authorities also exhibit a trait, common among specialists, of accepting that some feature specific to their period and place—say, the philosophical limitations of Greek science—offers the answer to what is really a general question. Culturally specific answers of the 'weak Greek science' variety are unlikely to be satisfactory when the question really falls into the class, 'what were the impediments to technical change in pre-modern economies?' They refer to regional and temporal correlates and not necessarily to fundamentals, for which a broad comparative approach is indispensable.

The obvious gaps in classical technology included a neglect of wind-power and steam-power and more surprisingly the limited refinement and diffusion of devices that had already been produced in an early form. These were the water-mill, mechanical reaper, crank, sailing-gear, and harness for horses. Recent research makes it plain that most technical 'inventions' of this type are in reality accumulations of refinements supplied by diverse hands; if the 'Eureka effect' occurs, it is less likely to deliver a final product into waiting hands than to signal an exciting solution to part of the problem. The lack of follow-up on so many embryonic devices in classical times suggests that, as we would expect, the total volume of inventive activity was low.

The explanations offered for the lapses of the period, the complete absence of some devices and the neglect of others, are various. They often amount to little more than lists of supposed disabilities of the environment of the day. One favourite is the availability of slave labour, but this equates abhorrence of the institution with the belief that it must have been inefficient, a position no economic historian of the modern period would take after the massive investigations which have been made of the profitability of slavery in the American South. The more pertinent points made in Oleson's sources are that a supply of slaves drove down the price of wage labour, with the result that the market for goods was very restricted. Certainly the market was very small, but would this necessarily have dissuaded efforts to *reduce* production costs? In any case, slavery was not a universal feature of the pre-modern world and cannot explain a general innovative sluggishness. The related argument that Greek and Roman élites so disdained manual work that they did not concern themselves with labour-saving innovations fails when we learn that there were after all changes of that sort, so that someone must have taken an interest.

Much is made of scarcity in the Mediterranean basin of sources of energy and natural resources, notably wood, coupled with high costs of transporting these commodities. High shipping costs, the result themselves of limited technical change in communications and transport, are of course part of what is to be explained and ought not to be advanced as their own explanation. The argument in any case ignores the possibility of using resources like coal on the spot and transporting instead the lighter and more valuable finished goods; it ignores the role of trade as a substitute for resources. No doubt resource scarcities raised costs, but they cannot be invoked as a cause of technical backwardness since, *ceteris paribus*, high prices for energy and raw materials would inspire the invention of substitutes.

Neither do other lacunae mentioned by Oleson provide convincing explanations of backwardness. The absences of patent law and limited liability were not crucial: later industrialization has not always depended on them. Economic growth has certainly not done so.

A recurrent theme, very widely espoused, is that the values and attitudes of the ancient world were inimical to growth. One claim is that there was a general cultural conservatism; but if such an attitude really existed it could probably be explained, like the characteristic risk aversion of poor peasants, as a function of prevailing economic constraints. It is unlikely to have been an independent cause of backwardness. A more specialized version of this argument is that advance was barred by the lack of an experimental tradition in classical science, reinforced by the fact that what passed for education was typically a training in rhetoric. In reality literacy and record-keeping were widespread by comparison with some parts of the world in quite recent years.

Underlying the argument is the unquestioned assumption that natural science was vital to the British industrial revolution, that therefore industrialization could not have taken place without it, and of course implicitly that growth takes the industrial form. At base the position is that 'the steam-engine owed more to science than science owed to the steam-engine'. This is contrary to modern views on eighteenth-century industrialization, in which, although formal science was not unimportant in a few industries, many technical changes took place that rested on no clear scientific basis. A lack of experimental science is insufficient to explain the generally low rate of technical advance in the classical world.

Another theme among the arguments that see inappropriate values as the key to backwardness is the claim that pre-Christian animism forbade manipulating the natural world for human ends, forbade, that is, striving for 'Faustian mastery' over nature. The corollary supposed is that without such a growth ethic there could be no mastery, and without mastery there could be no growth. It is fashionable to see the use and abuse of the environment and natural resources as results of Christianity's poisoned ethical chalice. This is a slippery argument which fails to explain a number of points. It fails to account for the long period in the history of Christian Europe when, despite the alleged attitudes, there was little growth. It fails to take into account the deforestation and soil erosion that did take place so extensively in pre-Christian and non-Christian societies, including those of the classical world, where no such ethic supposedly prevailed.

The assumption that there is something preternaturally malign about Christian attitudes to nature is an aberrant opinion of the 1960s and 1970s. It has more to do with the self-abnegation of Western intellectuals than with real historical differences between cultures or religions. The evidence tends to be philosophical statements in the Christian literature rather than comparative data on how Christian and other societies' actually treated the environment. As usual with literary evidence there is a severe sampling problem. In other words we almost never know how many people shared the opinions expressed and we never know what proportion acted on their beliefs.

The supposedly hard evidence adduced to demonstrate a special European or Western attitude towards manipulating Nature usually consists of the extinction dates for birds and animals in Europe's overseas empires and the island stepping-stones *en route* to them. These dates come from purely Western sources, which do not tell us what the extinction rate had been at the hands of non-Western, pre-Christian, peoples. Neither do they tell us what was the natural rate of extinction. Proper research design requires controls for these variables because the relevant figure is not the total rate of extinction but the excess contributed by 'Christian' actions.

Where comparative data do survive, for example from pre-colonial Hawaii and Henderson Island in the South Pacific, they tell a different story.[15] They reveal a previous extinction of birds at a level above any likely natural rate. Primitive farming typically expanded at the expense of deforestation, soil erosion, and pest eruptions, and because of poor technology and low densities of the human population it tended to use land and resources freely. Heavy use was not confined to large populations. The idea that there is something specifically Christian or European about this is absurd. The only peculiarly Western aspect of 'species-ism' is the tendency to bemoan it nowadays. Pre-modern societies lacked both the resources created by economic growth and the moral will to repair the damage they caused. Hunting societies probably brought about the 'Pleistocene Overkill' with its extinction of the mega-fauna. Poor peasants did not set aside nature reserves. There is no reason to think that the absence of the 'Faustian mastery' supposedly inculcated by Christian values meant that classical societies or any others treated the environment tenderly, and that it was this restraint that meant they missed their chances of economic growth.

Technical change, definitely, was not altogether forgone by the classical world. There were achievements in metallurgy, architecture (including waterproof cement and cranes able to lift huge weights), hydraulics, transportation (where draft oxen were substituted for coolie power), and warfare (notably the construction of siege and defence devices including projectiles capable of destroying at a distance). The projectiles depended on advanced calculations. There was even a rudimentary factory system in the pottery and glassware industries. Automata were made, and although they were toys, so were those in eighteenth-century Europe. In both places they testify to mechanical dexterity and control, including an understanding of feedback mechanisms like valves.

Rather than trying to explain the technical backwardness of the ancient societies which after all had this degree of mechanization, we should be trying to account for the induced innovation bias of the technologies that did develop. Where needs were thought to be greatest and the interests of the powerful were engaged, striking results were obtained. Progress was concentrated in the realms of war and the production of luxury goods. It was also marked in hydraulics, where Oleson notes successful responses to felt needs for pumps to irrigate crops, keep ships afloat, keep mines dry and working, and keep towns supplied with potable water (over those superb aqueducts).

Where the small élite with wealth and power was interested, respectable advances were thus made. The difficulty lay in creating enough new technology to bring the supply price of manufactures down far enough to tap what was otherwise a very restricted market. As in all poor societies, the 'mass' market was so small that the élite continued to ignore it in favour of investing in land or the self-advertising public works associated in Rome with political position.

The nub of the matter was the difficulty of shifting the attention of potential investors from rent-seeking activities to the preliminary investments needed to serve what was largely a potential rather than an actual market. To that degree the problem was a rather standard one. Failure was not a philosophical failure, nor yet a mark of philosophical merit (through the supposed absence of the Christian belief that nature was meant for man). It was not a resource failure, nor a sign that ancient society did not live by the laws of economics⸺ rather the reverse. The extent of the technical innovation that did take place shows that this was in no way forbidden by some absolute feature of the classical world, merely that innovation responded to the existing structure of incentives.

Chinese and Arab technological experience was much the same. Indeed, any idea that technical achievement eluded either the ancient world or non-European cultures is quite wrong. This can be realized in a moment's contemplation of the surviving monuments of prehistory, though their funerary, defensive, and martial biases are also obvious. Almost random examples will illustrate the record. Both India, in the Delhi pillar of the fourth century AD, and Europe, as shown by the cannon that Richard II installed in the Tower of London, produced iron which was corrosion-resistant. By the twelfth century exceptionally sharp and strong steel was used throughout the Islamic world.[16] This 'Damascus' steel was made in India, the very best blades, shields, and armour being forged in Iran. Yet even these metallurgical triumphs were latecomers on the world scene. As early as 470 BC, Greek colonists at Akragas in Sicily had been using iron reinforcing members 15 feet long and 5 × 12 inches in cross-section. They would have had no *technical* difficulty in making steam-engines or other heavy machinery, so J. E. Gordon tells us in his engaging book on materials science.[17]

Keynes's uncompromising view of a world for so long technically and economically unchanging utterly fails to square with the historical record. His was a 'Western Civ.' conception of history. There was no room in it for the profound changes being made in China nor for the evidence of a progressive drift of ideas from China right across Eurasia, until at length they were embodied in the techniques of the red-haired barbarians of Europe. Nor did Keynes find room for the plentiful evidence of multiple discoveries in India, Iran, and many parts of the Islamic Middle East, of which the news slowly swirled and diffused among all these cultures (China itself was greatly affected by ideas brought by Buddhists from India). The Old World, as Lynn White remarks, was 'a more unified realm of discourse than we have been prepared to admit'.[18]

To cite just one example of the complex historical geography of early science and technology, Derek Price reported the finding, in the wreck of a ship from Rhodes or Cos lost off a southern Greek island in the first century BC, of the Antikythera mechanism. This is a box with dials and an inscription on the outside, and complicated gear wheels inside.[19] It must have looked like a well-made eighteenth-century clock, Price tells us. The purpose would have been to mechanize astronomical cycles. This was a clockwork computer and others like it are known from scattered parts of the Islamic world, China, and India. Medieval Arab devices show every sign of deriving from the Antikythera, and similar devices were transmitted from the Arab world to medieval Europe, where they provided part of the background lore used in making other inventions in clockwork. Thus there was a diffusionist tradition in technical history, which is not however to deny the matching history of independent discoveries.

Striking technical advances of many kinds had sprung from many hearths of invention. Many were squandered on what amounted to little more than arms races which allowed this or that ingenious people to draw ahead and subdue its neighbours, but the instability of which meant that no one stayed top dog for ever. In other words the effects were redistributive, after a fashion, permitting the seeking of rents through plunder and conquest, but lacking a systematic upward effect on incomes. Additionally, for all the shining peaks, the plains between discoveries were bare and wide. Between one achievement and the next, in the absence of records to refer to or enough scientific base to build on, lay empty centuries, very long lags indeed.

The most notorious, or at least the most often cited, regression of technical level is the example of central heating in Britain. The inhabitants of miserably unheated English houses go today to look at the remains of underfloor hypocausts at the sites of Roman villas open to the public. They do so, for instance, at Bignor in Sussex, which has been a place of historical pilgrimage since it was excavated and opened in 1815, in which year the astonishing total of almost a thousand families visited it. Yet in the 1980s, half of English homes still lack proper central heating. Expressed like this, as it usually is, the example is not a particularly good one. Central heating was a distinct possibility in the nineteenth-century country houses that compared with Roman villas; even the orangeries were heated. For the rest, relative prices determine the matter. There was a genuine regression of technique, but it came much earlier, in Saxon and medieval England, where Roman precedents had been forgotten and even the rich did not benefit. Technical change, then, has been imperfectly cumulative.

This reinforces the interpretation which says that peoples in the past could (and often did) make major technical inventions, but failed to innovate many of them at the society-wide level. In the pre-modern world, technical change proceeded by granny-steps. Perhaps it still does, but the intervals were immeasurably longer then. As Diderot described the process of invention in the *Encyclopaedia*, by 1755 the process was at any rate cumulative: 'a third follows in the footsteps of the second, a fourth in the footsteps of the third, and so on until at last someone gets excellent results . . .',[20] but it is clear that this had not always been the case.

The deeper question concerns what difference *technical* innovation made to average incomes. Speaking of China's outstanding record, Perry Anderson is driven to remark that 'the whole development of Sinic imperial civilization, indeed, can in a sense be seen as the most grandiose demonstration and profound experience of the power, and impotence, of techniques in history'.[21] It was rare in early times for technical change to be translated into *intensive* growth. Despite this the greatest exception was Sung China between the tenth and thirteenth centuries AD, to which the next chapter is devoted.

No doubt there were other exceptions, virtually lost to us as poorly recorded phases in particular histories and prehistories. Douglass North is very confident about this. Between the eighth millenium BC and the first two centuries AD, 'there were also civilizations that experienced economic growth for lengthy periods', he avers, 'in Mesopotamia, Egypt, Greece, Rhodes, and, of course, the Roman Republic and Empire. There is nothing new about sustained economic growth, then, despite the myth perpetrated by economic historians that it is a creation of the Industrial Revolution.'[22]

Few episodes are however described in a fashion which would convince the sceptic determined to apply modern standards of measurement, but one that is persuasively described concerns Archaic Aegina. Thomas Figueira's study of the economy shows that it shifted from farming into a substantial involvement in trade in grain and slaves.[23] Aegina also re-exported Athenian pots and began to trade into the Black Sea. According to Figueira's careful estimates and controlled reasoning by analogy, 90 per cent of the population came to be fed successfully with imported cereals, paid for by the non-agricultural activities. Aegina was a trade and craft centre of considerable wealth in the last centuries before Christ. There is no reason why the rise in income from these pursuits and the structural change they made possible should not be seen as *intensive* growth. The author is careful not to claim that the level reached was equivalent to that attained by the commercial and craft centres of late medieval or early modern Europe. Some historians have made claims of that kind for parts of the classical world and, in the light of his evidence, Figueira's reluctance to follow them may be merely a bow towards those others, 'the primitivists', who have argued fiercely that the ancient world was *sui generis* and moving in no such direction. Regarding technology and economic structure, the primitivists seem to be wrong.

The instance of probable early *intensive* growth that is most plausible and impressive, apart from the Sung, came in the Abbasid Caliphate of Baghdad in the ninth century. Here Islamic society ascended to what was perhaps its highest peak, for Anderson calls this the richest and most advanced civilization in the then world.[24] Trade, urbanization, industry, and science all flourished. An urban merchant class grew rich; urban craft industries expanded; a commercialized sector emerged within agriculture, cotton becoming a cash crop. The lateen sail was invented and long-distance ocean shipping began. Paper-making was learned from Chinese prisoners-of-war. Science developed on the basis of astronomy, physics, and mathematics translated from the Greek classics. The range and scale of the changes did not, admittedly, match those that took place a little later under the Sung and there was no corresponding surge of output. By other historical standards, nevertheless, the Abbasid economy was noteworthy. There seems to have been some structural change, though political troubles ended the experiment before a long enough time had elapsed for the full potential to develop.

The record of technical and economic advance in the Abbasid and especially the Sung episodes demonstrates that the past was by no means changeless. The past becomes distinctly historical and cycles are detectable about the underlying trend of *extensive* growth. To return to something like an earlier metaphor, what is revealed is a world of *extensive* growth in which novelty repeatedly bubbled up and more than once boiled over into *intensive* growth. On the face of it, this is at odds with customary views of Western uniqueness. 'No historian has yet claimed that industrial capitalism developed spontaneously anywhere else except in Europe and its American extension . . .', writes Perry Anderson.[25] In those terms no one will. It distorts the endeavour to hunt for evidence of the sheep of economic growth only in the wolf's clothing of modern industry or capitalism, with which growth is imperfectly correlated.

The recurrence thesis is similarly at odds with uni-formitarian or extreme diffusionist views. Hodgson urged, as we saw, that all the civilizations of the Old World, which he called the 'cited agrarianate states', were advancing in parallel in productive methods and economic capability. He thought that this continued until at least the sixteenth century AD, when Europe happened to accelerate and outpace the others. The rest were nevertheless not 'frozen'; they were merely unable to match a particular spurt by one of their number. It is not quite clear how Hodgson squared his view of parallel gradualism, radically different as it is from Keynes's view of prolonged stasis, with his knowledge that there had been a renaissance of sorts in Sung China and one in Islam, both ahead of the Renaissance in the Christian West. He did seem to be aware that first one civilization, then another, took the lead.

Hodgson gave it as his opinion that 'the Occident seems to have been the unconscious heir of the abortive industrial revolution of Sung China'.[26] Taken literally this is a diffusionist view which could make Europe's later development less than fully independent. Technique was certainly spread at the individual level by traders and missionaries and at the societal level by empires that brought in better methods or alternatively sopped them up from the conquered. After the rise of Islam in the seventh century there was a regular east–west flow from China reaching as far afield as Europe, with the Islamic world as broker. After the Arab conquests, Chinese and Indian techniques spread much faster than before, once they had gained the borders of the Islamic world.

Thomas Glick concludes that the High Middle Ages were characterized by openness, not closure.[27] Paper-making, acquired from prisoners at Samarkand in the middle of the eighth century, reached Andalusia by the middle of the tenth century. Sung porcelain bowls reached Egypt, whence imitations were sold as far west as Andalusia, a form of re-export substitution. Iran, too, was an active source of innovation in trade, technology, science, and methods of farming. Technological ideas moved more freely than those of science, where ideologies sometimes barred direct adoptions—for instance, Chinese science was excluded from the Islamic Middle East, whereas Chinese technology was welcomed. The spread of low culture was a matter of economic calculus, but scientific ideas could run foul of state or religious policy.

By straining the diffusionist case we might even claim that the 'closed economy' of Tokugawa Japan was not independent of Europe because of earlier borrowings from the Portuguese and the surreptitious 'Dutch learning'. At a deeper level Japanese culture was in any case largely derived from China. But this is *reductio ad absurdum*, leaving nowhere wholly independent and giving no guide either to hearths of invention or particularly rapid adopters. Everywhere in Eurasia was remotely linked with everywhere else, but that is operationally as unhelpful as knowing that everyone is everyone else's seventeenth cousin. It distracts us from explaining what we have to explain, the occasional successful irruption of innovation. We are less concerned with the formal history of diffusion. That belongs to the histories of science or technology rather than economic history. In any case, there were recognizably independent discoveries in every major civilization to set alongside the undoubted examples of diffusion.

The true shift, according to the Hodgson thesis, could hardly have occurred before the present millennium. He thought that the limited size of the market and above all the accumulation of inventions would not previously have reached a sufficient, though unspecified, level. [28] Here, it seems, this least convention-bound and most stimulating of comparative historians did in two respects retreat before convention. He seems to have regarded the prize of economic growth as something awaiting the first society to succeed in engrossing a lion's share of trade throughout what he called the 'Afro-Eurasian-Oikoumene'. That would tend, conventionally enough, to make the Discoveries the source of Europe's growth. In accounts by the core-periphery or underdevelopment schools it is of course the necessary and sufficient condition, but this has been substantially discredited by O'Brien's calculation that extra-European trade in early modern times accounted for only a tiny fraction of what we might call Europe's 'gross continental product'. [29] If growth within Europe really did stem from an expansion of trade, the source was more likely to have been intra-European trade.

Hodgson also remained inclined to seek for positive features in Europe's history which would explain why it was the first region to dominate the world economy. He dated the pertinent changes late, as his insistence on the normal comparability of agrarian civilizations obliged him to do. The features he selected were, again conventionally enough, new methods of production and a concentration on industry that was abnormal by any previous standards. Here, too, he should perhaps not have gone against his instincts as an Islamicist and credited so much to the individuality of the West. Even great Homer nods. Europe's individual features were less likely to explain growth than to be secondary manifestations of it, adaptations of methods and organization to the stirrings of growth itself. They denote a great flurry of activity, certainly, but one which obscures the fact that growth was not unique to the West, as Aegina, the Abbasid and Sung experiences, and no doubt others, had already demonstrated.

Much of Europe's growing share of world trade may have been the freakish result of a conflict in a remote and distant place, the Chinese court. Great junk fleets had sailed from

China in the early fifteenth century as far as East Africa and were obviously capable in all technical respects of supporting a big trade expansion. In the event, the Chinese failure to pursue their voyaging in 1430 or to resume it in 1480 hung in the balance of factional infighting between naval and land army interests. The balance was tipped by what, in the context of world history, was a minor political decision. Admittedly it is possible that the natural asymmetry of the systems of oceanic winds and currents might have made it harder for the Chinese to cope with the Atlantic, and thus 'discover' Europe, than it was for the Europeans of 1496 to cope with the Indian ocean and 'discover' Asia.[30] Perhaps it would therefore have been less easy than is sometimes suggested for historical geography to reverse itself, but it was within the range of technical possibilities.

We confront here a shadowy debate about the momentum of world history, a debate that proceeds mainly by implicit assumptions, but very different ones. To give an illustration, when the Russian scholar, Khazanov, discusses this issue in his book on nomadism he takes the extreme position that Europe displayed a special dynamic at intervals as far back as the late Palaeolithic era.[31] Against this are ranged those authorities, like Hodgson, who claim that all the major civilizations were progressing equally, in slow motion and lock-step, until the acceleration of Europe at its Renaissance. Thus A. C. Graham, in a thoughtful essay on the history of science, concludes that the supposed stagnation of China is illusory and that change continued there, merely failing to speed up when that in post-Renaissance Europe did.[32] Graham is speaking of science, but there is some evidence that progress in technical innovation also continued in China, although, as Hodgson and others supposed, more slowly than the pace now achieved in Europe. Chinese agricultural methods continued to develop. The Chinese had water-driven mills spinning hemp and ramie (a plant with fibres used for fine cloth) in the fourteenth century, their earliest paper-mill in 1570, their earliest sawmill in 1627, and water-powered silk-winders from 1780.[33] However slow this may appear, and by the standards of early modern Europe it does seem slow, it does not at any rate denote technical stagnation. On the contrary it reflects a substitution of capital for labour continuing after Sung times.

On the other hand, plenty of archaic technology survived in the world—for example, the types of Arab sailing vessels used from the seventh century were resurrected in their dying moments only a few years back as the models for the ship Tim Severin sailed on the remarkable *Sinbad* voyage. (This traced the old Arab route from Oman to Canton.) At other times what seem to be antique methods or styles of artefact may be the result of regression. The idea that methods in the non-Western world were 'frozen' seems to have originated with Victorian travellers, whose snapshot impressions of technologies more primitive than in the West, or at any rate than the best in the West, led them to suppose like Keynes that no one else had changed since times too remote to contemplate. Travellers (and historians) are especially prone to overlook small but cumulative improvements in crop and animal selection. The bias of the literature towards non-biological innovation is over-whelming. Peasant agricultures are almost always regarded as conservative, but now that it is accepted that peasants after all are rational calculators, none more so, it should have dawned that they have always adapted their farming systems when the risk seemed justified.[34]

The differences between cultures and periods were more finely shaded than is usually assumed. They lay in rates of change that varied incrementally from time to time and place to place. State demands biased invention and innovation. The induced innovation bias shows up clearly in Europe even in the period from the fourteenth to the sixteenth centuries.[35] Population had fallen and there was little advance in agri-culture, but the demands of governments for weapons and coinage still drew forth developments in mining and metallurgy. It is tempting to speculate that part of what sub-sequently raised the rate of productive innovation in Europe was a fall in the share of governmental demand, and a rise in the share of private demand, for goods traded outside the locality. This may also have been a feature of economic change and monetization under the Sung dynasty and the Tokugawa shogunate, directing more of innovative effort to productive sectors of the economy.

The commoner feature of the pre-modern world was for power structures to favour such ends as the building of religious and funerary monuments and fortifications, which 'crowded out' private consumption. Talent was diverted to artistic, poetic, religious, philosophical, and astronomical endeavours: endless labour went into sterile computations of the movement of the heavens. I once saw a television programme in which the late Sir Eric Thompson, who had devoted his life to deciphering the inscriptions on Mayan temples, was asked what they all were. 'Calendrical piffle', he snapped back, a complete realist. Concentration on products for which there could be no mass demand and from which there were few spin-offs slowed an economic advance that from time to time was *technically* within the reach of some organized society. Kinglake is quoted as saying of the pyramids, ' "they were piled up into the air for the realization of some kingly crotchets about immortality—some priestly longing for burial fees; and . . . as for the building—they are built like coral rocks by swarms of insects— by swarms of poor Egyptians, who were not only the abject tools and slaves of power, but who also ate onions for the reward of their immortal labour." '[36]

The interest in *very* long-term technical change lies in poorly understood variations of its rate, in the induced innovation bias, and in the way it intimates continually burgeoning energies. There is no question that change did occur and recur across the world. In that case, one wants to ask, why was the rate of change so low and so biased against the productive sectors of the economy? The cause was evidently not lack of human ingenuity. It may have included values that militated against growth, though our investigation of the situation in the classical world suggests that this is not a convincing or independent explanation. Perhaps the difficulties lay in the market, in some general and crippling scarcity of factors of production, or in restricted demand? But those things too seem to have been secondary. What muffled the impact of technical change and made it sluggish was the social or political structure.

FOUR
The Case of Sung China

The history of early science and technology has been dominated for a long time by Joseph Needham's demonstrations of the scope of Chinese work. Needham has urged in many publications that China was the essential hearth of invention from which scientific and technical knowledge spread across Eurasia, ultimately to fertilize the history of Europe. The thesis has achieved the status of gospel, but there are signs now of resistance to the aggressive Sinophilia it carries within it. David Landes has derided as a *fantaisie* Needham's belief that the Chinese invented the mechanical clock and the Europeans merely borrowed it.[1] The horological traditions were different, as Landes convincingly shows. The Chinese measured time by the continuous flow of water, that is, by water clocks, whereas the Europeans taught themselves to do so by an oscillatory movement, a beat. The discovery by medieval Europeans that time could be parcelled out as a punctuated rhythm was a conceptual leap which put their clockwork ahead of any other, with rich implications for an admittedly fairly distant mechanical future.

The sources of science and technology were various. No individual civilization, culture, or country has permanently dominated the field. Nevertheless the early Chinese achievement was enormous, the greatest single contribution before modern times. We do not have to take quite literally Francis Bacon's famous remark that the three greatest inventions known to early modern Europe (printing, the compass, and gunpowder) all originated from China, to accept that the range of Chinese technology was nothing short of amazing.[2] The tool-kit included the abacus, as fast as the older hand-calculators, a compass, and astronomical and marine charts. All these date from up to 2,000 years ago. There was a single-span stone bridge built across a river over 700 years before the Ponte Vecchio in Florence. There were the iron-chain suspension bridges. There were drills for brine which could reach depths of 2,000 feet, using the method that was still employed in 1859 when Colonel Drake sank the first oil well in Pennsylvania.

Under the late Chou (before 475 BC) there was already distant trade, a growth of cities, and a spreading use of money. Among a rising class of rich merchants and employers, the ironmasters were prominent. During the Ch'in (256–207 BC) iron agricultural implements, especially ploughs, were widely adopted. The cities grew and communications among them were improved. The bankers were flourishing enough to make loans to the state.[3] There were large-scale firms using advanced techniques of production. Before the birth of Christ an ironmaster in Szechuan was employing 1,000 men. If one were looking for 'capitalist' entrepreneurs seemingly they had long since been in existence.

We can only speculate about movements in average real incomes at these remote dates. Despite some information about productive techniques, early economic changes remain shadowy, although all the signs are of a developed commercial and industrial life. It is unfortunate that the primary documents are typically unhelpful. Even for much more recent dynasties the sources consist largely of fiscal records which enumerate the population in order to tax heads of households. These documents tend to report the same population figures for long stretches of time. The reason for this seems to be that provincial administrators did not dare to report population decline, which might have been taken as a sign of their own mismanagement, and did not wish to report any increase, because that would have required them to pass on more tax to higher levels of government. Except when a new dynasty made a fresh survey, and not all did, the records are therefore seldom very helpful.

The Sung dynasty from the tenth to the thirteenth centuries AD is rather better documented. The 'economic revolution' of the Sung was remarkably early by any non-Chinese standards and, as far as the descriptive evidence tells, its scale was exceptional even by Chinese standards. It does appear to have been a genuine case of *intensive* growth. Under the Sung and almost certainly under the preceding late Tang dynasties the inventions listed above, with some additions, became part and parcel of a major industrial sector. As we shall see, Sung China came to produce more iron per head than Europe was producing in AD 1700 and also adopted, very widely, a water-powered spinning-machine for hemp which was as advanced as any Europe possessed by 1700. Folk technology, Kenneth Boulding calls it.[4] Some technology. Some folk.

Chinese experience reaffirms that the nexus between scientific discovery and technical advance was really quite weak. China seems not to have produced a sharp-edged, experimental approach of the type that really may lead to better technologies, which was the Greek legacy to the modern world even if the Greeks themselves did not much capitalize on it. Sung science and technology, like Greek science and technology, were rather autonomous spheres. While the scientific limitations of Sung China may eventually have hampered its economic performance, growth itself may surely have been able to induce (and provide the resources for) any later scientific advance which the development of future technologies may have required. For the moment, technology was more than adequate.

Sung technology and the performance of the economy as a whole were outstanding. The magnitudes do not emerge clearly from specialist writings, which edge back from tentative generalizations to a nervous protestation that the regional economies of China differed greatly from one another. This observation does not tell us much; we could guess for ourselves that there must have been a regional dispersion of performance. The more important point is that compared with periods before and long after, and compared with other parts of the world, descriptions of the Sung economy are detailed enough to show that it was very productive indeed. The clearest synthesis of work on the subject proves not to be by a specialist at all, but by W. H. McNeill, whose summary we may conveniently rehearse.[5]

On the face of it, the most astonishing performance was that of the iron industry. The Chinese had been using a bellows which gave a continuous flow of air for one thousand years, in other words their technique was already well developed, before early in the eleventh century they began to use coke in their blast furnaces. At the peak of coal usage (between 1050 and 1126) it was thus employed for smelting, something not paralleled in Europe until the eighteenth century. Iron output surged up. McNeill provides the figures from what he rightly calls some remarkable articles by Hartwell.[6] Output went from 32,500 tons per annum in AD 998 to 125,000 tons or more in 1078 (though elsewhere the latter figure is given as between 75,000 and 150,000 tons). Hartwell compares the level of China's output in 1078 with that attained in Europe in 1700: Chinese output then came close to the total production of Europe including European Russia (151,000–185,000 tons), and it topped the British output as late as 1788. Per capita output in China had risen sixfold between AD 806 and 1078, and at the latter date production was an average of 3.1 lb. per capita, in some northern market areas over 7 lb. per capita, compared with a range of output of 3.5 to 4.3 lb. per capita in the Europe of 1700.

In terms of real prices the effect was a major one. The ratio of the value of iron to grain (rice) in Szechuan was 632 : 100 in AD 997 and had fallen to 177 : 100 by AD 1080. The corresponding iron to grain (wheat) ratios in England were 223 : 100 in 1600, and 160 : 100 in 1700. Only the technical developments of the late eighteenth century decisively reduced the price of iron in terms of grain in England (down to 54 : 100 on the eve of the Napoleonic wars) below the Sung ratios of 700 years earlier. The astonishing statistical data for China on which these comparisons are based do not seem to have been challenged in print; they would have to be incorrect by a very large margin to invalidate the conclusion that the price of a major component of producer goods had fallen very fast indeed, down to levels reached in Europe only on the brink of the classic industrial revolution.

There was as a result a large and expanding consumption of iron, greater than at any other time in Chinese history before the nineteenth century. It was used for weapons, farm implements, and iron currency, but these three demands altogether were outclassed by the demand for industrial purposes. The extended use of iron tools in manufacturing and in the production of goods which were themselves made of iron could virtually have brought about a transformation of the economy by itself.

The vitality that created this surge in iron production affected many other industries, though more gradually. The most advanced technical innovation came in the textile industry, in the widespread adoption of the water-powered spinning-machine for hemp. In addition there were extensive cropping changes in agriculture and a big uptake of new, fertile lands in the south. The productivity gains that resulted had much to do with Sung prosperity; the interesting question is, what unleashed them? Part of the answer was a relocation of population that was seen as desirable in the political situation of the time. To that extent it was simply good fortune that a fertile option was available. The remainder, and the more fundamental part (since from time to time other societies have experienced windfall gains of new lands without anything like as significant a result), was seemingly the extension of the market.

By the end of the eleventh century the human population had risen to almost double its mid-Tang level, upper-bound estimates being 8.9 million and 19.9 million registered households respectively. (No secure multiplier is available by which to arrive at the actual population.) Because the net political area of China had contracted, notwithstanding the entry to new lands, population density had risen more than these figures imply.

Perhaps the chief novelty was the extent to which the land market had been opened up in the Tang period, by the ninth century.[7] The previous system in which land allocation had been controlled by the central government gave way to freer tenure, leading to the expansion of estates and an increase in tenancy. Government relinquished its function of allocating and re-allocating land in return for labour services and taxes in kind and instead took its taxes in cash. This hands-off policy facilitated the growth of the private land market; in the secondary works commonly available the political motives are obscure.

The private market would in principle have meant that land increasingly fell into the hands of the most energetic producers, who would presumably have wanted to put it to whatever uses the price system indicated. A freeing in this way of markets in factors of production, land, labour, and capital, is a significant sign of greater allocative efficiency. Factor markets are more fundamental than commodity markets. The changes in them, which unfortunately cannot be gauged in a precise way, give some indication of developmental level, although they are not a full index of productive change.

I urged in *The European Miracle* that a vital upturn in Europe's growth came when the private market in production was supplemented by the governmental provision of public goods. This is a 'render unto Caesar' thesis which finds the strongest economy to be the one in which a balance is secured between free markets and public intervention. The nature of that balance cannot be unambiguously specified; there would perhaps be no need for political debate if it could. I do not believe that the point of balance is unique, nor that it could possibly be long unchanged in any economy subject to real world stresses and fluctuations in its environment, but some historically unusual combination of public and private activity seems to have been vital for change.

There is evidence of vigorous public goods creation by the Sung, particularly in the communications sector, to go along with market expansion. With that balancing weight, and in a world otherwise typified by a rigidly non-market allocation of factors of production, the release of market forces was likely to add a powerful impetus. Other early states and earlier dynasties in China had sometimes created part of the infrastructure for growth, but without giving the market much institutional freedom. The Sung combination of state investment *and* greater market freedom may account for the release of productive energies. In addition, fixed head taxes were altered to property assessments and taxes on land under cultivation, and from levies in kind to demands for cash. Once output began to rise a switch to taxes in cash may have meant that the government share lagged.

Peasants were obliged to market part of their crops in order to secure the cash to pay their dues. Constant complaints of the shortage of coin may indeed reflect a fast growth in demand for money. Paper money was brought in and the total money supply expanded. A money standard no doubt brought about greater allocative efficiency with respect to human talent. It would have given thrusting individuals a better chance to work for hire and improve their lot than in a more traditional China where roles were ascribed, not achieved.

Distributional effects are another matter. Although as we shall see there was a socially widespread increase in private wealth, many peasants fell into debt and foreclosure extruded them into wage work, swelling the market in another factor of production, labour. Some moved to the towns and industrial or service employment where their productivity was higher. Others were induced to supplement their agricultural incomes by entering the commodity market as makers and sellers of home-produced petty manufactures. This meant they were participating in structural change of the type that is associated with an expanding market, rising average labour productivity, and rising average income, which amounts to *intensive* growth.

The Sung dynasty, which may have felt too weak to suppress its upstart merchant class, was nevertheless energetic enough to bring about the integration of the national market for commodities in which, naturally, the merchants traded. State action encouraged the take-over of more southerly delta lands and built canals running north–south, so that provisions could be brought to the capital, Kaifeng. Rivers were also canalized to make them navigable. Transport costs fell substantially. This proved a positive externality for private traders in bulk goods. The lifting of the dead weight of transport costs, typically heavy in the pre-modern world, was sufficient to generate regional specialization along lines of comparative advantage. The populace became used to a trading economy and many officials forgot propriety and engaged in trade on their own account.

Historically it was unusual for any very sizeable part of a peasant population to buy foodstuffs and pay for them by turning its own efforts to by-employments or growing non-food crops. Dependence on purchased foodstuffs is a historical Rubicon that the economy has to cross. We are impressed when we see it crossed by the Dutch in the seventeenth century. The risks of crop failure at the supplying end or political blockage of the trade routes are high, as the Dutch found. Within Sung China better communications made the rice supply seem safe enough for the time being, enough to persuade the peasantry to enter the market on a grand scale.

This growth in farm output within a market now better connected by fresh roads, canals, and canalized rivers, in what was still chiefly an agricultural economy, was very close to the heart of the Sung 'economic revolution'.

Many peasants worked full-time making paper, iron implements, and various other commodities. Others withdrew only part of their labour-time from food production, or only some members of a family withdrew. This was still structural change, because the effective industrial share of the total labour force, and of output, had risen, concealed though it may have been by the fact of the households remaining on the land. The occupational distribution in China under the Sung may not have been vastly different from that in Europe in 1700.

Peasants in the areas most favourable for rice-growing concentrated on rice, exchanging some of their output for the speciality crops or household manufactures of peasants elsewhere. Specialization created a large demand for hired workers in tea and sugar plantations, orchards, fish-rearing businesses, and market gardens. These and the cottage manufacturers were the ones who had been emboldened to rely on non-local grain for their subsistence. There is a marked similarity between this development and the emergence of alternate regions producing food and domestic manufactures in early modern Europe—until one shrugs off the ethnocentrism: Sung China's development was many centuries earlier, it was not like Europe, Europe was like China.

Rice from the new south helped to feed a rising pyramid of cities. State industries expanded and employed much labour, some of it in large workshops, especially in Kaifeng. In addition a wide range of goods came onto the market, the output of specialized private manufacturers with innumerable small workshops. There was a demand for hired labour in smithies, water-mills, oil shops, rice-cake shops, and the like. Some of the cities along the Grand Canal became large trading centres. Growing trade meant a need to staff the extensive transport system at a period when cargoes everywhere had to be man-handled in the most labour-intensive fashion. Both the larger urban population and the expanding labour force involved in distribution were parts of the structural change in which a growing proportion of the occupied population shifted out of agriculture. There was also the largest standing army the world had then seen. More than one million men had been withdrawn from the land. An increasingly productive agriculture was able to carry them.

The increased volume and variety of commodities manufactured for sale had to be consumed. Criticism of the extravagance of once-humble classes became vehement (and unavailing). Fashions in dress, furniture, and styles of building spread from the capital to the provinces. As McNeill wryly comments, 'if all this seems strikingly modern, I can only say that it was'.[8] Sumptuary laws were passed forbidding certain items to one class or another, but by AD 995 these laws were unenforceable. This was the first period in China's history when tea and pepper were widely consumed by the masses, a foretaste of the consumption patterns of England after the Commercial Revolution of the late seventeenth century.

The changes seem to have been a response to the relaxing of political controls and demands; the switch to taxation in money; and the improvement of communications. These things released a response in the Chinese people like taking a finger off a taut steel spring. The evidence lies in the growing prosperity and prestige of merchant and industrial groups, the production, trade, and innovation they sponsored, and the structural change and rising consumption that followed. The state was neither able to quash those economic changes it found socially undesirable, nor, it is important to note, did it cream off to the emperor and officials all the proceeds of change. Neither the state nor the 'prebends' could tax away all the gains, as both Weber and Ma claim they did.[9] Doing so would have destroyed the inducement for the supply response we actually observe.

Authorities differ on the scale of the changes, and the literature draws away into speculations as to whether or not modern science or sustained growth would eventually have emerged, or even whether the Chinese would have become 'capitalist'. These musings are beside the point. There was already an undeniable and transforming bubble of prosperity within the agrarian state; the Sung Chinese were already achieving *intensive* growth. 'In Sung and Ming China, as in Tokugawa and early Meiji Japan, there was almost no centrally-organized, large-scale, capital-intensive industry', writes Bray, somewhat belittling the Sung, 'Yet compared with medieval or early modern Europe consumer goods were plentiful, some of extremely high quality, but most designed for popular consumption.'[10] The point is that this *was* growth. That it was achieved by traditional methods of production, by the division of labour, by regional specialization, magnifies rather than detracts from the feat.

In the circumstances, Weber's view that the Chinese value system was responsible for a lack of development comparable to that in Europe seems irrelevant. Sung development had pipped Europe to the post. Weber of course did not have access to modern research. In any case, his opinion that growth was prevented in China by the absence of an ascetic, thrifty, and purposeful ethic of the type he thought so powerful in European economic history has been dismissed by Rodinson, Kautsky, and Elvin among others.[11] The dismissal usefully highlights some of the issues. As Elvin correctly says, an economic and ecological explanation is simpler in its assumptions, internally more consistent, and more amenable to empirical verification. It is not likely to be helpful to rely for an explanation on value shifts, in the sense of changes in unobservable preferences.

On the other hand it is not self-evident that new technology alone would be a sufficient explanation. Elvin himself seems to overemphasize the role of technical change, calling this, 'the central problem at the heart of the industrial revolution'.[12] Phases of technical advance recurred in history, as we have seen. These phases need to be explained in turn, and do not explain enough in themselves. The trick is to disentangle the conditions which fostered sufficient application of new methods to bring down the supply price of goods substantially and for a reasonable space of time, like the three centuries of Sung rule. What induced technical innovation on a few occasions like this, but more often frustrated it? The answer is likely to be found in the realm of politics and institutions.

How was it, too, that a promising start such as the Sung had given the world was finally frustrated? According to Robert Hartwell, 'why this precocious economic and industrial expansion did not lead to developments similar to the later and more famous Industrial Revolution of nineteenth century Europe . . . seems to lie partly in external factors such as the Jurchen and later Mongol invasions and conquests, and partly in structural limitations of traditional Chinese society'.[13] Distinguishing between these alternatives, or if they were complementary assessing their relative importance, is a task to which we will turn in later chapters.

Destructive conquest is an unsubtle matter. The more interesting question is why *intensive* growth, interrupted by the Mongol invasion, did not resume. It is important to be clear that a vast, productive, substantially commercial economy *was* rebuilt, not enormously long afterwards, and actually under the later Mongol Yuan dynasty. China was again bustling beyond the dreams of medieval Mediterranean commerce when Marco Polo paid his visit. Sinologists have not committed themselves to the opinion that average real incomes systematically rose after the Sung, so that the complex China they describe was apparently one of *extensive* growth only, regaining but not surpassing the level to which *intensive* growth had raised incomes under the Sung.

Even if the Ming and Ch'ing governments that followed were more interested in agrarianism and agrarian taxation, the high level of development and the degree of urbanization and trade that characterized their China sit oddly with the apparent lack of any further growth of the *intensive* sort. Very big regional developments, the geographical spread of productive agriculture, cities, commerce, all remarkable by world standards, are nevertheless not reported in such a way as to demonstrate that the condition of rising *average* per capita GNP was regained.

The puzzle of the stability of average real incomes in China after Sung times is one of the most significant issues in world economic history. China was still heir to its technology and still occupied its productive landscape, indeed added to this by renewed colonization further south. Yet population growth seems to have checked average income growth yet again without causing any tragic fall. What the homeostatic mechanisms were is quite unclear. The swings in population size and in political fortunes were hardly compatible with income stability, yet the verbal consensus among Chinese scholars seems to be that even the bloody transitions between dynasties, such as the twenty years of war in the seventeenth century when the Ch'ing wrested control from the Ming, were of little lasting economic consequence.

The somewhat limited growth-promoting investments that the post-Sung political system encouraged, together with further intensification of agriculture and the availability of a reservoir of fresh land in the south, managed to absorb the growth of human numbers. A Hodgson-esque view of this has been put forward. It is that, until eighteenth-century industrialization put Europe decisively ahead, the Sung achievements remained intact, lacking only the positive efforts needed to switch the economy back onto the track of *intensive* growth.[14] Whether the lack of further advance was because of the lack of fresh positive stimulus or because of the presence of some subtle depressant now emerged (or re-emerged) remains to be determined.

An Anatomy of Frustration

The Mills of God

The brutal fact of history is that tentative movements towards *intensive* growth did not succeed very often. Given the talent expressed in so many ways and places, and the obvious disadvantages of poverty, the striving for *intensive* growth ought to have been strong. What can it have been that typically kept it at or set it back to the level of *extensive* growth, where economies continued to grow bigger but could not sustain a rise in real incomes? We need to identify the depressive factors acting at large, before looking to see how they were defeated in the few triumphant cases.

These are dominating issues in economic history. They relate to the mechanisms that controlled the prospects for growth. A general explanation would enable us to link together the customary lack of income growth, the examples of recurrent creativity, and the cases in Chinese, Japanese, and European history where per capita gains were fully realized. We need, firstly, to winnow the range of possible negative factors for those most likely to have caused repression and to have brought about the occasional violent act of suppression.

What is the appropriate arena in which to look? There is a spatial hierarchy in economic history, rising from the exclusiveness of 'Little Englander' studies of the industrial revolution through broader Western European and American studies to the sweeping scale preferred by students of the 'World System'. Clearly the Little Englander approach will not do; England, or Britain, was not a closed economy and was, even as far as industrialization went, merely *primus inter pares*. And the broadest Western approach excludes the relevant Chinese and Japanese episodes.

The World System school has at least the merit of a larger canvas. This school is divided into two branches, both unfortunately still working on the assumption that all relevant change originated in Europe. One is Europocentric in that it sees growth achieved in Europe by 'unequal' trade at the expense of the peripheral, extra-European world. The other extends Europe's reach immeasurably and is more concerned with the effect on non-Western peoples than with the impact of trade and resource acquisitions on Europe itself. Neither pays enough attention to the possibility of independent growth elsewhere; the stress is on the dynamism and sinfulness of Europe.

The original concept that a world economy arose during the sixteenth century, separating itself into a core, semi-periphery, and periphery, was a fascinating one. It offered a chance for the subject to escape the industrial revolution format. The central notion was capable of being framed as a falsifiable hypothesis in terms of the relative number of hours needed for equally productive workers in different countries to obtain a given basket of goods. Without a demonstration of systematic differences along these lines, it must remain moot whether the divisions into core, semi-periphery, and periphery really existed, let alone whether fuel from the outer world was what drove the engine of European growth.[1]

On the extreme 'One-Worlder' view, which extends World System analysis to breaking-point, nowhere escaped the blighting influence of commercial contact with Europe. No internal circumstances made much difference to the fortunes of any other land.[2] This exaggerates the role of trade in far-flung farming and hunting societies before the nineteenth century and rests on the dubious proposition that the European engine drove the world. Neither World System view avoids a Europocentric stance or accepts that different zones may have had separate histories.

Yet such long-distance trade as there was before the nineteenth century need not be completely dismissed. The links between whole economies were weak, but in so far as any goods could in principle always be exchanged for others, trade was trade. This blurs the distinction between 'pre-capitalist' and 'capitalist' worlds. We do not have to press a 'One-Worlder' case back to prehistory, as in Jean Schneider's statement that 'the pre-capitalist world [was] systematically integrated through the operation of world economic forces',[3] to take the point that the division between trade in luxuries and trade in necessities can be artificial and that even the purely luxury trade of the remote past represented an ultimate exchange of values between distant areas. Schneider's suggestion that early Europe ought to be classed with other marginal, bullion-exporting, textile-importing zones, such as South-East Asia or West Africa, and not until recent centuries with China, acknowledges the ceaseless shifting of world economic distributions. There is no special privilege to Europe here! While this extreme 'One-Worlder' classification emphasizes far too much the role of low-volume trade in an overwhelmingly agrarian world, it does serve to remind us that economic history need not be the tale of a Nereid rising from a timeless sea of stagnation.

The proper arena for study is a crucial choice. Few data are available for the distant past from which to tell the true economic distributions, but one way to start is to consider the distribution of population, for which estimates are available.[4] Producing people is in some ways an alternative to producing goods and offers an indirect measure of economic performance. Large numbers of people also mean potentially large markets, including markets for information about technological methods of the loose kind that we have seen existed for a long time in Eurasia. Large societies also imply a degree of social and political co-ordination. Population was a limited but effective index of economic capacity, at least while incomes everywhere were low.

The period between about AD 1000 and 1750 gives us a frame of reference for both the main examples of *intensive* growth we want to investigate and the most important societies that showed no comparable achievement despite early promise. That span of centuries brackets the successful cases and allows ample time to consider why others fell behind.

Almost four out of five people in the world lived in five main societies in 1750; quite four out of five lived in at most seven societies. Where the remainder of the world's peoples were at all concentrated, the concentrations were small and scattered. These were usually outside the great landmass of Eurasia, and their isolation from the diffusions of technical and organizational best practices among the world's major cultures, at periods when rates of invention, innovation, and diffusion were low, may have been what kept them behind the times. The existence of its interconnected pool of ideas is one of the main reasons for focusing on Eurasia's past. World history was at its most active there.

In descending order of population size, the seven largest societies in 1750 were Manchu China (with 234 million people, almost one-third of those on earth), Mughal and the immediately post-Mughal parts of India, the European states-system, Tokugawa Japan, the Ottoman empire, West Africa, and Indonesia (with a mere 10 million inhabitants). In terms of population density the order was slightly different and Japan jumps to the head of the list, but no new societies are added. One another, the Safavid Persia of a slightly earlier date, might be added because of its bridging role in the history of Islam, which would give us at most eight societies to consider.

If we go back to AD 1000 we find that, although the majority were then very small, these same societies or their predecessors already contained about 75 per cent of the world's population. China, India, and Europe thoroughly outclassed the others, holding some 60 per cent of the total. They had been dominant in population as far back as 3000 BC.[5] India and China were also so impressive for their ancient cultural and technical productions that in them, more than anywhere, the earliest achievement of real growth might have been expected. Among the remainder, Japan showed the most conspicuous population increase between AD 1000 and 1750, but much of Europe also filled up during the Middle Ages.

Almost all these societies may be unfamiliar to Western students of economic history, but they are vital objects of study. It seems absurd to have to insist on the point in the presence of the world's chief peoples, but there are writers, such as Peter Munz and Hugh Trevor-Roper, who contend that history is by definition the study of the records of Western civilization.[6] If that is so, the definition should be changed. One may however confess to a sneaking sympathy with Trevor-Roper's acid view that the main function of African history is to show the present the face of the past from which it has escaped; this strictly limited sympathy is because part of the function of the history of the mainland Asian empires in this analysis will be to provide accounts of the negative forces from which Japan and Europe more readily escaped. Voltaire asked, 'if all you have to tell us is that one barbarian succeeded another on the banks of the Oxus or Jaxartes, what benefit have you conferred on the public?' The answer may be to help isolate, via comparative history, the key to the rise of something better, even if this turns out to have been largely the absence of a succession of barbarians.

Having said this, we can discard two of the smaller societies, West Africa and Indonesia. Both had low and low-density populations; neither was a great hearth of invention or originated a major political or religious force; both were at the end of the line as far as technological diffusion went. West Africa was unable to sustain the empires which intermittently rose in the Niger Bend, and was anyhow disrupted by involvement in the slave trade. The recurrent rise of political order there and some of the cultural attainments were remarkable considering the difficulties, not the least of which was a fierce disease-ridden environment. The creativity indicated by the Benin bronzes notwithstanding, West Africa did not permanently house a society recorded as achieving or sustaining growth. There was an underlying dynamism, but comparatively speaking a weak one.

Indonesia was for a long time a congeries of Hindu and Muslim states, eventually overlain by Dutch colonialism. The trade potential of the 'Indonesian Mediterranean' was not inconsiderable, but it was never fully realized, perhaps because of political instability. Separate coastal trading states eventually fused into a colonial enclave. This formed one half of a dual economy, the other half being the internal agricultural frontier. As late as the eighteenth century energies were being diverted into taking up fresh land, always an engine of *extensive* growth but not necessarily of anything more. All South-East Asia including Indonesia and the Philippines, half the area of Europe, held only one-fourth of Europe's population in 1400 and one-sixth in 1800. This population was scattered and in the 'early modern' period its commercial prospects were surprisingly slim. Many of its states were badly hit by the advance of malaria.

The exclusions leave only six major societies, even counting Safavid Persia. Among them, Europe and Japan achieved *intensive* growth and so had China under the Sung. This leaves India, the Islamic Middle East, and China under its later dynasties as the societies whose economic histories are at one and the same time of great world historical significance and likely to throw most light on the apparent obstacles in the way of growth.

'We have, then,' Yves Lacoste puts it, 'to explain why the scientific and technological advances made by the great states of Asia and Africa in the Middle Ages did not lead to a process of economic development comparable to that to be observed in nineteenth-century Europe.'[7] Given the geographical adjustments we have now indicated, this is a reasonable formulation: 'why not?' rather than 'why?' is the question. Lacoste continues, 'this is a very complex question, but also an extremely important one in that it determined the fate of the world for a long time to come.'

The world had seen definite change which had petered out or been blocked, and some definite cause of this has to be sought. Blanket 'traditional society' explanations of the type that used to appear frequently in books on economic development do not explain patterns of this kind. They brush the problem aside on the assumption that the poverty, restrictive folkways, and slow rates of change observable in much of the Third World during quite recent times had formed the permanent landscape of the past. Instead, as when Edward Gibbon wrote that the Byzantine empire 'subsisted for 1058 years in a state of premature and perpetual decay', there must once have been a condition of health on the heels of which deterioration followed. Rather than hypothesize primeval night followed by only one dawn, the need is to explain particular episodes of growth and particular relapses into the long shadows.

This task has usually been subsumed under discussions of supposedly permanent 'obstacles to growth'. Western ethnocentricity made the values and institutions of the less-developed countries seem foreign, distasteful, and incompatible with growth, but on closer consideration the question of obstacles is vastly more complicated. The concept of an obstacle is simply not solid. It is not possible to make a finite list of obstacles or to arrange them in a hierarchy. The point has been elegantly made by Albert Hirschman, who reclassifies obstacles in various ways.[8]

Among the 'obstacles' commonly cited as of the very greatest importance are values and institutions. Yet some of these turn out to be assets. A prime case is the extended family, commonly denigrated by Westerners who cannot believe that anyone would feel an obligation to his or her third cousins, or even, one might add, know such distant relatives. The Western assumption is that, where so many kin can make a claim on an individual's earnings, incentives must be reduced. The extended family's atmosphere can of course become poisonous as when any close relationship goes sour, and in India, at any rate, the acquisitiveness fostered in children makes each acutely conscious of his or her contribution to the joint family.[9] Yet the extended net of relatives and contacts has certain advantages from the business point of view. The prevalence of the extended family as a firm implies as much. It can be its own labour force, internally motivated, self-monitoring, without a need for much book-keeping. The material benefits, notably the 'insurance' of widespread networks of kin, seem to out-weigh any costs. Hirschman was ahead of his time in the 1960s in questioning the denigration of the extended-family system, but in the 1980s, in one of the voltes-face to which Western interpretations of the non-Western world have been subject, the extended-family system is being described as a *cause* of social stability, discipline, and growth in Singapore.[10]

The concept that values and institutions were what held earlier societies in thrall is deeply rooted in the literature. They were thought to explain why the Third World never had its own industrial revolution, and did not succeed in 'taking off' during the 1950s or 1960s. Hirschman however finds that in the modern world conservative beliefs have often vanished in the face of the cognitive dissonance set up by real opportunities of advancement. Old attitudes admittedly do not dissolve instantly in the presence of growth, there may even be a conservative reaction as the Iranian Revolution of the 1970s shows, and each episode has to be considered on its merits. Nevertheless the preponderant fact that growth has now been occurring for decades throughout most of the world shows that many a hindrance has evaporated in the face of opportunity or, as Oscar Wilde might have said, of temptation. Obstacles can be paper tigers: Otto Daimler thought the motor-car had little future because there were only one thousand chauffeurs in all Europe.

The most direct historical assault on the problem is in Walt Rostow's *How It All Began*. This has the virtue of an opening chapter, already mentioned, entitled, 'Why Traditional Societies Did Not Generate Self-Sustained Growth', to which the answer is quickly given that the pre-modern world failed to make a 'systematic, regular, and progressive application of science and technology to the production of goods and services'.[11] Although Rostow overplays the link between science and technology and underplays some phases in early history (what about the Sung?), he does see the need to probe beyond the lack of a regular flow of new technology. There was, he says, a conceptual failure, a weakness in the realm of ideas, not enough science was generated. Why was that? Partly because of a cultural failure, located mainly in the minds of rulers who saw no worthwhile pay-off to investing in increased productivity. Whenever their revenues fell short of requirements, they tried to squeeze the existing tax base for more than could be had and by so doing cut off the chances of growth.

This comes close to a viable explanation, except that there is no need to argue a cultural failure. Average methods of production in the ancient world lay well behind the production frontier; the diffusion of known techniques, such as the water-mill, was extremely slow, and this was surely a matter of high information costs rather than the lack of a scientific culture. At any given moment rulers (and millers) were responding rationally to the investment and revenue-raising calculus. Even in the longer run, rulers may have been rational in seeking rents rather than funding research, since in a growing economy their *relative* income position would undoubtedly have worsened. In other words political and economic conditions were the dominant influences on rates of technical innovation.

A variant of the argument by values places more strain on our knowledge of world history. This thesis is that Asian societies were in the process of becoming culturally introverted just before the first Western penetration. The claim appears in widely scattered and independent sources on the Islamic world, Hindu India, and Ming China.[12] All three of these societies are said to have undergone 'strange inexplicable experiences' at about 1500.[13] Typical comments about the phenomenon, conceived as cultural introversion, are made by Lacoste, already quoted here. In somewhat obscure ways it is said to have caused a shrinkage of trade, mainly maritime trade, as well as political conflict and isolationism.

The literature concerning the Ottoman world is especially full of remarks about cultural introversion and metaphors of dormancy. One is made by Vera Micheles Dean, who states that, 'after this [thirteenth-century] flowering the Muslim world "went to sleep" under the rule of the Ottoman Empire, run by Turkish military leaders and administrators who had originally come from central Asia'.[14] Compared with the splendours of Arab intellectual and cultural life in the Middle Ages, the subsequent regression was severe. A likely explanation is political chaos and, in the case of the Ottomans, the external defeats of their warrior state. The Ottoman empire did survive, but only to become the 'sick man of Europe' in the nineteenth century. It ceased to grow. The drying-up of sources of fresh land and plunder seems to have lain at the heart of its troubles, for a half-concealed, 'pie-slicing', internal scramble for shares of what remained followed its military containment. A new conservatism of values succeeded rather than preceded the encirclement of the empire by its enemies.

An authoritative statement of the cultural introversion theory was made by Nehru in his *The Discovery of India*. As Mancur Olson points out, Nehru was far more critical of Indian society than he was of British imperial rule, even though he was imprisoned by the Raj at the time he wrote.[15] Nehru's observation was that whereas prehistoric society in the Indus valley, around Mohenjo-daro, had been among the most advanced in the world, far ahead of Europe's, by the time of the Mughals in the sixteenth century AD the country was already ' "drying up and losing her creative genius and vitality" '. There was internal decay in intellectual life and technical methods and the economy was contracting. According to Nehru this was why such a large civilization could not resist Islamic aggression. The explanation he adopted was that the caste system was at fault.

Although, as Olson says, it would be unfair to lean heavily on the opinion of a gaoled politician devoid of scholarly resources, this view corresponds with that of many informed Indians. The difficulty with it is that no precise historical mechanism of change in the caste system is suggested that could account for this becoming paralysing by the time of the Islamic threat. Nevertheless, Nehru's opinion does have a latent chronological structure. He does not quite envisage Indian society as timelessly traditional; there is an implied history of the rise and intensification of the caste system, which was indeed so important and hidebound an institution that we will shortly give it a closer look.

The tightest codification of values occurs in religion. Examining the case that the prohibitions embodied in certain major Asian religions are at the very core of non-growth is the most convenient way of pursuing the matter. Many colleagues with whom I have talked hark back to religious motivations or sanctions as the final arbiters of economic change. This attitude, not always clearly formulated but obviously heart-felt, is an ironic last resort for an irreligious generation of economists. In the development literature, certainly, Islam, Hinduism, and Confucianism have often been described, from a Judaeo-Christian standpoint, as offering no stimulus and erecting actual barriers to growth. If these deeply revered systems of norms are not responsible then perhaps no beliefs are strong enough to be accountable and we should turn to more tangible factors.

Scholars with first-hand experience of Eastern faiths have dissented from the view that these must have impeded change. Maxime Rodinson, for example, concluded in a major work on *Islam and Capitalism* that a necessary relationship between Islam as a religion and any given economic system does not exist.[16] Islamic precepts are not contrary to growth nor during the last hundred years of 'capitalist orientation' can they be shown to have hindered it. Modern survey data tend to confirm this with respect to the malleability of Muslim values, attitudes towards mastering the environment, and achievement motivation.[17] It seems likely that varying political circumstances have more to do with the nature and growth orientation of any Islamic regime than moral dogmatism or inflexibility within the whole system.

There is obviously a core of precepts and beliefs in Islam but, as with other religions, it is unlikely that the practical application of this core has been permanent, irreducible, and unevolving over historial time. It would be naïve not to anticipate a feedback in which values and social context interacted and affected each other and there is therefore no reason to believe that religion permanently forbade society to adjust to innovation. Indian numerals, for example, spread rapidly through both Islamdom and Christendom, carried westwards by their sheer utility in navigation and administration. Once we accept that changing circumstances may bring out different aspects of a system, the independent explanatory power of the system itself is restricted. Certainly, the original spread of the Islamic faith was a triumph for all sorts of circumstantial reasons—political, military, social, and so forth—not merely in tribute to its intellectual merits, just as triumphant Christianity owed much to Constantine's Vision and his control of the Roman Empire.

Timur Kuran dissents from Rodinson's latitudinarian interpretation.[18] He argues that Islamic norms, created in a small society in the seventh century if not earlier, are anything but agents of progress. Officially norms have not changed since the tenth-century 'closure of the door of interpretation' and they do not contemplate, permit, or instigate some important arrangements which ease the workings of markets. For instance, they disallow insurance markets. Yet even Kuran shows that many of the norms are ambiguous. Their content has subtly altered, alternatives are appealed to, and they have not usually proved irreconcilable with growth and development today. Slipping around certain prohibitions must admittedly incur costs; the systematic under-use of female intellectual and business talent is a heavy cost in itself. These problems suggest the presence of a certain brake on the economy, conceivably even a lower average probability of independent growth than in, say, Christendom, but they do not mean that Islamic societies could never generate growth independently. There was after all the case of the Abbasid Caliphate.

Some telling points about these matters in the context of medieval Islam are made by Thomas Glick.[19] He urges that arguments about links between values and practices wrongly assume that values were homogeneously distributed among all strata of society. The relationship between values and action is often debated at an inappropriately general level, via the impact of values on something so abstract that Glick labels it national character. It would be wrong, he suggests, to assume that what determined whether or not an activity as potentially important as scientific enquiry could go forward were the values embraced by the modal personality. Decisions were taken by no such ideologically monochrome society. They depended instead on whether the élites of specific Islamic regions were willing to overstep the bounds of orthodox thought.

This conclusion opens the way to giving historical structure to an otherwise excessively abstract discussion. Relations between thought and action were neither preordained nor random, but patterned by the context. As Glick says (p. 249), 'The problem of medieval science is, then, less one of inhospitable cultural contexts and more one of selective barriers to its practice, each of which has a specific social or cultural locus.' In medieval Spain, Muslim and Christian scientists shared 'a basic identity' of interest. The key to practical effects always lay in the larger circumstances of the day.

Clearly, ahistorical debates about values and the economy are cloudy. As Dasgupta writes with respect to discussions of religion and action in Japan, 'no theorems follow from such intangible associations'.[20] We are not surveying a range of 'Asian' belief systems which were adamantine in more than the short run—systems which, supposedly unlike the Judaeo-Christian complex (rather 'Asian' itself, one might think), remained eternally hostile to material accumulation and change. It is better to think of religions, and other values and institutions, as filters through which action had to pass, to be slowed down or sanctified or winked at according to the occasion, but not as unyielding obstacles. Values and institutions may determine the form and probably do greatly influence the pace of change, but they contain their own inconsistencies and hidden flexibilities of the kinds nicely demonstrated for Islam by Kuran.[21] Although religions may appear to have been hostile at first, once a prospect of economic change was offered they tended to develop subtle vocabularies of Doublespeak and reshape themselves to accept part of Mammon's cold embrace.

Alfred Marshall was more alert than most modern economists to the way in which economic circumstances can soften the sternest moral precepts. 'Sometimes these forces break down the custom altogether; but often they evade it by gradual and imperceptible changes in the character of the thing sold so that the purchaser gets a new thing at the old price under an old name . . . customs . . . have ever been imperceptibly growing and dwindling again, to meet the changing exigencies of successive generations.'[22] To give a historical illustration, here is Glick's conclusion about the history of science: 'although general barriers appear to have existed (e.g. Muslim qualms about Greek rationalism, Western fears of Islamic sorcery), in neither instance were these strong enough to have affected anything more substantial than delaying actions.'[23]

Turning to Hinduism, the impression is reaffirmed of long-term or even medium-term malleability above a surface of apparent short-run fixity. Hinduism is acephalous and no courses of action are promoted or forbidden by a central priesthood. Hindu philosophy is said to accept any view of the world—as real and desirable, or real and full of woe, or simply as an illusion.[24] It would be useful to know, should the sources permit, just where and when each view has come to pre-dominate. The notion that the Orient, unlike materialist Europe, is motivated by other-worldliness is certainly mistaken. His-torically speaking this is a quite recent fallacy. The earliest Western travellers noted the intensity of the acquisitive drive in India, which one would undoubtedly expect to have been strong where the costs of poverty were so hideously apparent.

When we consider Confucianism, though this is a phil-osophy rather than strictly a religion, the nexus with economic action is shattered in a comical way. Once depicted by Westerners as quite incompatible with growth, Confucianism has lately come to be identified as the one common factor responsible for the ASEAN wonder economies of the 1970s. Admittedly, just how 'Confucian' these societies really are is disputable; Lee Kuan Yew has tried to infuse a Confucian spirit among Singaporeans, leading one to wonder what part it is supposed to have played to date in Singapore's spectacular growth.

This is a field where magnetic polarity reverses itself every generation. The attempt by economists to explain the superlative performance of the sinitic ASEAN countries, Singapore, Hong Kong, South Korea, and Taiwan, without making any reference to value systems, which until recently would have attracted little criticism from within economics, has lately been harshly reviewed by Hicks and Redding.[25] These authors complain that: 'the obsession from which economics as a discipline suffers, appears to render it inadequate when confronted with the world's confused array. Nor must we be taken to be advocating greater looseness in analysis, only more completeness.'[26] 'Objective' economic factors seem incapable, they say, of accounting for much of the observed growth. Existing interpretations certainly leave much in the residual. At best, economists' accounts come down to praising good policies, carried out in an environment of political stability, without explaining why policies of this kind were adopted here and not elsewhere or why other areas of stability failed to achieve equivalent growth.

Hicks and Redding therefore argue that because economic explanations are inadequate, non-economic factors must be what turned the trick. The source of ASEAN growth must, they say, lie in culture (their second article is called, 'The Culture Connection'). 'The almost perfect correlation between Chinese cultural heritage and economic success could hardly be due to chance.'[27] Confucianism plus materialism, i.e. post-Confucianism, becomes the kernel: valuing thrift, diligence, education, family, together with societal discipline and hierarchy, these things will make you rich.

Hicks and Redding have certainly exposed the inconclusiveness of narrowly 'economic' explanations and drawn attention to the perfunctory way in which economists have typically dismissed the possibility of non-economic explanation. It is less certain however that Hicks and Redding are wise to seize on culture and values as if they were a drowning profession's only straws. Like Weber in modern dress, they seem to wish to derive economic action from religion or values close to it, the reverse of Marx's derivation of such superstructural trappings from the economic base. Yet their culturist brew is adulterated with materialist ingredients.

One is the very materialism inherent in 'post-Confucianism'. The ' "restless materialism of the young in Hong Kong would make Confucius turn in his grave" ', Anthony Sampson is quoted as saying.[28] The cupidity of the merchants in Ch'ing China would have done so too; materialism is nothing new to the Chinese. The other adulterant is the political and social confidence of the sinitic ASEAN countries, reportedly based on the fact that Western imperialism's impact on the old cultures of the 'Eastasia edge' was only transitory. This is historically unconvincing. China never sounded more confident than when dismissing the first British ambassador at the very end of the eighteenth century, and she was not growing then. The purity of cultural explanation becomes lost in the folds of politics and greed.

The success of the Eastasia edge may have depended on the Ayres thesis applied in geographical reverse.[29] Just as Europe once developed its selective gleanings from the East, sinitic Asia, including Japan, found Western political and religious institutions insupportable and adopted only the technology, developing it unto the Fifth Generation. Both ends of Eurasia largely jettisoned the values of the other. Each adopted the other's technology. Both forged ahead in their day. From whose culture, values, religion, is the seedbed of growth formed? Why at one time and not another? It is more parsimonious to accept, with Robertson against Weber, that belief systems are produced or modified by opportunity: if as he says Protestantism was created by 'Capitalism' rather than the other way round, so too post-Confucianism may be a hybrid created by opportunity.[30] The creation of real opportunity lifts a great weight from the economy's shoulders and value systems stretch and breathe anew in the fresh air.

Besides values, a second major set of explanations of backwardness appeals to institutional rigidity. Consider law. A penetrating survey of the world's families of law by David and Brierly stresses the ultimate mutability of the decision-making apparatus.[31] Muslim law, they state, 'is immutable, but it leaves room for such things as custom, the right of parties to contract, and administrative regulation; it is therefore possible to reach solutions which satisfy all social levels and which will enable a modern society to be developed without prejudice to the law'.[32] Law is defended by the very elasticity of the alternatives to it. A strong hand at the tiller, whether political or economic, is able to bypass legal negations deriving from the 'closure of the door of interpretation' in the tenth century—a conservatism that had in any case stemmed from political circumstances rather than from inherent limitations in Islamic legal thinking.

Muslim law was what ruled in Mughal India, although a vast customary terrain was left to be charted by the multiform religious (as opposed to truly legal) precepts of Hinduism. In China, law suggested a mode of behaviour, never a set of categorical rules, and this worked by tacit bargaining, by *tâtonnement*, and in the final analysis by the suasion of the powerful. Once again, politics at base determined institutional workings. The content of 'law' would certainly have been made to adapt to changes in economic circumstances when they affected people of influence.

One institution which was apparently universal in the pre-modern world was the guild, and it may be worth considering just how restrictive it was. Typically, guilds regulated entry to trades and held down firm-size by limiting the number of apprentices a craftsman might take. They determined prices, qualities, and even quantities of goods that might be produced. In other words they acted as local monopolies protecting the incomes of their members, not least from mutual competition. There is even a story of 123 members of a Chinese gold-beaters' guild who jointly *ate* a fellow member who had offended by taking on a large number of apprentices.[33] Dog eat dog could obviously work both ways.

Guilds, though, were customary in Europe too and it cannot be claimed that they halted economic growth there. Rather, growth seems to have set up competition between European guilds and among their members, which led the institution to disintegrate. The true speed of the decline is masked by the persistence of guilds as social and dining clubs and for some welfare purposes. In China on the other hand, despite the competitive opportunities made possible by far earlier improvements in transport and communications, they survived in strength. The difference was that without *intensive* growth they were not subject to the same strains and temptations, and they were important to the interests of the political classes who accorded them support in the name of social stability and control.

English salt-manufacturing interests, for instance, were told in the mid-nineteenth century to forget any thoughts of penetrating the Chinese market as their superior technology had enabled them to do in British India.[34] The involvement of leading Chinese officials in the salt monopoly meant that it was going to be defended up to the hilt. Admittedly the junk guild, which was theoretically protected against foreign competition by an article in the Treaty of Tientsin, had been thrown to the wolves when the Chinese government needed foreign help against the Taiping rebels. This only shows that the regime looked on the opportunities which the guilds exploited as assets of its own, to be permitted for a rake-off or abandoned when it suited. Guilds in Europe were economic institutions and economic forces finally abolished them; guilds in China were at bottom the prisoners of politics.

Among potentially obstructive institutions we can pick out the Indian caste system as virtually the limiting case. Slavery and serfdom come to mind as even more abhorrent, but moral abhorrence need not imply an impediment to growth. Slaves and serfs will obtain little of their own product, but accompanying slavery or serfdom there may well be a growing average product, shared, all too gleefully, by others. There are striking examples of fast-growing slave states, notably Germany during the Second World War. Hideous the arrangements are, limiting the deployment of talent and restricting the size of the market, to put it in an objectionably anodyne way, but slavery and serfdom redistribute income without necessarily reducing total income.

The caste system, and even a system of guilds, is more general in its effects because in principle all entrepreneurs are embroiled, their investment regulated: the size of plant or workforce, the scale of output, the nature of the product, and what may be charged for it. Growth is traded for the 'insurances' of job security and reduced competition. 'In that civilization which seems the most profoundly impregnated by religion, it is industry which has fashioned the dominant social form', wrote Célestin Bouglé.[35] A more pervasive and ostensibly deleterious arrangement of society is hard to imagine. Ascriptiveness is at the heart of it and personal achievement is excluded in principle. Caste assigns occupations, marriage groups, and consumption behaviour on grounds that have no observable basis in merit (other than the circularity which ensures that individuals lack a kind of merit because they have had no chance to acquire anything other than their hereditary skill).

This is like the British class system but set in concrete. Even a couple of generations ago class in Britain would have needed the bolstering of tight religious affiliation, obligatory guild membership, and guild usurpation of all welfare functions, truly to match the restrictiveness of the caste system. Nevertheless there is a kinship between the systems. They are both orders of intense ascriptiveness with barriers to inter-generational mobility across internal divisions, as Olson emphasizes.[36] It is Indian specialists who, for reasons of their own, want to find caste *sui generis*.

Caste is a hypertrophied system of occupational classes which is tainted with ethnicity (in general the darker the skin colour, the lower the caste) and which extends into other crucial areas of life, such as choice of breeding partner and style of life. At any one date it theoretically forbids, and certainly exerts a brake on, mobility between jobs. Further, it depresses job performance. Attendance is what is required, more than effort. Collective effort is impeded where each worker may pollute the next by his touch. And the market is crimped in advance by sumptuary rules concerning who may consume what.[37] It ought not to be difficult, then, to accept that caste is the limiting case of rigidified institutions.

Traditional commentators, including the Brahmins who in British India were in the best position to articulate their rationalizations, claimed caste to be a system formed in remote antiquity and accepted by all as the way God, or the gods, had meant society to be. Less involved observers tend to think of caste as created by a hierarchy of tasks, with the occupations that have more recently come into being occupying the higher status. Can this be because learning new skills, plus the psychic costs of mobility, at first restricts entry to new occupational castes, thus raising their status return? This theory implies the rise of castes at specific periods, and the appropriation of jobs and status by the most powerful rather than the ancestrally most pure. It begins to introduce a welcome historical note into spurious arguments about timeless origin and function.

Most modern observers, at any rate Western ones, and at the extreme the Marxists, do see caste as little more than a façade for power relations. 'Ritual purity . . .', says Colin Rosser, 'merely expresses in a traditional idiom, "prestige and authority" based essentially on the harsh realities of the differential distribution of political and economic power within the system. As this distribution of power changes, so eventually—allowing for "cultural lag"—will modifications occur in the associated symbolic representations. . . .'[38]

Rosser has aptly caught the most probable situation, although others have pointed out that the system is nowadays actually strengthened by upward mobility as successful individuals and groups vociferously adopt symbols appropriate to what they claim to be their new status, a process known as Sanscritization. Caste may be changing less than the movement of certain groups and individuals within it may suggest. Nevertheless, it is changing. It has been changing for a long time now and certain achievement norms have been assimilated. It was remarked of Calcutta as early as 1917 that 'in these parts the social order is a despotism of caste tempered by matriculation'.[39]

M. N. Srinivas's brilliant study, *The Remembered Village*, contains several first-hand observations on the flexibility of the system.[40] The normal and habitual conservatism he encountered was stretched to meet new situations and this he observes is typical for many parts of Indian society. There was plenty of remonstration for transgressing the rules; a neighbour would look into a vegetarian's rubbish and note the chicken bones. Yet these transgressions happened and Srinivas concluded that 'what was remarkable was the *effortless* switching of rules as demanded by the occasion'. He showed that 'whatever the rules governing inter-caste contact, even caste Hindu–Harijan contact,· they were ignored in an emergency'.[41] Whatever the priest might say, powerful men disregarded the rules of purity when it suited them to do so.

The more it can be shown that caste responds to external stimuli, the more reason there is to disbelieve that even this most obdurate of systems exerts primary control over economic life. It may constitute an infuriating brake, yet it will not be quite capable of switching off a motor located somewhere else in society. The more it can be shown that the powerful manipulate the rules of caste for their own ends, the more we may suppose that periods when no symbolic changes are detectable will have been ones when economic incentives were not changing. We are not likely to find many such periods.

The exigencies of life are too numerous even for caste to give more than an appearance of the eternal. One of the commonest changes in India has been internal migration, which strains social rules and permits evasion. Occupational barriers which James Mill depicted as uncrossable are slowly crossed because not everyone can make a living at his hereditary trade. Caste may be the finest-mesh filter in the world, but a filter it still is, channelling economic change in the short run but adapting to it and adapted by it in the longer run.

Values and customary institutions were everywhere more tractable than they appear, given enough economic stimulus or release from the oppressions of the powerful—big provisos of course. Observant anthropologists in the thick of describing what seem to be specific and iron-hard customs have often commented on this. Thus Raymond Firth appends to a remark in his notebook, 'Shows how kinship system not a rigid, inflexible mechanism, but one which is elastic, capable of being adapted to meet new situations.'[42] Hirschman's suggestion is undoubtedly right. Obstacles are not solid. There are ways round some, others possess positive attributes, and many are little more than hard cultural glosses on harder economic reality. There are few grounds for finding in the values or institutions of pre-modern Asia final blockages to growth rather than brakes and filters that gave local coloration to change.

This is not to imply that the values and institutions we have examined had the opposite sign and actually initiated growth. Their function or latent function was to share out the available product, ensure stability, offer psychic repose, and provide some kinds of insurance. Given the earlier achievements of non-Western systems it is however tempting to go almost to the other extreme from 'traditional society' accounts of perpetual backwardness, and espouse instead a 'close to growth' hypothesis—to believe that only a superficial check held Asia back between, say, Sung times and the nineteenth century. The 'critical minimum effort' or 'big push' school of development economists in the 1950s and 1960s appeared to hold a similar view. It seems naïve, for the historical checks were really very powerful. But they did not lie mainly in values, institutions, or culture and away from the mainstreams of economics and politics. The fate of the pre-modern Asian economies was not, in the event, baked in the cake of custom.

SIX

Conquests

Culture, then, does not adequately explain the centuries of frustration. It may have something to do with the problem, but its intangible nature is hard to pin down. As it is usually presented, which is as a permanent, generalized backdrop to underdeveloped Third World economies, it does not offer convincing reasons why particular economies should have found themselves at particular dead-ends.

Can the problem be solved at all? Dr Johnson thought not. 'By what means', asked Johnson's Prince of Abyssinia, 'are the Europeans thus powerful; or why, since they can so easily visit Asia and Africa for trade and conquest, cannot the Asiaticks and Africans invade their coasts, plant colonies in their ports, and give laws to the natural princes? The same wind that carries them back would bring us thither.' Johnson's answer, through Imlac to the Prince, was that the Europeans were more knowledgeable. As to why they were more knowledgeable, the despairing answer was, 'the unsearchable will of the Supreme Being'.[1] The question is thus a classic one that has been raised since at least the eighteenth century and despite Johnson's pessimism has attracted many and various answers since then. In so far as these refer to the societies that interest us, the most prominent of the answers offered is invasive colonialism.

It is fashionable to attribute the ills of the non-Western world during the past, even the present, to European colonialism. But there is no general explanation here, because Asia's languishing began before the period of European intrusion. By that time much of the non-Western World was, if not asleep, more dormant than it once had been. In any case, European penetration was too patchy and limited and failed to restructure enormous areas, notably China. The early quantitative effects in no way matched the extent of qualitative contact. Colonialism simply came too late and too unevenly to account for the sluggish economic record of Asia—unless we are prepared to include the effects of the internal Asian colonialisms which followed invasions by the Mongols and later nomad peoples.

Consider the case of India. If we compare a certain strain of writing on the British industrial revolution with what Saran calls the 'Defensive School' of Indian historiography, we might almost run away with the idea that it was the British economy which entered the eighteenth century in a moribund condition and Indian industries that showed all the promise, only to be forcibly destroyed by the British.[2] There are no adequate Indian figures given to support this inversion of economic histories, and the view that after the British take-over there was net industrial decline in India seems simply to be wrong.[3] Despite early episodes of rapine and later outbreaks of snobbery (not really racism: the Maharajah's son was welcome at Balliol when an English worker's son was not), the West made a massive technology transfer to India and all the Third World. By the late nineteenth century the West had promoted vigorous export growth there.[4] The same cannot be said of the earlier empires, ruled from Constantinople, Delhi, and Peking by the descendants of steppe nomads.

Some time between the twelfth and eighteenth centuries, Eurasia from the Balkans eastwards to the China Sea, from all but the southernmost tip of the Indian subcontinent northwards to Muscovy, fell beneath Mongol or Mongoloid regimes. The last of these centuries brings us right up to the beginnings of industrialization in that fortunate promontory which escaped— western Europe. The Mongol fist smashed east and tried to smash south. In 1292 a fleet was dispatched to invade Java. In 1297 an army trampled Burma. The waves of slaughter and destruction were horrendous wherever the Mongols had their numerous successes, which was almost everywhere they went by land. The guesses are that 35 million Chinese were killed by the Mongols and 25 million by the Manchus, one-third of the population in the thirteenth century and one-sixth in the seventeenth century. On the face of it, conquest of this kind would seem ample to account for economic regression.

On the fringes of Europe, Poland and Hungary had been ravaged by the Mongols, but nowhere farther west. In the east, invasion fleets were twice launched against Japan, but unsuccessfully, and this other fortunate extremity of Eurasia, those endstop islands like Britain, housed the first successful economic growth in modern Asia. In the light of later developments, most tempting of all features of the invasion thesis is the way western Europe and Japan both escaped the Mongol and later conquests. For Europe this was a close-run thing, with the Mongol armies turning back into central Asia merely to settle an issue of succession after the death of Genghis Khan, and never returning. For Japan it was a closer haul still, but the 'kamikaze' wind scattered the Mongol fleets. Europe and Japan were the regions that slowly climbed the stairs of *intensive* growth and did so from their relative obscurity as borrower cultures at the opposite margins of the old Eurasian world. The coincidence of *intensive* growth at the extremities and reversion to *extensive* growth in conquered China and the rest of mainland Asia seems neat.

The death toll in China alone at the time of the Mongol conquest was so large that it must have obliterated economic life over wide areas. Because he initiated the attacks against Sung China, Genghis Khan has actually been referred to as a 'crisis of capitalism'.[5] Nevertheless, the salient fact is that China and the Chinese population did recover from this dreadful catastrophe within a few score years. Yuan China, that is, Mongol China under the Great Khan Kublai was again a bustling urban and commercial land. This was the country visited by Marco Polo, Marco 'Millione', and obviously it had reinstated a well-developed economy, although what awed a medieval Venetian might not have seemed quite so impressive to a Chinese of the preceding Sung period.

For Russia, which the Mongols also ravaged and where they ruled from 1240 to 1480, a century longer than in either China or Iran, Halperin strikes the following balance-sheet.[6] The overall impact was probably negative, but Russia did recover from the campaigns of 1237–40 and did survive harsh taxes and exploitation. After 1240, destruction in Muscovy was no longer indiscriminate but was used as a policy tool to reduce the power of certain principalities while fostering others more sympathetic to the Mongols. Although the Mongols killed savagely and razed whole cities to the ground, theirs, like other inner Asian nomad empires, did encourage the caravan trade with the East. This was a major cause of Russia's renewed urbanism and economic recovery.

In Russia and China the costs of Mongol invasion, though they were vast, were thus absorbed. On a timescale of a century or so the economies recovered, and in a distinctly commercial way too, not just as run-of-the-mill agriculture. This is sufficient to cast doubt on the impression that even the most destructive of all the invading hordes can be blamed for a long-lasting diversion of whatever original prospects for growth there had been. Luc Kwanten's may be the appropriate summary: the Mongols' main interest in conquering territory was the profit from subsequent taxation, not simply the loot and not the mindless bloodlust of legend, hence their concern with continuing political control.[7] Their habit and policy was to create terror and wipe out opposition by mass slaughter but the underlying purpose was rational enough. Conceivably, though Kwanten does not say this, they had a master plan for grasping at world empire under what they saw as a mandate from heaven.

It is in Iran, where the following times were so unsettled and discordant, that any serious case for a Mongol imprint would have to be made, and Iran is not really one of the major cultures with whose future we are concerned. The form of the argument, as Lacoste applied it to the Asian and African Third World as a whole, would have to be that 'their stagnation . . . proves to be a period of confused disorder and of unsuccessful attempts to put an end to the turmoil'.[8] This applied most of all to the Iranian experience after the Mongols and Tamerlane.

The record of destruction in Iran was frightful and is said to have been permanent. This was because the irrigation agriculture was wrecked, possibly due to salination of the crop land brought about when the dykes and channels fell into disrepair. Although it is now known that some irrigation systems were still being kept up at the end of the Mongol period, the initial impact had been colossal. Slaughter without mercy, almost genocide, was intended to enable immigrant Mongol nomadic herdsmen to replace settled peasants. From the 1220s the unbendingly harsh taxation policies of the viceroys caused a further slump in population, the towns to shrink, and the area under cultivation to retreat. Marco Polo in the late thirteenth century and the great Muslim traveller Ibn Battuta in the 1330s saw the results of a ruination that was in bitter contrast to travellers' reports of a society positively flourishing before the Mongol invasion.

The only hard quantitative data signal a decrease in the number of villages in three major areas of Iran between the thirteenth and early fifteenth centuries. That span includes the endemic political struggle and warfare which rocked in the Mongol wake.[9] The census of villages slumped from 972 to 140, a fall of 86 per cent, although the tabulation for the second period consciously *excludes* hamlets that are not listed at all for the starting period, which suggests incomplete recording at first and therefore a level of destruction that is not wholly revealed by the figures. The shock was a massive one, as is further indicated by the central Iranian treasury receiving 81 per cent less tax revenue by 1333–40 than had been coming in before the Mongol attack.

There seems little doubt about the cruelty of the Mongol exterminations or that they surpassed previous nomad attacks in their ferocity. In most regions Mongol orders to local commanders ran on the lines: subdue the population—if anyone resists, kill him—but settle our own men or get people back on the land and paying their taxes promptly. The invasion strategy thus involved some rational calculation. Even the talk among the Yuan about the advisability of wiping out the Chinese and performing the ecologically senseless feat of putting their land down to pasture does not seem to have been based on any prior, demented ideology such as drove German extermination policy in the 1940s. But in Iran the cruel Mongol pragmatism was at its cruellest. As Alessandro Bausani observes, 'the Mongol invasion, like an earthquake, affected the very geography of the country'.[10]

The traditional obligation to accept billetted official messengers became under the Mongols so burdensome, involving among other evils an epidemic of rape, that many peasants deliberately kept their houses in a dilapidated state to avoid being singled out. Although towns on .trade routes recovered quite fast and the Pax Mongolica did foster long-distance trade, this hardly amounted to a significant urbanization or a revival of much trade in bulk goods. The ruination at the start and the subsequent press of taxes held Iran back from the level of prosperity which had been evident at the beginning of the thirteenth century. New policies which permitted some conditional ownership of land only began to bring about a slight recovery from the 1290s.

It is common to lay complete responsibility for prolonged economic failure at the Mongol door. A modern high Syrian official is quoted as having exclaimed in earnest that, 'if the Mongols had not burnt the libraries of Baghdad in the thirteenth century, we Arabs would have had so much science that we would long since have invented the atomic bomb. The plundering of Baghdad put us back by centuries.'[11] Practising scholars have voiced much the same opinion. The historian Alessandro Bausani's view, not normally to be sneezed at (in 1970, long before most people, he predicted the failure of the Shah's policies), is that 30 per cent of the Iranian population remained nomadic at the end of the nineteenth century, and agriculture remains backward today because the nomad invasions halted previous developments. He contrasts this outcome with western Europe's escape from the Mongols, and even remarks that some Iranian cities were bigger before the Mongol invasion than they have ever managed to become since.[12]

Kwanten is more emphatic still, though he sets a somewhat tighter bound on the persistence of the effects: 'It was not until well into the reign of the Safavids, some three hundred years later, that the dire consequences of the Mongol invasion began to disappear.'[13] Tamerlane's immense destructiveness in his late fourteenth-century invasion of Iran is also implicated. According to Bausani this was responsible for smashing the irrigation canals, leaving some land uninhabited to this day, setting back the hesitant tenurial reforms begun by the Mongols in the 1290s, and instead restoring a nomad aristocracy on the original Mongol plan. The Mongols and Tamerlane between them are accused by Terry Reynolds of setting back the Islamic use of water-power; for centuries after the Mongols the number of water-mills stayed lower than it had been before.[14]

In the extreme case of Iran, what was it exactly that the Mongols or Tamerlane had done to set back or disequilibriate the economy? Slaughter and destroy is the obvious cry, and we know very well that they did those things. What we do not know is how exactly destruction or conquest can be held responsible for an inability to restore stable government many centuries later. A very precise kind of historiography, an explicit model of the long term, would be needed to establish the link. Explanations are seldom forthcoming. Indeed, few historians seem to recognize the logical difficulties of accounting for current events by reference to a shock long ago, but recently an attempt at a link has been made by the economist, F. E. Moghadam.[15] Instead of concentrating merely on physical destruction, she considers the consequences for market formation. She examines the effects on the land market of the redistribution of land to the military and civilian officers of nomad regimes. Conquests, each followed by large-scale confiscation, 'arrested the development of private property in land', and this would have diverted much of the revenue from farm operators to the regime, reducing individual incentives to maximize production.

Moghadam goes further and states that, 'with the exception of Western Europe, most other older civilizations remained subject to the conquest of nomadic dynasties well into the modern era. Thus nomadic conquests may be a general explanation for the absence of private property in land in these countries.'[16] Her argument does not account for Japan, which as she properly recognizes is left as an anomaly. Any scheme which could place Japan and Europe in one favoured category and the remainder of Asia together in a less-favoured one would be suggestive. It might be the starting-point for an explanation of the pattern of Eurasian economic history which interests us. Unfortunately for a simple scheme that depends on nomadic invasions, not only did Japan and Europe escape invasion, but so did Sri Lanka. That island was quite well placed for trade, yet it scarcely rose to become the Holland of south Asia.

There are other and stronger objections. Even for Iran, despite the rhetoric, development cannot be shown to have been permanently set back by the Mongol conquest. Moghadam's model is more subtle than that. Hers is not a simple inertia theory. It depends on invasions that repeatedly destroyed the private market in land each time dynasties began to lose control over their followers. New redistributions to 'the arbitrary tradition of the steppe' were what suppressed this market, not indelible harm done by the first shock. If anything, the re-emergence of a land market under each succeeding dynasty testifies to an underlying slow logic of growth.

China, India, and the remainder of the Middle East suffered less often. Even for Iran, argument based on the persistence of the effects of the Mongol horde or other invasions, at least in a crude and direct form, simply does not have the force needed to explain a lack of economic vigour lasting several centuries. That argument is probably the greatest instance in Asian history of reasoning *post hoc ergo propter hoc*.

The entire mode of reasoning by inertia is unsatisfactory.[17] We should not seek to find the cause of events wholly contained in some earlier event, like a butterfly in its chrysalis, without considering what forces prevented a return to the original equilibrium. In any case, Asian and Middle Eastern economies shook off the effects of the Mongols; China, especially, returned to a very passable form of *extensive* growth even before the end of the Yuan (i.e. Mongol) period. The special case of Iranian 'backwardness' was the result of repeated shocks each of which set the clock back. On the other hand, it remains apparent that nowhere in mainland Asia reached, or in the case of China regained, a condition of *intensive* growth before Japan and Europe did. Can we rescue a version of the steppe conquest theory by finding a more subtle carry-over?

SEVEN

Derivative Effects

Invasion and take-over by a new regime always administer a colossal shock to the economic system. Notwithstanding this, it must be admitted that in long perspective even the most savage assaults were not as damaging as they deserved to be and did not prevent eventual recovery. On the immense canvas we have allowed ourselves, even a ghastly interruption of life, such as the slaughter of 10 per cent of the population of seventeenth-century Szechuan after the fall of the Ming, paints only a tiny blemish. (Zhang Zianzhong proclaimed an independent kingdom, announced himself heaven's instrument of vengeance against sinful humanity, and killed one million of his subjects. A mere fleabite.)[1]

Some conquests were actually followed by spells of intellectual vigour and renewed productivity growth as the result of order regained, returning confidence, and the low taxes called for by regimes flush with captured loot. Akbar drew divines from many areas to his court in India, as he sought to encourage a new Muslim synthesis. Besides being a ploy of religious politics on the part of one who traced his descent from Genghis Khan and Tamerlane, this was a mannered consumption of luxury that the Mughals could now afford. Yet flowering periods of this kind tended not to last. Typically, during or soon after the first reign of a new dynasty, a tax survey and better system for collection would be organized and a substantial share of gross farm output would then be taken by the regime, including its local officials.

The Islamic empires were the chief fly-trap economies of this sort, in which revenues disappeared relentlessly in one direction, swallowed like insects in a carnivorous plant by the conquerors and their descendants. From the peasant's point of view it mattered less who took from them what we would nowadays think of as rent-cum-taxes, than how much was taken and how arbitrary were the demands. To change the

metaphor, these regimes were sponges that sopped up
resources already produced, whether or not they also prevented
some production in the first place. Given the low level of
average income, their 'take' could leave the peasant like the
one in Tawney's famous Chinese simile, like a man standing
neck-deep in water, whom even ripples may drown.

Drowning was all too likely in such unstable regimes.
Having created a great shock-wave as each arrived on the
scene, the Asian empires were in turn vulnerable to shocks of
various sorts. These included famines and other outcomes of
natural disasters such as droughts and monsoon failures;
military defeats or mere military stalemates, since either dried
up the supply of land and plunder with which to pay off the
regime's officers; and international trade fluctuations such as
downturns in world bullion supplies or unfavourable shifts in
the terms of trade. Some recent studies link the domestic
economies of early modern Asia to the international economy
through the supposed effects of denominating taxes in silver.
Difficulties at the mines in Spanish America meant that
silver soon became scarce, which made taxes harder to collect.
The relationships are unclearly specified, and the possibility
that regimes short of silver could have created money
substitutes is nowhere explored, but the model does highlight
the way predatory behaviour was intensified in the wake of
shocks.

Peasant-retained income was bound to be squeezed. Any
shock tended to set up competition for straitened resources
among members of the ruling élite and between the élite and
the sultan or emperor himself. The efforts of these groups and
individuals to maintain their real incomes reverberated
through society. As Ali puts it for Mughal India, attempts at
greater agrarian exploitation were counter-productive because
technology was not improving and the supply response was
rigid. The failure of efforts to raise landlord income led to
'reckless factional activities for individual gain, leading to interminable civil wars'.[2] Provincial breakaways began to
threaten. (The empires were far less centralized in practice
than they were nominally.) Even if collapse were staved off,
the regimes survived in some areas in appearance rather
than reality. Conflicts and uncertainty reduced productive

investment in assets of kinds that could be seized by tax-collectors and local officials.

If the costs of turmoil were high for agriculture, the operations and products of which were not easy to hide, they were higher still for the trade sector. Rothermund notes that for thousands of years the chief port towns in the potentially rich Arabian, Mesopotamian, Iranian, and north-west Indian regions changed much more often than in Europe because political mishaps were always causing trade to shift to new centres.[3] Trade in this region had long been a creature of politics, flourishing least when the state was weak. To give an example from the Mughal period, the strife after Aurangzeb's death meant that Surat, chief port for the pilgrim trade, declined within a few decades. The caravans from northern India went unguarded. A quick turnover of governors meant the merchants were soaked of their wealth without being protected in return. The richer merchants took to arming themselves, conflicts ensued, and trade diminished.

A modern economist, sheltering behind the *ceteris paribus* clause, might say that, because trade is a substitute for resources, no region would have been restricted to the resource endowment with which it started. Rational maximizers would have traded for what they lacked and for goods in which they did not have comparative advantage. This approach can be useful in countering the naïve physicalism which sees only absolute levels of resources, but when we realize that 'rational' trade did not always arise to maximize the opportunities presented, we see that market logic is only half the story. Asian trade, according to Simkin's impressive review of the evidence, was too political for the simpler theorems of economics to explain its full history.[4] From Curtin's review of cross-cultural trade, it seems that really long-distance trading links were only made possible by the simultaneous rise of large empires.[5] Each of these had some distinctive wares to offer; each had centres of demand among the élites of its cities. Periods of contact were however interrupted by longer spells of political breakdown which were presumably marked by reduced supply and demand and soaring costs of protection. Between the birth of Christ and the sixteenth century, the Han–Parthian–Roman trade, the Tang–Abbasid trade, and the trade between Yuan

China and the Middle East under the Pax Mongolica were the only long-distance flows arising from contact between major systems. That left a number of centuries when long-distance East–West trade went into abeyance. The central problem was the fragility of the international political order; simultaneous domestic stability in more than one major region was required before trade contacts could be built up.

Invasion and conquest were part of the Asian experience. Wickham urges that over Eurasia as a whole, 'it is [imperial] survival that is the norm, failure that is the deviation'. His point is that by falling into the hands of 'feudal' lords and never recovering, the Roman empire was the exception: most empires were in Asia—and they cycled and survived.[6] In reality they were *recycled*, the norm was the *reimposition* of empire.

Aristocrats and bureaucrats made niches for themselves within the Asian imperial state, but they did not capture it, and they never came to depend on or form a symbiosis with trade. There were interregna of varying durations after empires crumbled, and at those times ambitious lords built polities in the areas best placed to hold onto revenues that had formerly passed to the empire.

When men in revolt struggled to establish their position, they plundered. To this day some villagers in south Gujarat can point out where their ancestors used to hide harvested crops and other goods at the approach of the raiding Maratha chief, Shivaji. By the time of his death in 1680, Shivaji controlled 4 per cent of the subcontinent. He had imposed an elaborate administrative machinery which squeezed from that small fraction the equivalent of over 20 per cent of the revenue which the emperor, Aurangzeb, was able to raise from the entire remainder of Mughal India.[7] Less-favoured areas were repeatedly hit by synergetic political and ecological disorders. Indian history after the Mughals is now thought to have been systematically differentiated by region in this way, and not to have become, as older versions suggested, unrelieved anarchy as the empire collapsed.[8] Within the Ottoman empire, too, local fiefs seem to have arisen, but the empire held together. China definitely did.

Inside the state, as Adshead says of China, lay, however, only micro-entities like guilds, clans, and secret societies.[9]

There was even less coherence in the Middle East, and only the atomization of caste and village in India. These grassroots organizations touched production and exchange intimately but could only minimally represent themselves to the authorities. They were largely free of day-to-day direction or assistance from above, and the relationship between government and village economy was indirect.

The relations between government and the timing of economic growth have proved resistant to theory. It is difficult to state operationally what the relations may have been, and given the paucity and vague form of most historical evidence it is hard to support any particular idea. Few attempts have been made even to guess at the political structures under which growth may falter or fail. Two influential models may be mentioned.[10] Alexander Gerschenkron's view was that a big, state-assisted push of industrialization is needed and delay may mean that the *Sternstunden* (the crucial moments) will pass, opening the way for reaction, even revolution. Mancur Olson sees distributional coalitions arising when growth remains politically undisturbed for too long. Rent-seeking coalitions then carve up the existing product, restrict enterprise, and dramatically reduce the growth rate. Specifying the proper role of government at any given historical moment nevertheless remains a matter of art rather than science.

The 'traditional society' theory adopted by many social scientists to explain supposedly perpetual non-growth will certainly not do, in that, by definition, historical content is emptied out of it.[11] The 'obstacles to growth' approach, as it stands, is much the same and cannot fully succeed for the same reason. The matter became more mysterious still once Hirschman wrought his 'quasi-vanishing act' and caused 'obstacles' either to disappear or turn inside out.[12] Since Hirschman, 'obstacles' can be seen as socio-economic features with two faces, one favourable to growth, the other unfavourable. This leads halfway back to the opposite, positive feedback, rubric: that 'growth builds growth'. Of course growth does build growth, smoothing its own path by creating wealth, levelling barriers, and the like, except when it stops doing so, which is precisely what Gerschenkron and Olson were trying to explain. We are left unable to decide what has happened in practice—where indeed North and Thomas left us in *The Rise of the Western World*, with the idea that innovation occurs when expected net gains exceed expected net costs but not when they fail to do so.[13]

There is in principle a solution. This is to recognize that the ambiguity surrounding Hirschman's two sides of obstacles to growth might be dispelled with a more historical approach. Can the history of growth and development, then, really be made historical—or be made really historical? The answer seems to be affirmative, the same feature representing an obstacle under some circumstances and not under others. As a first move these circumstances may be identified by arranging episodes in the history of institutions (potential obstacles) chronologically.

The reason there is so little existing literature about the impact of particular politico-economic events on values, institutions, and growth, or vice versa, is the historian's habit of over-labelling. Many values, even whole religious systems, have ostensibly been present under similar names for hundreds or thousands of years. Many of the customs, rules, and embodied institutions—craft corporations, merchant associations, guilds, the craft system, and the like—seemingly have very long histories. Associations of merchants are for example listed in immensely early documents, and behavioural values which are still prized are mentioned in ancient sacred writings. This similarity lends itself to attributing fixed content and force to institutions and values over vast periods when no hard evidence warrants this. Better-documented cases show that real but shadowy fluctuations in meaning are always taking place, often in response to changes like the invasions and intensified struggles for revenue which we have discussed.

Undoubtedly there had always been rent-seeking behaviour, but there is no a priori reason for thinking that Asians and Middle Easterners devised institutions less promotive of growth than other people in comparable circumstances. What we observe in the Asian equivalent of the long early modern period is that the circumstances were likely to have had knock-on effects that changed institutions and attitudes and made recovery harder. The hardening of conservative values and rent-seeking behaviour as consequences of struggles over resources and group esteem were derivative effects that were patterned. A negative face revealed itself most in response to economic oppression, and made it harder for the economy to climb from the track of *extensive* growth to the track of *intensive* growth. Rigid values and defensive institutions were rational responses to the disincentives stemming from actual events.

The effects we are looking for are long-lasting social and intellectual conservatism leading to ascriptive behaviour that cramps the optimal allocation of resources, and new or greedier rent-seeking that replaces or hampers productive effort. These things are the arthritis that follows trauma and increases the minimum effort an economy needs to achieve or regain *intensive* growth. Rent-seeking is a political act. It refers to receipts above the opportunity cost of the resources—receipts obtained by 'politicking', and accruing, like some perverse halo effect, to the prestige or political influence of the agent. It means non-market allocation. A monopoly will earn rents if it can use political means to block new entrants from entering its industry.[14] No consumer surplus is created this way.

The secondary literature is not very helpful in giving historical flesh to these bare bones, but a few items turn up on inspection. One concerns the establishment under Mongol rule of the churches as powerful secular forces, and their persistence in the form of the conservative Buddhist and Taoist clergy in China and the Muslim clergy in the Middle East. The Ottoman civil service had some of its origins here. The legal system was reclericized under the Ottomans.[15]

In the post-Mongol empires, extortion and bribery often threatened to become ways of life. Fierce struggles for wealth and income broke out, running at the extreme to symptoms of social bankruptcy, such as banditry. An outbreak occurred in north-west China when the Ming (admittedly a native dynasty, but a very defensive one) tried to press more taxes out of an impoverished peasantry to fee its embattled armies in the north-east.[16] To choose another illustration, bitter competition for resources among the Safavid élite of Iran in the seventeenth century, when rulers tried to solve their problems with an expensive standing army, caused the *de facto* breakaway of some provinces.[17] In such circumstances defensive reactions by members of social institutions were to be expected.

Let us look more closely at the history of that depressing but important institution, the Indian caste system. We find that although the literature is chronologically uninformative it is not completely barren. The original Aryan invasion of the Gangetic basin had been followed by the reorganization of society on caste lines. The remnant 'taint of ethnicity' about caste does suggest that it originated in the imposition of successive overlays of conquerors, while subsequent southward missionizing by Brahmins spread the system into formerly tribal territories. The spread of caste between 1750 and 700 BC is explained in these terms by Kosambi.[18] According to him, the consequent paralysis of social will cost Indian society its ability to resist the later Muslim invaders. In addition, caste rules tightened after the Mughal conquests and again after the British take-over. From the point of view of the Muslim conquerors, the latent function of caste may have been to fragment Hindu resistance. The rules were still hardening well into the British period and it was a long time before policies were adopted that reduced some of the asperities.

Caste has a historical origin and caste rules have particular histories. As Srinivas has noted, the system was once much less restrictive than it became: Hindu trade and colonization could not have taken place throughout south-east Asia had the later prohibition on crossing the 'Black Water' (sailing the sea) existed in the Middle Ages.[19] Greater restriction, more ossification, and at the same time manipulation of the system by the powerful, are all consistent with responses to seizures of resources and restrictions of social space by alien conquerors. They can be seen as moves to preserve the remaining shares of social product and prestige in the hands of indigenous groups, all of whom had to some extent been marginalized by defeat. This is pie-slicing behaviour, and step by historical step it will have reduced the ability of society to increase the size of its pie.

Guilds are another significantly protectionist institution. Superficially they appear to have been universal in complex societies. Historians have labelled almost any association of merchants or artisans as a guild, whether or not it can be shown to have regulated business activities at all closely. There seems however to be no evidence that true guilds really existed in the empires of China or the Middle East at early periods, before late Ming times for example, or in Turkey before the second half of the fifteenth century. Both Ottoman and Ching dynasty (Manchu) guilds did come to regulate entry to occupations, adjudicate on quality of product, and oversee prices, but their ultimate independence from the state is doubtful or mythical. Variations in the enforcement of their rules before about 1850 can hardly be detected in the secondary sources available, even though most of these are based on intensive documentary research.

Most studies indeed draw the bulk of their references from the second half of the nineteenth century and extrapolate backwards to early times, portraying 'guilds' throughout as operating in a uniform miasma of archaism. Hard, dated early citations are scanty. Variations in the level of enforcement of guild regulations are quite obscure. Any evidence of the reorganization of guild rules, and of close control, thus tends to be drawn heavily from precisely the short and abnormal period after about 1850 when Western traders were penetrating the markets of the non-Western world. It comes chiefly from the port cities where Western merchants congregated, and often relies on Western testimony alone.

Signs of intense guild activity and efforts to police production and trade are just what we might predict in those focuses of trade competition and social stress. Ottoman and Ching guilds tried to suppress the rising competition among their members prompted by the entry of Westerners. They feared some members might manage to exploit it more than others could. Within a couple of generations the guilds had however dissolved in the face of competition and the Western modes of administering the economy that governments began to adopt. Once new types of administration and taxation could be copied from the West, governments lost interest in using the guilds and soon ceased to ratify guild arrangements.[20] After 1890 in Egypt and about 1900 in China the role of the guilds thus dwindled fast.[21] Market opportunity won out. Coupled with the withdrawal of state support, which they had previously received far more than Western guilds ever had, this meant the death of effective guild systems.[22]

These effects are interesting but they are not the ones we are investigating. The dissolution of the guilds in the face of greater market competition neither invalidates nor supports an argument about the intensification of their rules in phases of politically initiated competition for reduced resources, that is, after invasions. In any case, these guilds were hardly the pure economic institutions they may seem to be—they were extensions of the state.

Guilds in China derived their power from the state and they complemented the state without ever acquiring legal protection for their members. Only in the harshly competitive climate after the mid-nineteenth-century Taiping rebellion did they think of representing private interests. The power they had exercised over their members' livelihoods through controlling matters like credit, storage, tare, and weights and measures was a substitute for direct control by a bureaucracy that hardly provided everyday administration itself.

The powerful, persistent, and independent role of Chinese guilds suggested by Olson does not seem to be borne out by the sources and seems to be a labelling error, an anatopism in that he implies a role comparable to that of Western guilds in a place where it did not exist.[23] The guilds, as he notes, may have blocked some technical changes, but this was their response to the severe competition they eventually faced, or thought they faced, from the West. The effect cannot have been prolonged because the guilds themselves did not last much longer, and the whole episode involved a market penetration quite atypical of the political penetrations in China's earlier history.

There is no suggestion that the guilds were truly influential on their own account. Government officials were wary of letting guilds fix market prices, because although they were aware of the advantage of some price stability they were equally aware that monopoly pricing might give rise to popular discontent.[24] The guilds were to a limited extent able to look after their members' interests, but not by blocking new entrants. Instead they incorporated those who wished to join them, embracing and regulating these potential competitors without excluding them altogether. This they did mainly in the interests of welfare and state-approved order.

Under the Ottomans, guilds were controlled by the state everywhere except in Bursa. Instructions about the quality of goods, weights and measures, and prices to be charged, were actually issued by the government, not the guild. The aim was state control of urban labour—for security purposes, sometimes to direct workers to state projects, and above all for purposes of taxation. Ching government involvement was more cloudily indirect than this, but neither in China nor the Ottoman empire were the guilds capable of standing as independent producer organizations.

If the guilds held back the Ching and Ottoman economies, this would have been because government had seen in them a convenient means of social control and taxation. Government, then, was the ultimate restraining force. The fact that the Chinese state conceived of trade largely as a zero-sum game—what you gain, I lose—was its own source of restriction on the propects for *intensive* growth. There is no reason to suppose that the Ottomans thought very differently. What we find is that the sources do not tell us how 'guilds' responded to early invasions—but, then, they were not in the last resort true native institutions. They were steering devices to perform at a long remove functions which pre-modern states approved but were too indolent or inept to carry out through professional civil services. Conservative guilds were a cost attaching to indolent, rent-seeking political systems that used them as a roundabout means of economic administration. One might say that politics was the opium of these people and religion, after all, only a soft drug.

Round each corner the pre-modern state looms, its effects varying in different periods and different regions, perhaps never so decisively negative as an earlier historiography made out, but seldom benign and almost never positive. After the joyous release of smash-and-grab invasion, new regimes had no interest in obliterating economic activity, quite the contrary. They had every interest in milking the cow, provided she could be kept quiet. Keeping cows quiet became of almost equal importance to milking them, and with minimal delegated effort this was done. Societies were arranged to reward collaboration, by the guilds, by the Brahmin priests, and so forth. Even the Ming became conservative and agrarian and did no more for growth than did the alien regimes.

Thus far we have been discussing possible influences on GNP, on the assumption that any ossification in productive responses may be expected to have reduced its rate of growth. Average per capita real income is the quotient when GNP is divided by population. What about the denominator: the size of population? The links between fly-trap economics and the rate of population growth would have been via greater incentives or smaller disincentives for peasants to have large families. Only for Japan and Europe, significantly enough, is it usually claimed that peasants controlled family size, implicitly choosing income rather than an additional child. Musallam has admittedly argued that in medieval Egypt and Syria the urban middle classes did commonly resort to birth control in bad times and that this was acceptable within Islamic thought, but it is unlikely that the bulk of the population, which was rural, followed suit.[25]

Deliberate population restraint is not reported from the societies of mainland Asia. Whatever size family the stork brought may have been accepted *faute de mieux* or even with pleasure, as an adjustment to high risk and great uncertainty. For peasant producers it may have been sensible to consume any small surplus within the family rather than let the tax-collector have it, as a form of income and deferred indirect investment via more and better-fed children.

Perhaps, then, peasant demography was the spring of the trap in which most of the pre-modern world was rather willingly caught. Various other plausible motives have been put forward to explain why peasant families bred large numbers of children instead of trying to raise per capita incomes by limiting births. One possibility is that having a large number of children may have been a means of maximizing the number of sons, given that the sex of the offspring could not be predetermined. Sons were desired because in a surprisingly few years they would supply labour for heavy field-work. They offered hands to help recovery after disasters, say by rebuilding dykes. A motive even more frequently cited is that sons would provide some security in old age. These were insurance motives in a world lacking formal insurance markets, and the commonest Western view is that the inevitable price was the multiplication of poverty.

Non-Westerners clearly do not accept this on the basis of their own experience, especially as large families have positive social value to them whatever the true economic implications.[26] Unfortunately modern observations, made during a period of economic development and Westernization, are not necessarily representative of earlier conditions. The demand for children may actually rise in the early stages of economic development, to offset new risks and tap new opportunities.[27] This renders what we might call modern demographic anthropology a doubtful historical tool.

Since the Second World War the growth of human numbers in the Third World has been a great bogey and has spawned a literature ranging from the coolly analytical to the 'population bomb' variety. Obviously one can list ways in which unbridled demographic expansion may add to the difficulties of raising per capita income. Yet everywhere except in parts of Black Africa the vast increase in population in recent years has been accompanied by *intensive* growth. The resultant level of real incomes over much of the world is not yet nearly enough for decent living and certainly does not match the expectations that have been aroused, but if we believed the alarmist writers we would have been seeing incomes fall rather than rise.

Although they are not as fashionable in these days of doomstering, models can be built in which a large and rising population facilitates growth instead of depressing it. A literature associated with names like Ester Boserup and Julian Simon points out the positive contribution that population growth can make. Once again it should not be hard to think of ways in which this may happen. On the assumption of a normal distribution of intelligence, the supply of gifted individuals will grow to the point where, *ceteris paribus*, it may attain critical mass for solving a country's problems.[28] Simon and Steinmann show formally that the larger of two populations will always have the higher output per worker, because of scale advantages in learning-by-doing.[29] The trouble is that this does not automatically happen, or at least it did not do so in the past. A larger population does *not* by itself guarantee a more productive economy and rising incomes. These results depend among other things on the institutions and relative interconnectedness of society. Nevertheless it is far from certain that population growth as such actually held incomes down.

Boserup's theory is described by Simon as a population-push model, in which, while the invention rate is independent of population growth, the adoption of new techniques of production depends on a rising population. Further population growth presses the available stock of inventions into use. This may work for straightforward subsistence or near-subsistence agricultures but does not seem to hold where matters become more complicated. Institutions and markets make a difference. The obvious alternative model is the Malthusian one, invention-pull, where inventions (innovations) succeed in pulling up output and enable more people to be supported, but are eventually overtaken and exhausted by the pressure of human numbers. Once again the argument needs the economist's let-out: 'other things being equal'. Such models are useful as ideal types. They clarify some relationships, but by neglecting the institutional and political setting they leave the final outcome indeterminate. Will talent be mobilized, will rates of invention and innovation keep ahead of population growth? These questions cannot be decided by the court of population studies alone. The political context is and was crucial.

EIGHT
The Lethargic State

At the time of the oil shock in 1973 I remember reading that although geologists probably knew where the world's larger hydrocarbon deposits were, many lesser fields must still be unknown. Only 4 per cent of drilling had been done in less-developed countries, apart from the Middle East. Economic history suffers from a similar geographical imbalance in what has been studied and in its most exciting prospects for future work. Whereas Europe has been studied in depth, far less research has been carried out on Asia.

The absolute number of publications on Asian economic history is of course vast, and rapidly increasing. No individual could hope to read more than a fraction, but the point about relative proportions still holds. In addition, Westerners who engage in Asian studies have Eastern languages to contend with, and this imparts a bias to their work in favour of close textual interpretation. Few such scholars—there are of course some great exceptions—display much interest in economic history or write about it in ways that throw light on the sorts of questions a comparative economic historian might want to answer.

One of these questions concerns the degree of involvement of the Asian empires in the international economy. An older opinion, that European imperialism was directly responsible for the 'under-development' of an Asia in reality little visited let alone monopolized by Europeans, has been manipulated to get round the miniscule European presence. It is variously argued nowadays that trade naturally favoured the Europeans; that European demand for luxuries out-competed Asian buyers and caused a politically destabilizing inflation; and that fluctuations in the supply of silver brought in by the Europeans reacted adversely on Asian society. These approaches rely on the undemonstrated existence of a significantly reciprocal international economy a long way back in early modern times.

This vein of recent historical writing represents the opposite pole from depictions of pre-existing centralized states as the villains of the piece. Belief has weakened in all-determining command economies of the sort envisaged by work on the 'Asian mode of production', brought to prominence by Karl Wittfogel's *Oriental Despotism* (1957). This draconian command-economy model was made credible to non-specialists by visions of enduring oriental slavery—from the use of whips on the hordes toiling to build the pyramids to the use of whips in the streets of Peking under the Manchus. These stark pictures are misleading, but nevertheless the impact of the regimes was likely to have been great. For Safavid Iran we are told that land revenue was sometimes 'as little' as 25 per cent of annual produce.[1] Estimates for Mughal India vary between central government levies of 33 per cent and 50 per cent of gross farm output or even national product.[2] A prima-facie case might be made out that governmental and élite shares like this would have 'crowded out' productive investment, although this does not imply complicated financial models of the type the phrase nowadays connotes. It is also possible to think that the initial seizure of large shares by conquerors will have had a resource-squeezing impact leading to derivative effects of the kinds discussed in the previous chapter.

The élites in pre-modern societies spent heavily on conventional luxuries and no doubt squandered and immobilized much of their income. The questions are, how large was the share taken by central governments or their adherents; was this total 'tax' share productively employed; and how much was typically left for Asian peasants to invest? The conclusions that the ruling élites as a whole consumed rather than invested are open to exceptions, such as the promotion of irrigation schemes at certain periods by provincial gentry in China, but seem to hold as generalizations.

Central governments lacked a growth ethic (they had a power ethic), and in any case they lacked budgets proportioned to the development needs of sprawling, primitive landscapes. Abandoning the notion of universally grasping authoritarian regimes that quashed all prospects of growth, but convinced that blaming underdevelopment on the Europeans is less historical judgement than rationalized modern politics, we arrive at the possibility that pre-modern regimes were too indolent, unknowing, and ill equipped to bring about growth.

The Islamic empires most warrant the appellation 'fly-trap economies' since so much of what was produced in them flowed in one direction only, into governmental and élite hands. Governments invested in productive ways no more than a trumpery share of their receipts. Resources were appropriated for military purposes and for consumption by the ruler, his entourage, and officials, and there is no sign that the élite in the provinces spent its money very differently. The direct benefit of this to the economy was little more than the formation of a market for luxuries that encouraged particular sets of merchants and artisans. As Raychaudhuri says of India, 'the Mughal state was an insatiable Leviathan: its impact on the economy was defined above all by its unlimited appetite for resources.'[3] We need not enter the debates about the fluctuating relations between central governments and the provinces, which mainly meant that at different times different shares of revenue reached the innermost recesses of the trap, to see that we are dealing by and large with economies where ruling groups imposed deadweight costs on producers.

In Akbar's reign at the end of the sixteenth century, 82 per cent of the entire net revenue of the Mughal state passed into the hands of a mere 1,571 persons.[4] These privileged beings can have felt little impulse to alter a system that treated them so kindly; growth would have reduced their relative advantage—small wonder that the potential economic managers in that society lacked a growth ethic. Looked at in this way the 'agency' costs associated with pre-modern government are seen to have been very high. From the viewpoint of economic management, far too much of what the state and ruling class took was misapplied.

Unfortunately for generalizing about 'Asia', the share of national product appropriated by Chinese governments and governing élites was too low to have accounted for the suppressed performance of China's economy; the share was not more than 8 per cent in Ming or Ch'ing (Manchu) times.[5] If crude appropriation in China is to be rescued as a serious argument, the regime will have to be taken at its broadest, that is, including the local gentry. The grey area surrounding the scale of the 'taxes' extorted by this wider group and the nature of the evidence mean that it may never be possible to estimate it closely. Local officials will have had no wish for Peking to realize just how much could be squeezed from the system. Although the distinction between rent and taxes customary in Europe was not made and this may exaggerate the resources taken from the countryside, the case for taxation crowding out investment in China must undoubtedly remain weaker than in the Ottoman, Mughal, and Safavid empires.

The concept of taxation was not our modern one. Whereas we envisage taxes as collectively agreed and enforced payments for a bundle of public goods, taxes in the pre-modern world were primarily levies by rulers on the ruled. States provided little more than the elementary governmental functions of defence and order. It would have been in the state's own interest to provide more background 'insurance' against disasters. European states increasingly did so, but Asian states were much less active. After Akbar, the Mughals had no permanent system of famine relief.[6] The ever-normal granaries of eighteenth-century China did thoroughly outclass their European equivalents, but neither China nor other Asian societies seem to have devised the quarantine or the *cordon sanitaire* that did so much to limit the spread of bubonic plague and cattle plague in Europe.

Even in China, famine relief measures deteriorated badly after about 1810–20, at a period when Europe's competence in relief measures was exemplified by the energetic response to 1816, the 'year without a summer'. European governments at large had handled remarkably well the harvest and disease shocks that coincided during the early 1740s.[7] In some Asian emergencies limited income-redistribution did take place—the Safavid regime, for instance, redistributed revenues in times of drought and other disasters—but these measures seem to have been less reliable than the provision for the poor in Europe. As Samuel Johnson said, 'a decent provision for the poor is the true test of civilization'.[8]

The demands of rulers' consumption on limited central funds could be heavy. Conspicuous consumption by the later rulers of Yuan China led to real budgetary difficulties there.[9] Under the Ming, imperial expenditure became oppressive and in the mid-sixteenth century this curtailed the sums left for genuine disaster relief. In 1561 while the emperor and his current favourite were drunkenly romping they overturned an oil lamp, set fire to their bedding, and thence to the whole palace. This 'had' to be rebuilt at once, which was done by using materials intended for the reconstruction of the audience halls of the Forbidden City, burned down in 1557. Much heavier taxes had to be levied to recoup.[10] There is no suggestion that demands like these led to the fall of dynasties and there is no means of measuring how far they replaced more productive outlays, but they do give a clue to the priorities of the rulers concerned.

There was after all a long line of central Asian conquerors who became folk legends because they were red-handed mass-murderers; the last on the grand scale was probably Nadir Shah who sacked Delhi in 1739. Wars of succession were endemic, too, like the one in which Aurangzeb took power from his father and slaughtered his own brothers. Scant force was required to drive risk-averse peasants, who had enough natural disasters to contend with, back into subsistence farming; to frighten merchants, who lacked standing in societies originally based on warrior hierarchies, and cause them to consume their assets or keep them in 'liquid' forms like jewels; or to separate from their estates landlords who were state officials rather than hereditary owners. Men like the *jagirdar*s of Mughal India could not usually bequeath the *jagir*s they held, and lacked much incentive to invest in the land. Instead they milked the peasants while they could.

There are plenty of instances of governments directly frightening off capital investment. Bernier's account of seventeenth-century India, where householders did not repair their property for fear of attracting the notice of the tax-man, is among the best known.[11] Any society founded so recently on the naked violence of conquest was perhaps likely to resort to force automatically. Mughal provincial governors were sometimes tortured on suspicion of falsifying the tax returns. Again, this applied less in China than elsewhere, but it would be astonishing if customary rather than formally legal methods of collecting taxes did not depress *some* investment even there.

From a modern or Western standpoint one is surprised at the extent of market activity that took place in these circumstances. Commodity markets did work despite haphazard means of settling disputes. The Mughal court system was in theory comprehensive and is said to have been more sensitive to the variety of Hindu legal practices than the British Raj. In reality it was corrupt and used trial by ordeal or direct force to settle matters. Litigants could often buy decisions favourable to themselves.[12] The issue is not whether some classes were in practice excluded from using the courts, as indeed many people were in Europe, but what degree of impartiality might be expected even by those who came before the law. While perhaps only semi-arbitrary (the suspicions which substituted for hard evidence may have had some basis in observation and shrewdness), typical Asian justice was necessarily uncertain.

A modern person tends to expect that a lack of secure government and proper state and legal regulation of the economy would reduce activity or cause chaos. Yet markets did work. Moreover, private arrangements within merchant associations, castes, guilds and the 'native place associations', which the Chinese formed when away from home, offered substitutes for functions we would expect government to provide, including the reduction of transaction costs by establishing systems of weights and measures and agreeing exchange rates among local coinages. The issue is the subtle one of just how inferior these substitutes may have been. There is no means of computing the hidden costs, and it cannot really be claimed that because Western governments took certain measures and Western economies became more developed, the key must have lain in the lack of that particular type of provision. Yet the suspicion must linger that arbitrariness cost something, perhaps a lot, though much more in the Islamic empires than in China.

The view is emerging in the literature that the root cause of under-development was less the grasping state than the state's under-government. As Fox says, 'agrarian states were often less than the sum of their parts'.[13] They definitely spent too much of what they took on armies, palaces, high living, and debauchery. Yet it is still arguable that neglect rather than expropriation was the greater hurt. Sometimes the thesis is

quite specific: governments neglected to supply negotiable
instruments of state credit, backed by the public revenue,
certified by the majesty of the law.

Feuerwerker has traced what was missing in Chinese government to the early success in presiding over a vast, complicated
economy with a standard of living that was respectable by any
pre-modern standards.[14] He speculates that this drained away
the incentive for governments to intervene further. Feuerwerker
sees no logical need to explain why there was little advance
beyond this point. He takes the position that real growth is
abnormal even in the modern world, being limited to 'a
minority of the earth's nations'.[15] This is wrong. GDP per
capita has been rising throughout the World Bank's sample of
ninety countries since at least 1960 and much earlier in many
cases. Annual average percentage change has been negative
only for certain countries in Black Africa and only since 1973:
it was − 0.1 per cent for Africa from 1973 to 1980 and − 1.7 per
cent from 1980 to 1985. This was a tragedy, but it was
restricted to the one continent and, speaking in averages, was
much more than offset by gains elsewhere. In low income
countries as a whole, GDP per capita went up at an annual 4
per cent between 1980 and 1985. Economic growth is *not* the
exception.

Feuerwerker takes the view that growth has been not merely
abnormal but uniquely European. Yet his own observation
that pre-modern economic fluctuations have had too little
attention compared with the 'more fashionable problem of
modern development' shows what the true issue is. We cannot
afford to dismiss the long stretches of *extensive* growth, so
different from stasis or stagnation, as non-problems of history
—their deadness 'over-determined', in Feuerwerker's phrase,
because any one of a multitude of hazards may have been killing
off the prospect of *intensive* growth burgeoning within them. His
admission that the pre-modern world saw no '*sustained growth*'
or '*continuous innovation*' shows that we are indeed studying
economies which sometimes hibernated but did occasionally
burst into life in places far apart in space and time and quite
dissimilar in culture.[16] *Intensive* growth and *extensive* growth are
Siamese twins and should seldom be severed for the purpose of
study.

The issue of pre-modern growth is the real one and, even though I disagree with his assumptions, Feuerwerker deserves the fullest credit for making a more direct approach to it than almost anyone else. He goes on to sketch an ingenious solution to the puzzle of the divergence between European and Asian economic performance, in terms of what European governments came to do and Asian governments neglected. (This surely explains Asian non-development in precisely the way he criticizes as over-determined, that is, in terms of one *specific* lack among many possible causes.) He starts from the notion that European governments of the seventeenth and eighteenth centuries devised funded national debt. They made government bonds and annuities into investments that were as safe as land. Landed families certainly did diversify their portfolios in this direction.[17] Asian governments, on the other hand, never thought of negotiable instruments as more reliable sources of revenue than direct taxes. Chaudhuri makes a similar point with respect to Mughal India.[18]

The activist role of European governments certainly included the state extension of capital markets, although one would not want to base an explanation of economic growth on this alone. Lending to the state may have been secure, but even respectably interventionist European governments spent much of the money they borrowed on war and diplomacy. In any case, we must confront the fact that private agencies in Manchu China and Mughal India (the merchant associations in China and fraternities of bankers in India) seem to have substituted for many functions that were eventually taken over by government in Europe.

Admittedly, Chaudhuri makes the essential further assertion that the Indian failure to define the merchant's position at law meant that in the popular mind commerce remained tainted by usury, engrossing, and monopoly, and as a result was practised less than it might have been.[19] If so, this may challenge the idea that the private sector could adequately substitute for government. Feuerwerker himself puts in doubt the adequacy of the role of Chinese merchant associations.[20] It would be misleading to set all this against the other possibility—that pure private enterprise changed the face of Europe, and that rather than more efficient government in Europe, the key was a more efficient private sector. The presumption must be that European government and business both became more efficient, in a complex synergy. Even private markets could not work without the specification and enforcement of property rights (and much more) for which governments alone possessed the authority and sanction of force.

The emphasis laid by Feuerwerker on a particular mode of credit creation, the bill of exchange, seems more appropriate. In Europe, merchants rather than the state promoted it. This comes close to the position that the difference we are all trying to identify was not so much that in Europe the private sector substituted for government, but that it did so more efficiently there than anywhere else. In any case, governments themselves were also more active in Europe. Successive improvements in the legal specification and enforcement of property rights, helping the rise of a mortgage market, together with a whole web of commercial laws and legal precedents were what altered the investment climate, at least in common-law Britain. The joint-stock company and limited liability came of course far too late to explain growth and ought to be seen as growth-adapting changes. Nevertheless, the earlier legal changes seem formative.

The Chaudhuri–Feuerwerker approach plays back a particular version of European economic history. This is risky because it depends on the accuracy of the portrayal of events in Europe, about which no consensus exists. One sometimes wryly feels that economic history is an effort to explain events shown by the next round of research not to have happened. The approach is also risky because it places on a single difference the immense burden of proof that this, finally, crucially, was what divided West from East. The implication is of a chronic inability on the part of Asian economies with already quite developed trade sectors to cross the last divide to the 'capitalism' or 'industrialism' of eighteenth-century Europe, or more precisely Britain, as if the growth divide can only be defined in this way. Given that a commercial sector has often emerged within a past economy without transforming the whole, it is conceivable that something was being omitted, but this does not guarantee that the final step had to be the governmental creation of financial instruments. Eighteenth-century procedures and forms were not the only ones possible.

The deeper question is why the growth rates of the Sung were neither regained in China nor attained elsewhere. Most large societies of proven creativity could surely have turned their hand to creating a suitable array of economic institutions given enough incentives and political security.

Locating the divergence between Europe and mainland Asia in the role of the state is thus not absolutely certain to be correct, for all that this is the historical tradition. Whether the state has been unduly permitted to overshadow other considerations has for China become the subject of a debate under the catchy title, 'The State of the China Field. Or, the China Field and the State'.[21] Nevertheless, the conclusion we have reached ourselves, and for the other Asian empires as well as China, is that one way or another the state had much to answer for.

The problem of Asia, as Rothermund expounds it, was the inability of trading interests to match the revenues the state could obtain from the land. Only this could have given the merchant classes a position from which to bargain for a change in the rules of the game.[22] Perry Anderson says, 'all these Islamic States, like the Ottoman Empire itself [and Mughal India], were essentially warrior and plunderer in cast; founded on conquest, their whole rationale and structure was military.'[23] The ancient civilization of China, however, more than half digested its invaders, so that immediately below the blanket of similarity a distinction needs to be made between China and Islamdom. 'Asian development cannot in any way be reduced to a uniform residual category, left over after the canons of European evolution have been established . . .', declares Anderson, 'It is merely in the night of our own ignorance that all alien shapes take on the same hue.'[24]

We could complicate matters further—anyone can do that—but the serious issue is just how much may be squeezed into a still parsimonious pair of boxes, Islamic and Chinese. Our desire for simplicity in argument may be self-defeating if the highest common factor among the conquest empires is small. Even two Marxist scholars, to mention them alone, take opposite sides about the appropriate degree of generalization. Perry Anderson agonizes over the theoretical implications of his inversion of orthodoxy in which a different superstructure for each state determines the economic outcome. On the other hand, John Kautsky notes that social forms were quite regular across the ancient empires, and sets out to generalize about the pattern.[25] Capitalism was the convergent form, it was pre-capitalism that differed from place to place, says Anderson; what pattern is shown by the regularities, asks Kautsky. My preference is for an intermediate position. There are funda-mental similarities among pre-modern systems and among modern ones too, but for some important purposes we need to subdivide both categories. The primary subdivision of pre-modern Asia is between Islamdom and the Chinese empires.

Accidents and exigencies beset all governments. Their condition and behaviour alters over time like the condition of the realm. In the Islamic empires a high degree of state-induced uncertainty was added to the sloth of economic policy, and there was a tendency for government to crowd out invest-ment when its political difficulties required extra revenue. The role of the Mughal empire in the economy was 'practically non-existent' according to Datta, though this refers only to the direct role.[26] Security for merchants was reasonably assured until the breakdown of the eighteenth century, but neither under the Mughals nor in the surprisingly stable kingdoms that sprang up afterwards in Bengal, Awadh, the Punjab, and Hyderabad did merchants acquire influence as a class or attract rulers to undertake measures that might have system-atically promoted economic growth. As Rothermund observes, a country with a parliament which buys a king and gains a say over taxation, English style, has a better chance of assuring continuity of purpose than one where merchants could only bribe governors whose personal power was like snowflakes in the sun.[27]

In Ming and Ch'ing China the economy may actually have been stronger than the state, continuing to expand with little encouragement beyond what Feuerwerker calls a 'perceptible lubricating effect'.[28] As Morse long ago observed, the Ch'ing or Manchu State was a taxing and policing agency which inter-vened directly in the business world only to assure the profits of officials and for ethical reasons, not on grounds of economic management.[29] Moreover, the suggestion has been made that from late Ming times the state was withdrawing from public works and welfare areas in favour of a more active role for private interests (with its approval and under its umbrella).[30] There is evidence from Ningpo of a secular shift from official to private involvement in fire-fighting and water supply, flood works, dredging, and even the building of emergency granaries.

The belief that the Chinese economy took a downturn after the Sung seems to be out of favour. Modern sinologists entertain no 'crowding out' thesis and they also place surprisingly little emphasis on uncertainty created by the greed of government or élite. A label for the condition of the economy may be Martin Heijdra's 'non-growing dynamism', although in our terms this was actually growth of the *extensive* variety.[31] As to government, the needle was stuck. It was not very active, preferring to manage from behind a bamboo screen—for instance, via the guilds.

The system lacked the sharp sectoral boundaries of the developing European economies. It was a unitary mass, responsive enough as a whole—that is, allowing for regional variation—to feed, clothe, and house a vastly growing population at levels to be compared with those in late medieval or early modern Europe. Commerce expanded, the cities grew. One great asset was the lower overhead cost of trade in areas near the great waterways with which China was endowed or had earlier equipped herself. There was no need in such a self-maintaining system, Feuerwerker suggests, to resort to the demographic restraint that Europeans imposed on themselves by way of late marriage and considerable spinsterhood.[32]

This scheme for China is closest to an under-government model. With little separation between state and economy and in the presence of huge population growth, the system retained a high level of per capita output without raising it any more. A vast society that had already attained respectable income levels by Sung times continued to walk along that ceiling for century after century, scarcely falling off, but not pushing up the limits. Administrative weakness had much to do with this, at least under the Ming. Corruption was rife, the palace was extravagant, and the quality of bureaucratic and financial administration deteriorated from the levels of Tang, Sung, or even Yuan times to the extent that Huang describes its main problem as 'its superficiality'. Worse, there was 'a commutation in reverse' as the regime demanded tax in grain instead of money and aimed at stability at the expense of potentially productive change.

A bureaucratic society without the European aristocratic challenge did not provoke the court to change.[33] There was a comparable weakness of challenge and response in the Islamic empires, which did not even have the same bureaucracy.

What explanation would be acceptable? The pronouncement by David Gellner that because at about AD 1500 China and Europe were technologically on a par we need a *cultural* analysis of their divergence seems misplaced.[34] The technological comparison is dubious; the agricultures in particular were very different. In any case, as we have noted before, Elvin is right to say that an economic and ecological explanation is simpler in its assumptions, internally more consistent, and more amenable to empirical verification. There is nothing to be gained by assuming *initially* that economic action cannot be explained by reference to economic inducement.

The problem of China's *very* long-term economic performance remains with us because the sources are almost intractable and the necessary research has not been done. We can only try to sketch an outline consistent with current opinion. The private sector remained responsive without regaining the originality it had evinced under the Sung. Government embraced business at arm's length, a contortion very different from lending a helping hand. The state's own rather minor investments in the infrastructure were enough to maintain the proportions of the economy, to produce history's greatest case of balanced *non-intensive* growth.[35] It was a nice balance, almost incredible in the face of the fluctuations within the overall growth of population. As much as anything, the internal farm frontier in what is now southern China enabled a peasant society to be replicated until at least mid-Ch'ing times.[36] This meant static expansion on the grand scale, contributing to an economy that widened rather than deepened.

The field is beset by an extraordinary Western delusion of cultural stasis in China that might be called the 'China Con'. This elevates continuity in the high culture and supposed harmony with nature above changes in the low culture which were unavoidable for coping with population increase. Perhaps, as we have now stated several times, average per capita real incomes did not shift much in the centuries after the Sung. This is not likely given the swings within the increase of population but, if sinologists will not commit themselves to much change in either direction, an assumption of no income change is the parsimonious one. However, something had to change under the massive pressure of population, and almost every other economic magnitude seems to have obliged.

The received view is of scientific, technical, and economic development in China long anticipating the West but subsequently modified very little. This is found in descriptions of the antiquity of Chinese culture, the perpetually high productivity of wet rice agriculture, the continued use of the same Confucian classics for two thousand years, the enduring power of the state, and the changeless style of architecture.

There are four related problems here:

1. Did China discover and invent much in the way of new technology very early? The answer is yes, though the achievements of some other cultures can be too easily overshadowed and China herself was sometimes an importer of ideas, for example, via Buddhist missionaries from India.

2. Did China supply Europe with most of its key inventions? The answer is probably not, although there were important technology transfers. Truly independent European invention is not always easy to demonstrate in these circumstances, which makes it possible to over-emphasize the Chinese role. Europe's ability to innovate is in any case more salient, given the existence somewhere at home or abroad of an accessible supply of inventions.

3. Did China become fundamentally changeless after the Sung, undergoing only unprogressive 'cycles of Cathay'? The answer is no. The appearance of stasis depends on a fanciful image of continuity in the high culture, symbolized in that Chinese coins record only the reign whereas European coins are dated to the year. In reality the stasis has no more authenticity than the willow pattern plate—which was Western orientalism, designed in England in 1780.

The proper symbols of imperial China after the Sung are not the pagoda and weeping willow, but forest trees falling. Accommodating China's population involved the adoption of dry-land crops brought from America in the 'Columbian Exchange'; the frontier movement to the south to take in new farmland; warfare against aboriginal peoples like the Miao who were in the way; great migrations; and a huge bill in the form of deforestation, erosion, silting, disasters, and waterborne disease. It also involved continued technical changes of kinds forgotten because one or two spectacular early innovations like water-powered spinning-machines did retreat, because the invention and adoption of some others have been masked by the now much faster rate of change in Europe, and because Chinese agricultural intensification is too easily overlooked.

Two pieces of evidence of subterranean change have been found in research by my graduate students. Shen Gensheng has found that the service life and repair intervals of a big sample of buildings did not remain constant and unimproved over the post-Sung centuries, and Deng Gang has charted the accumulation of technical advice in successive generations of *Nong Shu* or agricultural treatises. What is indeed needed in Chinese history is more work on the investment and inventive/innovatory processes that coped with the growing numbers of people.

4. What comparisons are appropriate between the achievements of Chinese and European society? Comparisons are clumsily expressed in the existing literature and seem to give rise to resentment on the part of sinophile Western scholars rather than to fresh thought about appropriate criteria. It has never been clear why anyone's *amour propre* should be bound up with the poorly recorded antics or accomplishments of our forebears, oppressed and organized as they were in societies for which, given the unidirectional arrow of time, we can have no responsibility. Do Chinese and Western astronomers co-opt the stars into home and away teams?

An essential difference between the two historical systems of China and Europe lay in the mix between state action and the market. Both societies employed both means of handling economic problems, but not to the same degree. China's famine relief arrangements under the Chien Lung emperor eclipsed those of Europe, but this success depended on the ability of the state to organize food supplies and that ability did not last. Put not your trust in princes. While it lasted it may actually have depressed incentives for peasant farmers to produce and market enough grain. Europe's greater reliance on the market dissolved more of the problem before it needed to be relieved. Prevention is better than cure.

Chinese agriculture, her 'gardening', is often taken as admirably efficient because it supported such an increase in population; but it did not do so without adopting dry-land crops from elsewhere nor without violent and continuing year-to-year fluctuations in output. The confusion here is between technical efficiency and economic efficiency—and the ecological costs of both wet-rice and upland dry-crop agriculture suggest that even the technical efficiency was marred. For all the different philosophical tradition, one does not sense in Chinese reality the restraint of environmental damage that Conrad Totman once demonstrated for Tokugawa Japan or the positive concern to remould the environment for the sake of public health that James Riley has shown for Europe.[37]

China was not self-evidently a balanced system that did not need to employ its great triad of inventions—the compass, gunpowder, and printing—in the disturbing ways they were used in the West.[38] It was not outside history in the way of timeless literati cultivating long fingernails, but was bursting at the seams with real people struggling to make a living. *Extensive* growth did occur. Fixity and actual regression in governmental functions probably suppressed some of the potential for *intensive* growth, but cultural conservatism and antiquity should not be mistaken for mere spiritless repetition in the Chinese economy at large.

At the end we should generalize again and try to comprehend the common elements of the Islamic and Chinese systems. Invasions in themselves left few enduring physical scars on either. What they left were strengthened conservative institutions and values that made renewed growth more difficult. Whether or not the original tax 'take' was large and later conflicts about resources bitter, a strong performance was discouraged by the reinforcement which unprogressive governments were pleased to lend to unprogressive institutions.

Indolent governments with or without large budgets, and always lacking the models and will to create growth, found the divisiveness of caste and the uncompetitiveness of the guilds convenient methods of social control. They subtly restricted the movement of the market's invisible hand, probably unthinkingly, because the disproportions of rapid growth would have been unthinkable to them. Although some Asian governments took less out of the economy than has usually been claimed, it is at least as much to the point that none of them put much back. They failed to create a financial or legal context in which trade and industry might flourish and become independent of luxury demand. Pre-modern Asian governments could not conceive of maximizing growth or the common good. Instead they abused or neglected the economy as they pleased. This deviation from the goals and methods of a hypothetically dispassionate manager may be seen as imposing heavy 'agency' costs on the economic system. The whole complex of greed and lethargy was sufficient to smother the prospects of re-growth.

Growth Recurring

NINE

Japan

Japan and Europe implicitly raced the empires of mainland Asia as Aesop's tortoise did the hare. In other words, they stole the march by plodding. A latent tendency for growth existed everywhere and history offered multiple opportunities for it to be expressed. The case of Japan shows as well as any that the numerous negative factors could be overcome and the process at last brought to fruition. 'Any commercialized empire . . .', says John Kautsky, 'could conceivably have developed an industrial economy, as Japan in fact began to do.'[1]

Favourable conditions for growth took a long time to evolve in both Japan and Europe. Viewed on the canvas of world history, or at least on that of Eurasia, success amounted to the reassertion of growth tendencies apparent in earlier times, but now welling up in unexpected places. Had growth been the rather sudden and discrete event portrayed as the industrial revolution, it might be clearer what sort of variables we should consider; they might be more conventionally 'economic'. Instead, the ultimate sources of change in societies as different as those of Japan and Europe were subtle and problematic and, as much as anything, by-products of evolving political structures.

The prolonged and indefinite character of the change makes it hard to sum up. Growth may have been possible everywhere, or at any rate very widely, but it was not inevitable. Even in the most undisturbed circumstances, merely to accumulate effective techniques or organize production and exchange would be a slow business. Difficulties were plentiful, inherent in initial poverty and ignorance and in the violently rent-seeking nature of pre-modern politics. There seems no way of telling from prior history that the political situation would have permitted growth, more or less at the same period, at the opposite extremities of Eurasia. We have to eschew the conclusion prompted by hindsight, that because the difficulties were overcome in these particular places it was certain that the problems would have yielded.

The proposition that some people in any society will strive to improve their material lot, and if unimpeded may well succeed in doing so, contains its own dilemma. Where growth did occur the impediments must be judged too weak to have stopped it; where there was no growth the impediments must seem too strong. The danger of circularity is obvious. Can we escape this by making an independent estimate of the strength of the negative factors? Given that the resistance to growth seems to have been a tricky interaction of poorly recorded political and institutional factors, the task is very difficult.

Are we therefore in no better position than advocates of an industrial revolution? After all, their belief requires them to find some novelty capable of bursting through the cake of custom—like Sir William Browne's Tories, admitting no argument but force. Their assumption that the initial case of growth was unique means they can have no range of comparative cases to help isolate the source of the change. Our assumption, that historically speaking growth was on the cards unless it was actually frustrated, depends on persuading the reader that this was the case. But we ought not to baulk at this, because the need for persuasion is a normal part of historical reasoning—like the Whigs, we admit no force but argument. Scientific clinchers have no place in the art form.

Nevertheless, although both arguments ultimately rest on persuasion, they are not equivalent. The case that growth needed the creation of some novel positive force is not as easy to credit as that it unfolded when negative forces evaporated. The likelihood was very great from what we know of them that the steppe conquerors of Asia would impede growth by economic rapacity, mismanagement, or sheer under-government.

Even if we concede the possibility that each customary 'obstacle' to growth had its advantageous side, we will need to show that in Japan and Europe the disadvantageous sides were eroded by specific historical processes. A couple of successful results are just not sufficient evidence that removing barriers meant growth would result: after all, some new push-force *may* have started it off—some 'laser-beam miracle' along the lines implied in most work on the 'causes of the industrial revolution'. Luck there undoubtedly will have been, but it probably helped to account for the speed and shape of growth as much as for its original occurrence. The basic tale is one of processes that reduced rigidities, or enabled them to cancel one another out, without throttling change by creating fresh bottlenecks. These processes must also have produced economies resilient enough to withstand the shocks of the natural and political disasters to which Europe and especially Japan were subject.

The task is twofold. Firstly, we have to show that *intensive* growth did emerge gradually in early modern Japan and Europe, and did so independently, that is, that Japanese growth may have been helped but was not begun by the borrowings from the West after 1868. There are no modern-style statistics on the rise of average per capita GNP with which to do this, but that should not deter us. There are many historical issues in an economy on which no good figures exist, and many modern figures are not what they seem. As Sir Josiah Stamp once observed, 'the Government are very keen on amassing statistics. They collect them, add them, raise them to the nth power, take the cube root and prepare wonderful diagrams. But you must never forget that every one of these figures comes in the first instance from the village watchman, who just puts down what he damn well pleases.' In any case it is scarcely possible to reduce political and institutional factors to a few numbers.

Early modern evidence is not quite as poor as this may suggest. Since about 1970, research on Japanese economic history has rescued the Tokugawa shogunate (1600–1868) from its previous reputation as a stagnating prelude to the imperial Meiji rule which followed. Far from being a decaying feudalism, Tokugawa Japan was a developing economy. The extent of development is still being debated, but it is no longer plausible to deny the trend.

Our second task is to identify the processes which transformed or washed away impediments to growth. While to do this in a fully documented way would require the services of a team of specialists, our sketch must at least persuade the reader of a prima-facie case for thinking the changes were real. They need to be shown as the logical opposites of the suppression of growth taking place in the contemporary Islamic and Chinese empires.

Growth in Japan had distant beginnings and is perhaps easier to trace over several centuries than in Europe where, until recently, the industrial achievement was greater. The task may be simpler because Japan is a single country with a more homogeneous culture. Her example serves to push into the background some of the changes in the more familiar European case, which are often taken as if they were *general* causes of economic growth or industrialization. When we find that some of these 'causes' were absent or unimportant in Japan, we can see that they were not universal factors after all but were simply attributes of the European form of growth. The case of Japan obliges us to recognize the straightforward but often forgotten fact that solely European features cannot be necessary conditions for growth.

Until the recent revisionist phase, it was widely believed that economic growth did not start in Japan until the Meiji restoration. This meant that many studies cut in sharply about three-quarters of the way through the nineteenth century. Ohkawa and Rosovsky once complained that 'before 1878 statistical deficiencies are nearly insurmountable'.[2] Evidence other than aggregate series was discarded because it could not produce a comparable line on the graph. The compelling but less formal tale about the Tokugawa period (and before), which qualitative evidence has latterly been made to tell, was almost ignored; worse, it was implicitly taken to be a tale of non-growth. This narrow insistence on aggregate statistical data confirmed its own underlying assumption, that growth began when it could be measured on a single trend-line, after Meiji. It was a self-fulfilling prophecy.

The lengths to which this approach used to be carried are shown in a rhetorical question by Rosovsky. He asked, where should one start an analysis of Japan's transition to MEG (Kuznets's Modern Economic Growth)? In answer to his own question he declared that historians have a professional interest in sketching preparatory activities way back in the past, and 'this somewhat superficial element of continuity is terribly bothersome for those whose primary purpose is the study of an industrial revolution'.[3] No doubt it is.

Quite apart from the methodological unreasonableness of restricting the enquiry to a period chosen in advance and to a particular kind of evidence, ignoring earlier Japanese economic history has indeed proved mistaken. Much of the relative ease of the Meiji achievement is now attributed to the start which that history gave it. Meiji started at what is described as a high level for a less-developed country, and although this is somewhat tendentious, in that Japan had long been a developing country in her own right, it does draw attention to the gradualism of the case.

The Tokugawa shogunate that arose victorious from the civil wars of the late sixteenth century was itself heir to a surprisingly vigorous economic system. Throughout the Middle Ages the population had been rising, from 5 million in the eleventh century to almost 10 million by 1300 and 18 million by about 1600. This increase rested on a growth of agricultural productivity sufficient not only to permit total numbers to rise but to support and raise the living standards of an expanding non-agricultural group of clerics, traders, and warriors. The emergence of this group seems to have represented genuine structural change, not merely the squeezing of a greater surplus from the peasantry. And decentralized politics with plenty of armed resistance succeeded in keeping most of the gains out of the hands of would-be national leaders, until the time of the Tokugawa unification.[4] It may seem surprising that income gains continued to be made during the political tumult of the sixteenth century, but that sort of thing happened in the history of Europe too. The progress individual *han*s had made under the Sengoku *daimyo* during the sixteenth century goes a long way towards explaining Tokugawa growth, since the unification brought together in one market a number of already vigorous units.

The Sengoku lords had been investing heavily in irrigation works on their domains, continuing and enhancing the vitality of even older trends. The index of the total area of paddy-fields rises from 91 in about AD 930, to 100 in *c.*1450, and steeply to 173 in *c.*1600.[5] Under the Tokugawa the gains were greater still, the index reaching 314 in *c.*1720. Thereafter the areal extension was much slower, and reached only 322 by 1874.

The gains on unification were considerable, and the Tokugawa take-over in 1600 needs to be approached with as much respect for the prior achievement of the Sengoku as does the better-known Meiji restoration of 1868 for the achievement of the Tokugawa. Five major influences on early Tokugawa growth may be picked out: (*a*) the unification itself, which released the constraints on the national market inherent in *han* separatism; (*b*) the huge and rapid growth of the new capital, Edo (Tokyo), to the status of a 'millionaire' city with its implications for the size and nature of the market; (*c*) the settlement of the samurai in the castle towns, with its implications for enforced production to supply them with tax rice; (*d*) the imposition of the *sankin kotei* system whereby provincial lords, the *daimyo*, were obliged to reside under the Shogun's eye in Edo for long periods and therefore spend much of their rents on city living, with all the implications for the market of this too; and (*e*) the exceptional responsiveness of agricultural production, partly released by the break-up of communal farming and its replacement by nuclear family farms more sensitive to commercial incentives. Summed up, the stern Tokugawa political settlement unintentionally released a powerful variety of market forces.

On the other hand, one of the biggest depressants on Japanese growth in this period stemmed from another political act—the policy of *sakoku*, the closed economy, whereby for security reasons the shogunate cut the country off from foreign contacts. Almost all foreign trade was stifled, leaving only a small and heavily shuttered window at Deshima off Nagasaki through which the Dutch and Chinese could bring in foreign goods and take out Japanese exports. While this had the intended result of a more stable internal order, it put off-limits overseas markets that Japan had already shown herself able to penetrate—for weapons, as one example.

Perhaps even more important for the remainder of Tokugawa life, *sakoku* virtually abolished access to foreign models in any sphere. The 'Dutch learning' to which scholars found access in the more relaxed later Tokugawa times did begin to fertilize science in Japan, but the absence of political models and competition may have proved a greater economic depressant than the closure of external trade. Unlike a European country, Japan was not a member of a system of competing and colluding states, perched as she was in political withdrawal well off the coast of China. Other things being equal, development would be slower than in Europe.

Domestically, Japan was not badly placed for trade because she had a long coastline, although the roads were poor, even the great Tokiada highway. On the face of it the central government, the *Bakufu*, was not active in creating in respect of communications and other matters a European-style framework for market activity. Without a significant foreign-trade sector, the merchant class did not become as important as in Europe. There, market-building acts by governments were often responses to representations by members of the merchant class, who as agents of prior growth were able to induce further growth through their increasing political influence. Merchants did not catch the ears of the Tokugawa shogunate to quite the same extent.

Yet although in Japan political influences of this kind were weaker, the absolutism of the shogunate waned after about 1650. The samurai class was moved to the sidelines and its members either became indebted to the merchants or eventually took up trade themselves. Forces favourable to growth were able to make headway after all. The expansion of the civilian economy in such a warlike society was indeed an outcome of the Tokugawa pacification and unification, which released depressants on a growth that had already been evident during what Europeans call the Middle Ages.

Tokugawa growth has been described as 'phenomenal' by an author properly contrasting the period with preceding rather than succeeding ones.[6] Between 1600 and 1850 agricultural output almost doubled. Since population rose only by about 45 per cent, a considerable increase in output per head must have occurred. This was the result of an expansion of the arable acreage, already noticed, but also of the diffusion of technical innovations, individually small but linked and cumulatively impressive. Purchased fertilizer was applied heavily, treadmills and Dutch pumps moved irrigation water, new crops like sugar cane, sweet potatoes, peanuts, and maize spread. These new crops were mostly American and originally part of the 'Columbian Exchange'. Japan closed herself off at a fortunate period, after she had received some valuable imports via Portuguese traders. (When they were thrown out as trouble-making Christians, the Japanese kept the Arab horses they had brought to upgrade the stock of their own little Mongolian ponies.)

The development and spread of new rice varieties figured prominently in the agricultural improvements, as did better tools. Much is now known about the intensity of innovation at the village level, the local entrepreneurs involved, and the didactic books that transmitted their ideas through an abnormally literate society. The observed increase in average farm output, even output per head, is quite compatible with the evidence of serious famines at the regional level and two or three affecting the entire nation. These famines punctuated the economic diversification that followed the long-run rise in productivity, but they did not halt it.

The Japanese had early become inventive and experimental, in agriculture and many other activities. In the fifteenth century Japan made high-quality weapons and sold them in South-East Asia. Once the Portuguese had introduced firearms these were imitated and improved. Problems with the firing mechanism of the musket that had defeated European armourers were solved here.

Productivity growth produced results in three important directions: urbanization; regional specialization and structural change; and the standard of living and life expectancy. City growth was prodigious during the first half of the Tokugawa period. Fewer than thirty medieval settlements had held over 5,000 inhabitants each, but under the Tokugawa there came to be more than 160 places of that size, with a proportionate increase of really large cities.[7] Without draining other cities, Edo (Tokyo) mushroomed from a fishing village to a millionaire city.

Later in the period there was some de-urbanization, at least to the extent that the largest towns and cities shrank in population, but this was not evidence of reversed structural change. In the eighteenth and early nineteenth centuries, village economies were taking on urban functions, diversifying into distribution and retailing. 'One could argue', says Totman, 'that urbanization continued, too [like commercialization], but that it did so in the countryside—and at the expense of large towns and cities.'[8] Seventeenth-century

Europe had seen a similar movement.[9] In both Japan and Europe, urban-style growth was thus temporarily transferred to rural domestic industry, industrializing large tracts of the countryside. Locating industry in the countryside paid because it avoided the high overhead costs of town-building as well as the high cost of urban labour. It was industrialization by the back door. Any hiatus in structural change was thus apparent rather than real. Manufacturing industry continued to expand throughout the early modern period in both Japan and Europe, whatever its precise urban or rural distribution at any one time. Labour time continued to be withdrawn from farming into industry, whether labour was housed in the cottages of the countryside or in the towns.

The spatial patchiness of cottage industry meant that regional specialization was developing. There was a corresponding patchiness in the spread of cultivation, notably the construction of new rice paddies. The administrative units, the *han*s, varied in intrinsic fertility and also in distance from the main city markets. Some were less able than others to share in the increased production of rice. To cover tax demands or their own consumption they needed to buy rice on the open market and accordingly required an alternative source of income. Echigo province, for example, managed from the end of the seventeenth century to develop a sizeable hempen cloth industry. There, especially in Uonuma county, in one of the harshest, most isolated and agriculturally unpropitious environments in the country, the farm population spent the long winters weaving native grasses for sale. Output had reached 200,000 rolls of cloth per annum by the end of the eighteenth century. By 1814 the local linen dealers challenged the Edo drapers, and by the 1850s they were selling direct to the city markets. Of silk fabric entering Edo by 1859 only 10 per cent came from Kyoto, which had once held a virtual monopoly. The rest came from rural districts.[10]

In the fertile rice-producing districts of the Plain of Japan, crop-growing was productive and not all the available labour was needed to grow food. Female labour in particular was released from field-work and its availability for by-employments attracted complementary investment by merchants and the richer peasants, so that these districts too housed cottage industries producing lacquerware, fans, parasols, toys, footwear, paper lanterns, and the like. There was nothing in principle unusual about the emergence of rural domestic (and workshop) industry, which happened in many parts of Eurasia, but the scale of the Japanese development was outstanding. There was a very big growth of domestic trade in food, city night-soil as fertilizer, and small manufactured goods.

Students of Japanese economic history for a long time reacted to the phenomenon of uneven regional activity by implying that it was symptomatic of a low general level of development.[11] This was unreasonable, in that the inequalities were evidence of regional specialization. Some degree of regional specialization, with the attendant benefits of trade, typically accompanies rapid national growth and may be a prerequisite for it.[12] It is associated with structural change, that is, the widescale withdrawal of labour-time from farming. As with urbanization, rural domestic industrialization testifies to the increase in productivity on the land which alone can release labour and labour-time from food production.

The demographic background to this was a rapid increase during the first half of the Tokugawa period and near-stagnation during the second half. The reduced population growth in the latter period did not in reality halt the growth of the market, and the continued rise in output surpassed the rather small increment of consumers. Susan Hanley has urged that by the early nineteenth century the average quality of life was as high as that in contemporary Britain.[13] She bases her conclusion on calculations of life expectancy. Totman has also made much of the restricted environmental costs imposed by the Tokugawa style of growth, but as mentioned in the previous chapter he has since adumbrated a more dismal version of Tokugawa life.[14]

In the course of a paper informed by concepts drawn from ecology—something much to my own taste—Totman tries to strike a cost–benefit balance for the Tokugawa economy. His result is negative. The picture is of a society facing Malthusian limits, pressed into poverty by the weight of its own numbers on a biological resource base that it could not extend through foreign trade, because of the shogunate's ordinance against overseas expansion, nor exploit through more technical change.

This view may be in harmony with that of some political historians who wish to concentrate on the record of peasant risings in eighteenth-century Japan; it is assuredly not consistent with the work of 'revisionist' economic historians. There are indeed reasons for thinking that Totman's dismal environmentalist view is mistaken. The problem lies in the criteria. The boldest conceptual innovation is the anxiety entertained about damage (perhaps) done to the non-human biota by economic growth. Whilst there may or may not be an ethical case for worrying about this, it is not in itself pertinent to what happened to the living standards of humans. The concern seems to stem from reading backwards the fashionable but speculative case that modern humanity is threatening the carrying capacity of the environment.

In any case, the concern about what happened ecologically under the Tokugawa is inconsistently applied. Totman admits that the rural economy recovered from eighteenth-century difficulties by early in the next century, and he retreats to the assertion that no such recovery could last, claiming that the new equilibrium, which he calls 'maximum' utilization, would inevitably have brought periodic catastrophe. There is no inevitability about this at all. The period over which output is to be maximized needs to be specified before 'maximum' acquires meaning. The whole pessimist case is flawed by confusion among the various criteria by which the Tokugawa economic performance is to be judged: whether short or long periods are relevant; whether we are discussing the welfare of *Homo sapiens* or a welfare function for all species (which could never be constructed, given the complexity of ecological interactions); whether supposed but unknown increases in labour input per unit of output vitiate any growth attained; or whether we should be swayed by unknowable attitudes to the (supposedly) harder work needed to secure this higher material output—which it is admitted the Tokugawa peasantry did obtain.

Revealed preference would surely say that the peasants valued a higher living standard if they put forth the effort to get it. Life was complicated; not all movements were in the same direction; all periods within the Tokugawa dynasty were not exactly the same; but little is to be gained by comment on particular costs to particular groups if the items cannot be added up. Consistent, whole-society (and inter-country) criteria are needed. Most surprising of all, Totman in his concern for the fate of non-human organisms recks little to the Tokugawa achievement of a larger human population and longer life expectancies.

Hanley has summed up the work of the revisionists who portray what was a high standard of living by any pre-modern standards. Even a critic, Yasukichi Yasuba, strongly supports the optimistic view in general, objecting only that the quality of life, measured by life expectancy, daily calorie intake, and material consumption, was still considerably lower than in the exceptional case of England.[15] Yet neither Hanley nor Yasuba really indicates much advantage to either leading country. According to Yasuba's data, which derive variously from years between 1765 and 1803, Japan was evidently not far behind the England of that period in terms of per capita income, wages of cotton-spinners, life expectancy, and stature (this last being seen by recent research as a sensitive indicator of well-being).

Tokugawa Japan did not of course fulfil all its potential. What economy has? The shogunate was immensely concerned with its political security, though increasingly forced in practice to rely on offsetting changes that might well have been destabilizing. The natural resources of the northernmost major island, Hokkaido, were secretly surveyed, but almost no development was permitted for fear of an internal colonial war against the Ainu inhabitants. A fearful regime, running what in terms of personal liberties was something of a police state, found itself presiding over an economy whose energies thrust upwards into *intensive* growth. Perhaps growth was an alternative to politics, at least to the more destructive kinds of rent-seeking. The *Bakufu* government was repressive, formal, and arbitrary, but in the areas of life that mattered for material advance, including many that affected the physical (or biological) quality of life, its actions did not stand in the way of an extraordinary achievement.

The question is, should the multiple, complicated, inter-acting 'roots' of the Japanese response be emphasized, or the easing of political pressures that made room for it? Do we want a genetic explanation in terms of earlier history or

Japanese predispositions of almost a 'national character' kind, or one that rests on the nature of the structural forces that produced the new equilibrium? In measurable respects, Japanese culture does seem to have been remarkable: consider for example the high level of popular education and literacy at early dates. The problem is that evaluations of the importance of such matters are *post hoc* and may amount to little more than saying that this was a society which was fortuitously (and fortunately) different from its neighbours on the Asian mainland, including China from which it had borrowed so much after the Taika reforms of the seventh century. A little reflection will show that we need both kinds of explanation. We must look at the history that preceded any period in which we are interested because only this can indicate the menu of possibilities from which the Japanese could realistically choose. But we need to know something more: we need to know what forces affected the choice at any one moment and whether they were truly new constructs or, as they seem to be, the decaying of old constraints under the unlikely umbrella of Tokugawa control.

In social forms Japan was of course different from the parallel case of successful growth in Europe. Nothing is easier than to point to dissimilarities between Japan and Europe, not merely in the fancy dress which always makes 'them' seem unimaginably alien to 'us' (whoever we are, whether people in different cultures or people in different periods of history, or *a fortiori* both), but in presumably significant aspects of political organization. Yet for the historian there are useful tools other than the microscope. As Joseph Strayer says of the Japan–Europe comparison, 'if at every point of comparability one is to drop down into a lower level of specificity to look for differences one can never get beyond a fascination with differences alone'.[16] The economic outcome in Japan and Europe was sufficiently alike in measures that concern rude mechanicals like economic historians to make us suspect that the social dissimilarities may not have been decisive. The bedrock processes must have been working in much the same directions, despite surface differences in style and appearance.

Some similarities there were. In a rigidly formalized scheme not unlike that whereby Louis XIV required his nobles to remain at Versailles, wasting their rents on conspicuous display and subject to close surveillance, the shogunate kept the *daimyo* (regional lords) on a tight rein. Under the *sankin kotei* system, they were obliged to spend half their time and a large share of their revenues residing in their palaces at Edo. This helped to expand the urban market.

Moving the 'potted plant lords' around, obliging the samurai to live in the castle towns, instituting the great sword hunt to disarm the countryside, ejecting the Portuguese, telling overseas Japanese to stay away, forbidding foreign trade, persecuting Christian subjects, relegating the imperial line to ceremonial status, setting up a spy system, and watching the checkpoints around Edo for those signs of revolt, 'guns in and women out', all these make Tokugawa autocracy seem severe enough. How did any room to grow emerge in such a society? What was to prevent the *daimyo* from squeezing wealth from the peasants like lords almost everywhere else in the world? What prevented the stern Tokugawa on top from squeezing lord and peasant hard enough to press out any margin of resources that might have been available for growth?

Growth emerged because behind its stern exterior the absolutism of the regime proved surprisingly weak. Internally pacified, much of the initial impetus spent, Tokugawa Japan sat back. By 1732, 60 per cent of the *daimyo* supporters of the shogunate had managed to settle permanently on lands they were to hold until at least 1868.[17] Effective lordly power rose, notwithstanding the rigidity of form and show of stability in high politics.

Nevertheless, the central government was not always inactive. It was at the same time less powerful and more interventionist than it seemed superficially. Hideyoshi quickly abolished the checkpoints around Kyoto, broke guild monopolies, and made trade more free. Local *daimyo* also took it on themselves to free trade by abolishing toll gates. Between 1600 and 1650 the government undertook massive building construction and flood-control works. It issued, and time and time again reissued, enormous numbers of regulations and admonitions concerning the economy; so did local urban and rural administrators. The absolutist states of Europe did the same. These orders were designed to maintain urban safety and included complex rules for fire-fighting, sanitary arrangements, and size limits on buildings. Large judicial and policing bodies were formed in all cities and big towns. Instructions appear about planting trees, harvesting crops, access to water, the allocation of seeds, and emergency stores of grain. All these types of injunction were sometimes echoed at village level, where they amounted, in Totman's words, to 'purposeful self-regulation'.[18]

Vigorous public efforts were made to solve one of the major problems of pre-modern urbanism, the massive fires. The efforts were never wholly successful, but officially ordered fire-breaks in Edo do seem to have reduced the average destructiveness a little as time passed (see Table 9.1).

Table 9.1. Relative Average Lengths of the Track of Major Fires in Edo, 1650–1874

Period	Average length of track
1650–74	100
1675–99	122
1700–24	89
1725–49	142
1750–74	128
1775–99	75
1800–24	69
1825–49	80
1850–74	80

Source: K. Yamagawa, 'Fires in Tokio' (1881), 71–81, in T. C. Mendenhall, *Report on the Meteorology of Tokio 1879–1880* (Tokio: Tokio University Press, 1880–1). Areal measures rather than length of track are not available.

Examples of the effectiveness of official promulgations are easier to find where they affected public life than where they concerned private market activity, but this may be an artefact of the sources. The greatest 'policy' gains seem to have come about from the original unification by the Tokugawa of the 'local centralisms' of the preceding lords, who had already been progressive enough to commission cadastral surveys of their domains. Differences in rice output among these domains inspired trade; so did the isolation of some of them from the sea and hence from supplies of fish and salt. The Sengoku *daimyo* had already begun to build their domains into larger trade areas. Between 1620 and 1660 the Tokugawa unified them and secured their trans-boundary trade.[19] The new regime also standardized measurements, including the dimensions of the *masu* (the square containers used in trade), unified the scales by 1665, and unified the coinage, thereby pursuing the work of the Sengoku lords to its logical conclusion in a single market area.[20]

Events conspired. The break-up of clan communal farming units into nuclear family farms seems to have been a major spur. Released from agriculture, many peasants began migrating to the cities, and many who stayed on the land took up by-employments on a big scale. Neither the *Bakufu* nor the lords could stop this. They had unleashed forces beyond their control, and in any case their revenues benefited. The older view that only the Meiji government could facilitate growth tended to obscure the extent of growth 'from below' during the Tokugawa period and before.[21] Competition in a widened market meant substantial gains from the division of labour, including naturally from the regional division of labour. By the nineteenth century what might be called proto-newspapers were reporting provincial disasters that threatened to have commercial repercussions in Edo and elsewhere, which testifies to the integration of the market.[22] Cotton-processors in Osaka, to cite one of Totman's examples, could not stop competitors in the city's hinterland from capturing part of their business; neither could the silk merchants in Edo stop rural producers selling there.[23] The consumer was the beneficiary.

Views differ as to the degree of centralism brought about. According to Bolitho, the Tokugawa *Bakufu* lasted for 265 years, but scarcely earned its immunity from civil turmoil: 'Beneath the veneer of centralized government lay all the ancient traditions of regionalism, reinforced by the daimyo institution, strong enough to keep a distant government at bay, sufficiently diffuse to prevent under normal circumstances the emergence of new coalitions.'[24] There was no outside model of centralization, no outside threat to compress political structures into national unity. In the event just enough seems to have been done to achieve national economies of scale while leaving the *han*s in competition with one another.

The *Bakufu* undertook a number of commercially unifying acts and a number that were stabilizing. After the serious crop failures of 1782 and 1783 it did take up, so Bolitho concludes, 'a position appropriate to a national government', ordering the sale of all domain rice stores.[25] This was important. *Han* policy had been anisotropic, that is, elastic in one direction only.[26] *Han*s that normally produced a grain surplus were willing to sell in average or good years, but sought to avoid unrest at home in bad seasons by storing against their own emergency needs. The Tokugawa were at any rate strong enough to demand a system in which sales were made in good and bad years alike. After all, the disorder of food riots in the cities and deficit areas was something they wished to prevent.

The results of rising productivity flowed sufficiently to the Japanese producer to reinforce change. The benefits of this were clear enough to the local lords for them not to stifle the process. Here we have political fine-tuning able to bring into being a system in which individually centralized *han*s retained their economic autonomy but were nevertheless linked in a national market not unlike the grander linking of the nation-states in the European states-system. Perhaps convincing explanations of Japanese and European growth have eluded us because of balancing acts like these. What were being balanced were sets of incentives and disincentives of a largely institutional nature, with interacting effects that are hard to describe and almost impossible to quantify.

The Tokugawa were never willing or able to raise the rice tax above the levels set when they made a survey in the seventeenth century. Hence the proceeds of subsequent growth fell into provincial and peasant hands more than in most historical societies. This was ironic in a country that laid so much stress on internal control; but growth and control turned out for a long time to be mutually permissive. It is hard otherwise to see how the shogunate could have survived the veiled but fundamental changes beneath. Provincial prosperity however led to distortions in the distribution of wealth that eventually proved fatal for the shogunate because the outer *daimyo*, least loyal, farthest from Edo, on the poorest lands, remained lightly taxed as their domains developed, and were able to play a disproportionate role in the overthrow of the Tokugawa.

Compared with some European states, the Tokugawa may have done rather little in the way of active economic management, but as we have seen they did remove some of the checks on the growth that was already apparent before their day. The more active Meiji removed many more checks, but they were not the ones who began the process. Even the Tokugawa had taken over a society where they could act as broker for a tier of regions quite able to sustain and magnify their growth if they were brought together, offered the opportunity of big urban market growth, and otherwise mostly left alone.

Collectively the *daimyo* held one another and the *Bakufu* in check. Thus in Europe the nation-states checked each other and checked the pretenders to real overall power in every age (the Holy Roman Empire, the Papacy, the Habsburgs, Napoleon . . .). By the last Tokugawa century, hereditary bureaucrats ruled in Japan. Changes in substance continued, veiled by the curtain of custom where there were so few models for change in the social style. Limited changes in national style should not obscure the changes in substance that were taking place. Merchants and financiers who profited from the fact of growth were able to administer further nudges because they had attained some, though formally unacknowledged, influence.[27]

Japan and Europe were both derivative cultures, borrowers, far back, from mainland Eurasia. It was this which helped them eventually to share in and further develop the common heritage of Eurasian ideas and technology—but the mainland shared in that too, more abundantly and sooner. Japanese and European growth took place at approximately similar periods; but the systems were essentially isolated from one another, so how are we to account for their coincidence of timing?

The most obvious *Zeitgeber* or timing device, the long build-up of technology in Eurasia, scarcely seems powerful enough to dictate chronology to an interval as short as a couple of centuries or so. Viewed in the long and broad, what was happening was however a virtual recrudescence of growth of the kind once seen in Sung China and hinted at many times elsewhere. Growth might have been expected earlier and more easily somewhere in mainland Asia or the Middle East, in larger societies that had created much of the technical apparatus of the late pre-industrial economy. Their prime stumbling-block was the centralized politics of conquest, in its effect on incentives. The advantage of the peripheral positions of Japan and Europe was that offsetting currents in their separate political lives permitted *intensive* growth to slip through. A common technological heritage offered the chances. Politics made the chances real, and it was politics that influenced their timing.

TEN

Europe

Europe is a more complicated case than Japan because of the number of political units involved—not just countries or nation-states as we now think of them, but in the past a great array of kingdoms, principalities, bishoprics, and so forth. Yet these constituted an economic system or at any rate a group of economies with enough in common to be treated under the one head. European specialists jib at the idea. Undoubtedly there were immense differences in experience from place to place, and however the units are grouped, some big fractures like that between eastern and western Europe are certain to remain.

Europeanists nevertheless tend to be specialists in the history or current affairs of one country or another, or at most of a region like the Mediterranean basin or Scandinavia. They are usually too close to the trees that make up the continent to see it as a single wood, however distinct it may have been as a whole from other continents. They make a virtue of this stance, naturally protecting their investments in the study of given languages or cultures, by insisting that not to do so is to become superficial. But different questions invite different levels of response, and some answers and patterns show up only when we stand back from the detail, as world historians should, and survey Europe at large.

For the purpose of studying the long run there is good reason to rise above national histories. Until a few centuries ago the nation-state did not exist and the separate countries did not occupy their present bounds. It is better, then, to look on Europe, and before that Christendom, as a single culture-area set apart from other cultural or religious zones like, say, Islamdom. Because of its internal similarities and cross-contacts, Europe began early to form an economic system in which change in one part tended to diffuse to or at least be imitated by the other parts. Peasant farming may seem to have trudged along everywhere in the world unaffected by differences in government or trade, but Europe's rain-fed agriculture distinguished it from both desert and monsoon Asia. Even agriculture was not exempt from a slow diffusion of new ideas or new ways of taxing and administering the land.

There was, altogether, an informal levelling-up process at work in Europe, much of it through the migration of skilled people who are always the chief means by which technologies are transferred. Alien communities survived for a long time in many places, socially apart but acting as centres of imported methods and new industries. In Norwich, for instance, the Strangers included Walloons, Jews, and Netherlanders, originally involved in the cloth trade, and R. H. Mottram records how he heard the last sermon in Dutch preached there as late as 1900.[1]

Can we detect real growth across early modern Europe, before the industrial revolution of the late eighteenth century? Any conclusion must be inferential rather than statistical, for no adequate national income statistics exist or were ever kept. Early governments did not collect data at the aggregate level. There were no regular censuses before Sweden's in 1749, let alone figures on national manufacturing output (those for eighteenth-century Britain are mostly derived from the excise on trade). Even for the eighteenth century and later, ingenious proxies and heroic extrapolations have to be used to identify and trace the movements of many economic aggregates.

It would be no worse in principle to adopt a similar approach for assessing their course during early modern times. This has scarcely been done. Historians prefer the narrower certainties of direct record, while economists prefer the apparent relevance of more recent periods. The samples of interest rates so far published, for instance, are too spotty to be convincing at the continent-wide level. Material which does exist is however consistent with a long-term rise in investible funds, and this presumably helped to drive growth; given the volume of economic activity, the fall in the rate of interest is unlikely to have been the result of *reduced* demand for capital.

The major indirect signs of growth are probably in life expectancy, for which we have a few data indicative of a long-run rise; various non-monetary indicators; technical innovation; and structural change, this last being largely the product of off-setting increases in rural domestic industrialization and urbanization. Although large sections of the peasant population and the poorest urban dwellers will not have shared many of the gains until quite late, investigations of the household goods of several European populations show that by the middle of the eighteenth century living standards and domestic equipment had improved, and the medieval gap between the super-rich and the rest had already begun to be closed.

Entirely new consumption items had by then come into widespread use, like books and sporting guns, many items of furnishing, and the very subdivision of houses into upstairs and downstairs and separate rooms. Former luxuries like tea, coffee, sugar, and tobacco, unknown before the seventeenth century, were typically being consumed by many people every day. Some of these goods were substitutes for native European products (in much less elastic supply), like sugar for honey; many were deleterious to the health and not the untarnished blessings they were thought to be; but changing habits suggest a change in taste that had been satisfied and an expectation of realizable changes in preferences in the future. People perceived themselves as better off, and in the sense of commanding more, better-made, and sometimes exotic commodities, they were, well before what is conventionally thought of as the period of industrialization.[2]

The capital stock of the continent had clearly increased and improved. No sensible reader of contemporary works could think otherwise. Even if we cautiously remember that population had grown and gains per head might not have much outpaced capital works, this conclusion seems to hold. There were more roads, bridges, docks, canalized rivers, and buildings than there had ever been. The quality of materials and construction had also improved, and if we examine the range and quality of tools and workplaces available before the industrial revolution, say in Diderot's *Encyclopaedia* of 1765, the development of productive techniques becomes clear. It had been going on for centuries, not necessarily right across every territory of each incipient nation-state, but at least in key districts in many of them: note, for example, the impressive multiplication of mills and forges in the Rhineland and other upland areas since the Middle Ages.[3]

The currents of technical change flowed from far back in time, and in Europe they gradually accelerated until faster rates than elsewhere were reached. 'While the list of Chinese applications of water power is moderately impressive,' concludes Terry Reynolds after making his monumental survey, 'it does not compare to the European accomplishment, particularly in the period from the eleventh to sixteenth centuries.'[4]

As the age of industrialism approached, but still before it arrived, greater gains were realized in manufacturing. One of Diderot's plates shows the production of Japanned tinware on a flow-line, that is, with the processes subdivided and each carried out by specialist workmen. The entire job was not done by one man and his apprentice, as in the medieval stereotype. The advantages of a division of labour were appreciated, and were to be celebrated a little later in Adam Smith's account of the pin factory. Output was greatly increased by breaking tasks into repetitive parts, simplifying them, and reducing the time spent moving worker and materials from one activity to the next.

The method had not spread to all industries. Many workshops were too small to give much scope, and larger units had seldom begun to compete them out of business. In the middle of the eighteenth century there remained plenty of room for further growth by the division of labour and the extension of known techniques, without the invention of steam-powered machinery, the main adoption of which did not come until late in the nineteenth century. The progressive application of simpler procedures had long since started to make a difference to European industrial productivity.

Mass production had already begun to come in in a few places. The customary example is the development, by the Taylors at Wood Mill on the Itchen in Hampshire, of a lathe to cut identical ships' blocks (that is, pulleys for rigging). This was an early stage in the emergence of interchangeable parts manufacture. Other improvements were appearing in various areas of Europe, and they were communicated from one country to another faster than ever before, as entrepreneurs and skilled workmen responded to the increased tempo of activity. There is no reason to wonder at the ease with which so many places were to adopt textile-looms and steam-engines from England. They were already technically advanced by world standards and their methods were, historically speaking, already in a state of flux.

One need only glance at the splendid plans of Swedish sailing vessels in the *Architectura Navalis Mercatoria* of 1768 by Chapman (his family was originally English) to notice the complexity and scale that a major industry like ship-building had attained by that date. A comparable degree of improvement had affected many sorts of articles in everyday use. Housing, to cite another major example, was becoming much more fire-resistant in the northern half of Europe during the seventeenth and early eighteenth centuries. Styles of building in non-flammable materials, brick and tile, were spreading from the Netherlands and the North German ports. They meant better houses, easier to keep clean, and significantly less vulnerable to fire, hitherto a source of loss that has mostly been ignored except for odd cases like the Great Fire of London.[5]

The manual fire-pumps and leather hoses used to fight fires were also improving in design, though they were toys in the face of a real blaze. Most progress came through the better building materials. The pumps and piping for domestic water supplies were getting better and being adopted in more districts of more towns. Street lighting and interior lighting were improving, too, since whale-oil lamps were supplementing and replacing rushlights and candles. These matters may seem small, but they can be multiplied many times over, and if we compare them with what went before, rather than with how they look from the vantage-point of our own comfort and security, the progressive amelioration of life becomes plain.

It is less significant that these changes did not affect everywhere and everybody at once and did not come in at all rapidly by nineteenth- or twentieth-century standards. There are always lags in technical diffusion; the distaff remained in use in Italy at least as late as the Second World War, and I saw the flail still used for threshing in Germany in 1955. This merely demonstrates the prolonged overlapping of change.

Better methods, materials, and finished goods were already spreading in 'pre-industrial' Europe on such a scale that they were clearly raising average standards of well-being. Some very significant items were widely diffused socially and geographically before the middle of the eighteenth century. Clocks and watches are good examples. The price of a watch in England fell from £20 to £1 during the century *before* Adam Smith wrote *The Wealth of Nations*.

In long perspective, Europe was a continent that had absorbed Asian and Middle Eastern science and technology and energetically added much of its own. Historically, its total population had not been large or dense compared with India or China, but in the centuries following the Black Death it filled up again and did not pause at the fourteenth-century level. In important respects this expanding market was ripe for development. Geologically and ecologically Europe was varied and offered incentives for a criss-crossing trade in everyday commodities between regions that were variously endowed and had different costs of production. The coastline was long and irregular and there were many rivers that were either naturally navigable or could be made so with relative ease. This favoured the expansion of long-distance trade in bulk goods which were very expensive to cart any distance over pre-modern roads.

Given a promising, if partly derivative, history of ideas; rivers and coast conducive to bulk transport; and a favourable political history (to which we will shortly turn), it is not surprising that population growth produced a rise in real market size. Compared with several other Old World societies, Europe may have expanded and grown rather late. But when it did, technical change had somewhat matured, and its rapid advance needed mainly a political context that did not discourage the innovator and entrepreneur.

During the early modern period, particularly in the seventeenth century, there was a great expansion of rural domestic industry. By 1700 the percentage of the population employed full-time in agriculture had fallen substantially in the most advanced economies, Britain and the Netherlands. Dutch capital was being invested from Russia to Italy in a wide range of activities, bound up with transfers of 'best practice' technology. In this way the urban commercialism of the

London–Amsterdam axis leavened an agrarian continent. During the eighteenth century any faltering in the rate of growth in Holland, the leading economy of the previous century, is a tribute to wider growth as other nations sought to exclude Dutch products, encourage import substitution, and cut out the Dutch middleman by trading directly with one another.

Growth was thus long under way by virtue of diffusing best practices, seizing economies of scale, and extending the division of labour. Some part of the structural change that resulted came from the growth of the tertiary sector. The number of bureaucrats swelled.[6] Somebody else was now productive enough to feed these people. Not all the increased government activity was fruitful or even new (some of it replaced functions of the medieval church), but part of it was. This was nowhere more evident than in greater efforts to ward off disasters or minimize their effects.

Regularization by the early modern nation-states of the quarantine, adopted by Italian cities in the Middle Ages, seems to have been forceful in reducing the chances of further outbreaks of the plague. Bubonic plague was thereafter confined to the Ottoman end of the Mediterranean where quarantining was not introduced until the mid-nineteenth century. Coping with the occasional plague outbreak that occurred when someone broke the quarantine rules, as at Marseilles in 1720, required administrators to risk their own lives. That many did so reflects a better-organized public life with passably modern expectations of certainty and order.

It is obviously hard to be sure just how honestly and effectively measures like the quarantine were carried out. There would always be individuals and commercial interests that sought to cheat. The governor of Gibraltar wrote in 1805 about the complaints of merchants concerning the imposition of a quarantine, 'I am much afraid that Mr. Turnbull and the merchants and traders of Gibraltar are inclined to expect such Facility to their Commercial Intercourse as is inconsistent with . . . the prevention of the return of the Disease.'[7] The state however had its eye on safety in the longer run, and its policy prevailed. Disaster management was indeed a form of insurance on the part of the state. Minimizing losses from negative shocks and stabilizing the context of economic action became things governments were willing to do to match the efforts at maximizing output made by the private sector, where initiatives were also taken to achieve healthier living conditions.

City and state as well as market contributed to economic growth in Europe. Progress was not merely a matter of the invisible hand, but of a fortunate balance between a freer market than before and public intervention that was intended to help at least some of the interests of commerce. Plainly the degree, efficiency, and disinterestedness of intervention varied across the continent, but the general tendency, and the astonishingly satisfactory balance, are not in doubt.

Governments and civic authorities began to supply more public goods, such as roads to open up hinterlands and help unify the market. The Absolutist states have had an unfairly bad press with respect to the vigour with which they began to intervene in economic life. All in all, a process of economic growth, admittedly meandering and uneven, did spread across Europe. The existence of regions and classes that continued to elude this diffusion does not detract from the fact of a rise in average well-being. Furthermore, given the definition of a public good as one from whose use no one can be excluded, the poor especially stood to gain from public investment. The role of the authorities was largely an enabling one. Within the framework they helped to construct, private productive activity—following the abolition of the guilds, common-field agriculture, and serfdom—was able to bring about *intensive* growth.

The question is how to explain this maturing of the political context of growth in Europe. Explanations of *very* long-term change of this kind are rarely found among the descriptions in the history books, except by remote implication. It is indeed unclear what shape they should take. Some of the schemes put forward urge that Europe was different from the rest of the world from very early, even prehistoric times, in ways that may be presumed to have facilitated growth.[8] One feature of Europe to which reference is often made is its Christianity. The causal links between religion and economic action however remain uncertain, and those who are convinced of Christianity's role have not explained how it could have been on the scene for so very long before it evoked demonstrable economic growth. The trickiness of long-run explanations stems from the difficulty of separating from fundamental causes those facilitative changes which mostly affected the rate of change and the specific forms growth took in Europe. Such general features as the environment and religion seem more likely to have affected the form of growth rather than to have brought about economic growth in the first instance. The timing of the onset of growth requires there to have been some real means of actuation, and this is seldom specified by proponents of geographical or religious explanations. This may be an acknowledgement of the length, gradualness, and complexity of the process.

The most fruitful approach seems to be via the consequences of political structure. European peoples are the overlay of one early westward population movement after another, though successful invasion ceased a long time ago. In the tenth century AD the attacks of the Magyars, Moors, and Vikings were all beaten off. In the thirteenth century the Mongols turned back from Hungary and Poland. In the sixteenth and seventeenth centuries the Ottoman attempts to invade were defeated.

Unlike much of Asia, Europe therefore long ago ceased to experience destructive invasions or (and this is more important) the imposition of alien regimes. Equally, no indigenous attempt to take over the continent and rule it as a single empire ever succeeded. Every time one of the larger polities threatened to engulf its neighbours a coalition of others arose to maintain a 'balance of power', so that the very need to ensure balance became an article of diplomatic faith. Europeans always remained rather separate peoples within a common culture, and although for many centuries the trend has been towards fewer and larger political units, in the Middle Ages there were hundreds of polities. The underlying decentralized structure has its roots in the original ethnic mix, reinforced by the high costs of conquering and retaining a hold on a topographically and linguistically diverse landscape.

We still have to explain why Europe's numerous kings and lords do not seem to have taken as much revenue out of society as did the conquest dynasties of Asia and the Middle East. An economist's preference would be not to resort to common speculations about supposedly enduring cultural differences, but to consider the costs and benefits likely to have affected the behaviour of rulers. To generalize about this over a number of centuries, or about crude, long-term differences between 'Europe' and 'Asia'—both portmanteau terms—is obviously hazardous. At any one moment there were several types of regime in both places. Nevertheless, only by risking some generalization, by offering a kind of idealized summary, can we hope to see the patterns formed by innumerable and sometimes contrary events.

The heart of the matter is not simply how Europe escaped both conquest from without and the rise of a unitary empire from within, but why its many kings and lesser lords tended to extract less and return just a little more than rulers elsewhere. The difference in the share of income levied was no doubt slender, but it seems to have grown over time. Growth itself left larger incomes in citizens' hands. Bernard Shaw somewhere remarks, 'I am a bandit, I live by robbing the rich. I am a gentleman, I live by robbing the poor. Shake hands.' Why was it that European 'gentlemen' allowed the margin for a developing economy to slip past them? While some may have been schooled to the asceticism of old money, restraint never accompanied the first winning of a fortune, was not universal, and could not be relied on. Competition for subjects and power among the states and between kings and nobles seems in the end to be the answer. It abridged the worst behaviour—not much, and only on average, but more than in the other great societies of the world.

More resources, too, began to be returned by acts of state policy. From the seventeenth or eighteenth centuries, governments interested themselves in political arithmetic and economic programmes. No matter that they could not always carry out their intentions, or that their aims were often ill-informed or misconceived, and more concerned with state-building than directly with welfare, the tendency was there. A political society was being constructed in which private market activities were tended by the state rather than immediately milked. This necessarily introduces a positive variable into the growth and development equation.[9] Nevertheless, it is possible to see the emerging positive acts of European governments as growth-adapting—as adapting to and promoting growth primarily released by the removal of constraints which arose from the continent's competitive politics.

Why the competitor-states did not bring their world down in the flames of war is an immense puzzle. The close-packed political units formed a different chess-board from the sprawl of the great empires, and it was perhaps noticed that the costs of expansion were especially high. Territorial expansion certainly did take place in Europe, as the number of political units was eventually collapsed into the format of a few nation-states, but the opposite poles of a single empire or anarchy were both avoided. Adverse coalitions no doubt dissuaded some of the ambitious, but luck too must have been involved in avoiding fragmentation or total consolidation. Small states elsewhere, in Indo-China for example, offered no such check on the greed of their rulers.

The reliance of Europe's rulers on mercantile sources of income increasingly permitted their merchant subjects a voice in the affairs of state. Writers emerged from the bourgeois ranks to press for policies that would promote further change. Where merchants gained a say in parts of Asia it was as individuals dependent on favour and not as a class. It is because the difference between Europeans and others was one of degree rather than kind that it is so difficult to assess, and impossible to measure. The difference was in modal behaviour, shifting only gradually, sometimes wavering, varying from place to place within each system. Out of it finally emerged the managerial European state that desired to raise its economic strength, because this was seen by the ruler as an arm of his power and prestige—one on which he eventually became dependent.

In the less *dirigiste* countries of north-western Europe, mercantile interests gained the biggest say, however hidden they were behind the costumier's confections of court and army. Private entrepreneurial forces marshalled themselves under the encouraging umbrella of states that had become apprised of the gains from growth. Mannered snobberies dominated 'society' but not its bank balances. Commercial realities came to influence, if not yet to control, states willing to reduce uncertainty, provide a stable setting for contract, and no longer inclined to treat business as a larder to be raided. The reinforcements of growth overcame the worst backlash effects. The market became strong enough to dissolve defensive institutions, like the guilds, committed to sharing out work at whatever cost in forgone opportunities. Once these processes were under way, the environmental advantages of Europe could come into their own. But competitive politics that cancelled out rapacious interests were what had first released the continent's immense potential.

ELEVEN

Summary and Conclusion

One danger in economic history is a mild form of anachronism, in which the goal is historical explanation of the modern economy, but the stylized version of what is modern is already out of date. In Chapter 1 we suggest, more than half seriously, that the implicit terminus of industrial revolution studies is the Britain of 1907. That Britain has obviously vanished. Even the economy of the 1970s is passing away, and with it any conceivable 'modern economy' of the individual nation-state as aimed at by the textbooks.

'I wish to argue', writes Peter Drucker, 'that the world economy is not "changing"; it has *already changed*—in its foundations and in its structure—and in all probability the change is irreversible.'[1] Drucker refers to three shifts, the detaching of primary production from the industrial economy, of manufacturing production from manufacturing employment, and the loosening of capital movements from trade flows (with capital movements rather than trade now driving the world economy, and in a volatile way). Relationships taken for granted in industrial revolution studies and the like are therefore doubly behind the times. They do not plausibly lead from canals and cotton to the world of electronics, plastics, and hypermarkets; and they do not direct us forwards to the choppier seas of Drucker's world.

An obvious response would be to update our agenda, to strike off earlier periods and roll forwards in an ever-moving carpet of 'relevance'. That was what the 'take-off' school did when it dropped the years before 1750 into a pit of medieval nothingness. It was however unwarranted intellectually and unfortunate for the pedagogic standing of economic history. A better approach is to rise above the moving target of the modern economy in its latest descriptive manifestation and try instead to identify conditions favourable to the birth, or influential on the rate, of economic growth *in general*. Ancient experience and wide comparisons may teach us as much about fundamentals as modern macro-economics does (not more, but as much, and different things).

Orson Welles sardonically said, 'in Italy for thirty years under the Borgias they had warfare, terror, murder, bloodshed—they produced Michelangelo, Leonardo da Vinci and the Renaissance. In Switzerland they had brotherly love, five hundred years of democracy and peace, and what did they produce . . .? The cuckoo clock.'[2] Economic historians are people who understand the romance (and utility) of the cuckoo clock, its innovation, diffusion, falling price, and mass appeal. Greed, piracy, war, treasure, blood and thunder, are all part of the subject too, but at bottom we are people with a vision of the good life that is essentially Swiss, bourgeois, tranquil. We are against avoidable human misery. We probably think that, despite the hideous entropy of history, a judicious combination of good government and working markets could have reduced it. *Pas d'argent, pas de Suisse?* Anyone who thinks that growth is near saturation in the developed world, or a crassly materialist concern, or that redistribution alone will bind up the world's wounds, should read 'When Croesus Rules' in *The Economist* (7–13 March 1987), Geoffrey Moorehouse's *Calcutta*, and the more formal account of the desirability of growth in Sir Arthur Lewis, *The Theory of Economic Growth*.[3]

The present book thinks growth is very important. It is a new sketch-map of how and where it came about. It implies that large-scale maps like those of the British industrial revolution are not placed helpfully with respect to the smaller-scale map of world economic history. This is not to challenge the ruling paradigm by saying that the existing maps are all wrong, though British industrialization was longer and flatter than most of them show, as much as to point out that they tend to isolate and exaggerate the one episode. The reader is invited to re-orient and see modern British, European, or Western experience as representing one type of growth—industrialization —and, because of the similarities within the West, not much more than a single form at that. Our perceptions will have to shift in the hope of ever arriving at a theory of what causes growth.

In other words the book tries to reconceptualize a central part of what historians and social scientists have always studied. It is better to have a rough sketch-map of where you are than an intricate chart of somewhere else. To fill in the details, even from secondary sources, would be tantamount to writing the economic history of the world. That needs to be done by someone with larger resources of every kind. Here we merely try to indicate the outlines such a map might assume.

After Emlyn Williams had won a Scholarship to Christ Church in 1923 he still had Higher School Certificate examinations to sit. He went to catch the train back to Wales. 'I looked out at the fustian station, peered at the corner of the sign "Oxford" and thought, mine . . . I started to read, like a novel, easily and with affection, my notes on the Causes of the Industrial Revolution. Ugly people joined me and I loved them all.'[4] That was over two generations ago, but a continuing tradition for British school children does not guarantee that the puzzle can be solved in the guise in which it is set. Many references to the industrial revolution are of course not historical at all, but make use of the label for symbolic purposes. The other great shibboleth is the Fall of Rome. *Ex cathedra* pronouncements about what caused either of these happenings should instantly put us on our guard. They are almost always specious.[5]

The 'facts' in conventional accounts of the industrial revolution may be correct within the normal parameters of scholarly debate, but this is beside the point if the standard model's assumption that economic growth began in this way is misleading. Are those facts the most relevant ones? Many of them refer to a bewildering range of supposedly unique propulsive factors in the Georgian economy, but on closer inspection look more like secondary, culturally specific, and growth-adapting changes than anything decisively new. Massive efforts to measure the economic variables connected with early British industrialization may be justified for the purpose of writing British economic history. They are not the most appropriate for illuminating economic growth as a general phenomenon, even if their semi-quantitative sources mean they can be made more precise than the approximate magnitudes which alone are computable for earlier cases.

Conversely, the 'facts' underlying the analysis in this book may be inaccurate on a number of points. Perhaps that is unavoidable where a non-specialist blunders through reports by so many specialists on individual societies, when so few of them are well-honed for the economic historian's purposes. But it is not devastating if the new framework is one that directs us to study appropriate patterns. While the text is dependent on secondary sources, with all the hesitations that ensue, it is the conception and interlocking of the picture that is important, not each piece of the jigsaw. The vision of gradualism and changes in pace around the world is meant to be judged as a whole. A general thesis like the one put forward here can be amended but cannot truly be falsified on the basis of individual points. For example, the precise extent of *intensive* growth in the cases we have discussed is secondary to the fact that there was some such growth.

From 1958 to 1970 or thereabouts I read every word being published on the agricultural history of England from the sixteenth century on. I enjoyed it and wrote a lot about the topic. From that experience I got a shrewd idea of whose statements were properly warranted by the evidence, who were the copyists, and who were the plagiarizers of ideas. Each tired assertion and agricultural misconception in the general history books and works on development economics stood out like a sore thumb. I learnt very well how the generalist can irritate the specialist; but the irritation is reversed when the specialist will not place his or her work with respect to the broad issues, and there is nothing like rural history for avoiding those. Since about 1972 I have been reading in the vastly more diffuse literature of world history and have come to see that broad patterns do not have to fit tightly at each specialist corner, desirable though that may be, to articulate larger truths or send the reader off in interesting directions. At that rarified level, beyond any individual's complete grasp, the purpose must be a different kind of mapping.

The main disadvantage I have felt in writing this book is not what one might think. It relates little to the surface disabilities of a virtually monoglot English speaker, to technical incapacities in history or economics, to lack of skill, time, or resources. Instead it relates to ingrained point of view, and not to political or religious attitudes, but to something deeper. I was born and brought up an Englishman during a period of English history which was by world standards abnormally at ease. Astonishing as this may seem to those who experienced the Slump when I was a baby, the war when I was a small boy, and the post-war austerity which lasted throughout my schooldays, it was a calm society. This is not middle-aged nostalgia. I felt it then. It was codified for me in the books of John Moore, whom I came to know and love, and who wrote about a small country town such as the one in which I grew up.

The last outbreak of war and the last outbreak of plague in my ancestral Wiltshire village were both in the year in which my great-great-great-great-great-great-grandfather was born there, 1645. Such freedom from disaster is almost unimaginable in world terms. By the time of my youth crimes of violence against the person were at a seven-centuries' low.[6] This level would have been unheard-of in much of the world and inconceivable to most people's ancestors. My society was class-ridden, but it was orderly and passionless. It is this which may unfit me for writing world history, for I secretly believe in the perfectability of our species and the possibility of sustained economic growth. That is a *very* long-run view, but the processes recurrent in the *very* long run are what I am trying to assess here.

Australia turns out to be a better base from which to survey world history than one might suppose. A British culture anchored off Asia, with poorer neighbours than Britain and geo-political surrounds that are beginning to fray, gives a different perspective on what matters. No one is more fascinated by Old World detail than myself, but it is a mesmerizing vortex of puzzles, drawing one deeper and deeper into the minutiae of the historicized landscape. In newer lands the opportunities for amusement are fewer but the distraction is less. 'The breezes have nothing to remember and everything to promise', Rupert Brooke wrote about Canada. Australia is a tablet even less scribbled on.

To make sense of the strands of history it is vital to distinguish between industrialization, capitalism, Modern Economic Growth, *intensive* and *extensive* growth, and economic development. The opposite point of view is expressed by Irfan

Habib: 'It is a reasonable assumption, however, that for all societies other than those of our own day, the only possible road to modern industry lay through capitalism; and it may therefore be taken for granted that the proximity to or distance from true capitalistic relations that a given premodern or modern society maintained offers a valid criterion for judging its capacities for growth, so that, in essence, *the two questions may be treated as identical.*'[7] Once the questions of growth and capitalism have been tied together in this way all hope of tracing their separate histories has been lost. The more strands which are run together, the more blurred the subject becomes. This blurring means prejudging the results of the historical enquiry itself.

Habib is not directly concerned with economic growth. He continues: 'A rather more difficult question is one of definition: What do capitalistic relations consist of?' Habib adopts the Marxist definition in which anyone who owns tools which he employs someone else to use is a capitalist. 'This definition, in effect, restricts capitalism properly to the economic organization that became dominant with the coming of the Industrial Revolution', although Habib is immediately obliged to sweep in to his net and consider the preceding development of a 'money economy' along with the machine industrialism he wants to define as capitalism.[8] It is more satisfactory to concentrate on *intensive* growth than to equate it in advance like this with the diverse forms in which it may appear, capitalist, industrial, or anything else. That must obscure the sources of growth as growth. The early, multiple, and non-Western histories of growth are especially likely to be obscured by the smokestack of Western industrialization if proper distinctions are not made and evidence is not sought wherever it may be found. Describing the Sung, for example, in almost-but-not-quite-capitalist terms does not help at all.

Once we have established that we are looking for evidence of *intensive* growth, our first assumption is that there was indeed a propensity for growth. Some people in every large society have worked to invest, invent, innovate, and so improve their material circumstances; recurrent moves in that direction by whole societies become historically probable. This assumption is 'universalist', although not universal in that it does not need to assert that every individual is a 'maximizer', merely that this kind of behaviour is common in human populations. What it does not accept is that there are innate, unobserved differences between sizeable groups of any race, colour, gender, and so on, which would explain why some peoples have achieved growth and others have not.

The assumption, then, is non-racist, non-sexist, and so forth, and ought to be heart-warming. I also think it is correct; it is drawn from reading a lot of history. But it is not an ideological assumption in the sense of deriving from someone else's ideology. It simply seems economical to make the assumption, and to derive actual behaviour from observed changes in the constraints surrounding it. I do not assert in a Pollyanna-ish way that *intensive* growth is pre-programmed, only that a tendency for growth is one of the behaviours that seem to be. Growth is not guaranteed to overcome the countervailing forces of sloth and greed, and even if it does, the lag intervals may conceivably be centuries long, swallowing up whole periods of history. *Extensive* growth may be the only result. To that extent the assumption need not be heart-warming at all.

'Surely', remarks Stefano Fenoaltea, 'the *differentia specifica* of the cliometrician's cast of mind is the refusal to recognize systematic differences in casts of mind: not so much because we do not believe they exist, as because the challenge we pose ourselves is precisely to explain observed differences in behavior by observable differences in opportunities *without* appealing to unobservable differences in preferences.'[9] Without writing cliometric history ourselves, or indeed knowing how the matters that interest us might be more than roughly quantified, Fenoaltea's seems a reasonable starting-position. The propensity for growth will assert and reassert itself, *ceteris paribus*, and the question becomes, what were the constraints lurking in the *cet. par.* clause?

This assumption reduces the length of the lists of 'necessary' conditions common in the industrial revolution literature. They are time and place-specific, correlates of the advanced society of eighteenth-century England, and no more assuredly general than the vaguely 'Western' traits listed in economic development texts. (A complementary type of argument traces under-development in the Third World to the *lack* of some feature found in the West, when even there that feature was as likely as not an adaptation to a pre-existing advanced level of development.) The necessary conditions for economic growth may be few and much the same as the sufficient conditions. They usually take a long time to operate, but can sometimes appear quickly, depending on the prior build-up of technology and the speed of political release or active encouragement of the division of labour.

Is this too vague a prescription? Economists must not think they can isolate the economy from its matrix. Precise circumstances are hard to call. One is reminded of Lenin's explanation of the Russian Revolution as a fusing of disparate tendencies 'with remarkable coherence'. Perhaps growth can occur only within an 'optimality band' where factor and commodity markets are freed and the government is neither too grasping nor too weak. These conditions cannot be specified in any way measurable with the will-o'-the-wisp historical records and the rigid economic models at our disposal. At this early stage of comparative history, this fact should not be fatally depressing; at least it keeps us on the tightrope between descriptive histories where the theory is always smuggled in and theoretical exercises tested only against episodes carefully selected from history. Comparative history cannot finally determine the causes of growth because history ran too few experiments with too many variables, but it is the best control on the confusion.

Equally, or almost equally, our second assumption of a widespread tendency towards rent-seeking may explain the suppression of growth. It allows for external shocks and is a more general propensity than the internal formation of Olsonian 'distributional coalitions'. Accordingly we examined the history of some major societies to try to assess how far internal social or cultural obstacles, as opposed to political or external forces, repressed their potential. These societies lay in mainland Asia during the early modern period (playing fast and loose with both geography and chronology) and were political societies chosen on the basis of population size, as one proxy for potential, and earlier achievement as another. They were the main contemporaries of developing Japan and Europe.

A historical observation takes third place. This is that the British industrial revolution was by no means the only case of economic growth. A Tory councillor in Swansea objected to a Falklands War computer game because it gave the British only a 50 : 50 chance of a successful landing. We reject the kind of reasoning which would arrange the rules so that growth must have occurred first in Britain. We are on safe ground; growth, by any reasonable definition, did not.

The procedure adopted follows the advice of the nineteenth-century algebraist, Karl Jacobi, that when a problem is unyielding we should try turning it upside down to see if an explanation can be shaken loose. The problem of the causes of the industrial revolution, and by identification or extension the problem of growth, has been stubborn enough. Hence the idea of turning away from the search for a push-force. My feelings about that after years of reading are summed up by the rhyme,

> As I was going up the stair,
> I met a man who wasn't there
> He wasn't there again today
> Oh, how I wish he'd go away.

We do not know whether any push-force worked at all. What we have are loose correlations and allusions to a mysteriously greater responsiveness to changes in factor prices. On the other hand we do know, as well as we know anything, that some negative forces can suppress growth.

It may seem forlorn to try to account for something that did not happen. The argument against the attempt, most succinctly expressed by A. C. Graham, is that there are no grounds for choosing among an infinity of negative possibilities.[10] This seems thin. A great number of simultaneous positive, or potentially positive, forces is always at work, and that has never dissuaded historians from picking and choosing among them. There may appear to be an asymmetry between attributing building a house to work by the builder and accounting for it not burning down by observing that no one dropped a cigarette butt, the wiring was not faulty, no bombs were dropped, and so on *ad infinitum*, to follow Graham's example. But that is not really so.

What we are trying to explain is why some houses did not get rebuilt at certain times. We already know (to make our analogy fit switches between *extensive* and *intensive* growth) that houses had been built previously, sometimes in the same place. We could attribute building to actions at many different levels, from changes in the mortgage rate, to changes in the zoning laws, to family formation rates, to individual investment decisions, to trowelling by the bricklayer. An equivalent forensic may surely be applied to selecting from a menu of negative factors and urging, as best we may, that some were more likely than others to have blocked building. All we are trying to understand is a lack of building in particular places at a given period, when building was going on elsewhere.

In practice, argument proceeds from the removal of constraints more often than is recognized. The form is to attribute a process or event to the ending of something else, rising productivity, say, to the disappearance of guild restrictions. Such arguments tend to be supplementary: the forcing-open of bottlenecks is advanced as necessary, but seldom sufficient, for growth. Our position, that in the absence of constraints growth was likely to come about, is not admitted. By implication it is denied, sometimes strongly, in the literatures of economic history and economic development which paint (all too accurately) pictures of the miseries of poverty, but read into them hopelessness and moral inertia. Instead, we find the reasons for suppressed growth not in the absence of desire or effort but in grasping by rulers and governments and the secondary consequences of their acts, as well as in their failure to create institutions conducive to change. These negative factors, the shocks and the referred pain from them, need more evaluation in the context of particular histories, but by and large they were the nub.

How to escape these forces? In Europe, Marc Bloch long ago said, the key lay in binding the ruler.[11] There had to be a dispersal of power to many centres, so that market forces could push their way through, the way weeds crack paving-stones. There had to be some inducement for rulers and governments, and at lesser levels the lordlings, to offer services and commercial protection to their subjects, in the expectation of sharing in the proceeds of market growth. When they looked down their royal and aristocratic noses, they did at last learn to see their subjects as clients, however much they might have affected that all they could see were inferiors.

What, then, is to be made of Japan? The answer seems to be that beneath its enamelled exterior, the fullest power of the Tokugawa shogunate was constrained by the *daimyo*, but they could not mount an open challenge to it until after the first rude clarion call of the West in the 1850s. No matter: a balance had been struck in which the market unexpectedly hollowed out autocracy from within, many of the samurai for example having over the centuries turned themselves from warriors into merchants. The economic challenge had already been made, even if an overt political one had still to await the stirrings of the Meiji Restoration.

Formulated in this way, Japanese and European history seem to be matters of accidentally contrived balances of forces. Indeed, why not? Political struggle and political solutions across the world were multiform. The evolution simply tended to a balance in two parts of the world which, at a particular historical juncture, had escaped the knock-on consequences of invasion from the steppes. Remember our canvas—the world geographical sweep and the many centuries in which events could work themselves out—and our supposition that the propensity for growth would be steaming away beneath the rent-seeking jockeying and strife. It is not as astonishing as it seems that *intensive* growth might bubble once more through the *extensive* growth porridge, in more than one place and as a result of a happy abridgement of the worst forms of political greed.

This was 'Smithian growth', essentially brought about by the several forms of the division of labour, supplemented by an array of pre-machine technologies. Industrialization was still to come. But Smithian growth meant big proportionate returns. All growth is at the mercy of the politicians, but this variety with its basis in improved skills (human capital) was surely no more vulnerable to political interference than was the 'Schumpeterian' industrial form (dependent as that was on fixed capital which could be commandeered or destroyed). As it was, growth did now persist long enough, with more of an accumulating technical and scientific heritage than the Sung had, to spawn industrialization.

This scheme may smack of Adam Smith's 'natural progress of opulence' theory. Growth was not however an automatiç blessing from 'peace and easy taxes', instrumental though they were in permitting a 'natural' desire for it to well into action. An additional, positive, role for various public authorities was involved, springing not from altruism or popular expectations but out of the impetus political competition gave to succour one's own economy. Political conflict and competition in the pre-modern world were usually destructive, the replacement of one band of brigands by another. Situations that gave some sign of quietening down, with the contenders exhausted and no side able to gain a decisive advantage, must have occurred in other times and places, only to be destabilized again by new intrusions of strife. Beyond some scarcely fathomable limits, rent-seeking conflict and the propensity for growth could each crowd the other out. In Japan and Europe political competition diverted enough energy into fostering market growth for long enough to make a real difference, to change the history of the world, no less.

The framework is a general one but it has a number of advantages. It comprehends more cases of technical innovation and *intensive* growth than an a priori industrial revolution approach can do. Descriptively, then, it is broader and takes a more realistic view by not confining the genesis of growth, as it were, to eighteenth-century Lancashire. It is not ethnocentric. It is not time-bound. It directs attention to known negative forces in history, rather than to push-forces the power of which has not been independently demonstrated. Because it encompasses more than one case it offers an opportunity to those who wish to formalize theory; no single industrial revolution, no single anything, can underpin a theory of growth, since theories have to be generalizations of multiple cases. The dominant alternative is a 'take-off' or 'great discontinuity', after which everything begins at once. That theory was of great cold war convenience, since it could be made to imply that growth is attainable virtually overnight, without long spells of institution-building and a balanced evolution of private markets and public power.

'Decisions on these matters also imply a political stand on more current affairs . . .', asserts Suraiya Faroqhi, speaking of the controversy over the Asian mode of production.[12] So they may, but they do not *necessarily* do so. Hermeneutical suspicion is just that, suspiciousness. Over-politicized individuals may not be able to conceive of an attempt at disinterestedness (the confusion of the term nowadays with a lack of interest is no doubt indicative), but that is a problem they should not try to export. All social scientists have personal origins and values, but this need not be imprisoning. It is whether we try to allow for our bias that counts.[13]

A similar caution is needed in dismissing conventional economics as value-laden. Only at the speculative edge of philosophy need that be a great problem. There are plenty of antiseptic concepts which can help to cut through a great deal of historical confusion. 'Comparative advantage', say, or treating labour for analytical purposes as a factor of production, are hardly the discardable baggage of 'neoclassical' ideology, neither does their use commit anyone to a given modern political programme. To argue that they must do so is a complete, and offensive, *non sequitur*.

The Asian empires discussed here are all long dead. They are not in my mind surrogates for modern Russia or China, or (courtesy of the Ottomans) modern Islam, any more than the guilds are surrogates for trade unions. That would be illiterate. Any modern government offers so much more in services (and control) as not to be comparable with the indifferent and ramshackle tyrannies of the past. Appeals to the past for specific contemporary purposes are usually spurious. They are analogous to tracing one's ancestry through the male line only, ignoring the biological, social, cultural, and economic implications of the female line. Investigations like that find nothing more than they seek.

Appeals to a rounded history are another matter. Yet history is so complicated, so unlike today in the appearance it presents, that any lessons to be drawn from it must be abstract and teach only at one remove, through illustrations of the nature of debate and the deployment of evidence, good for the mind, good for context. Some very sensible words by D. C. M. Platt and Guido di Tella are in order here: 'as economists and historians retreat respectively into specialisation, and antiquarianism, within continents, in countries, by periods, by themes, and even by ideologies, it does no harm to look around and perhaps to detect influences more powerful than those immediately within grasp.'[14] One needs to know some pre-nineteenth-century history and comparative history, for instance, in order to judge fairly whether change in the West was unique or a variant of a universal thrust.[15]

Japan and Europe were the residuary legatees of a much larger world that might have grown (and has grown since, following their example).[16] Archaeological finds are constantly showing today that many productive techniques are far older than ever was thought. As Hodgson observed, the supposed millennial torpor from which the East has awoken in the twentieth century was in reality a condition of slow change.[17] This translates as *extensive* growth continuing over the period when Japan and Europe were entering *intensive* growth.

We need a powerful means of explaining why change had failed to raise average per capita GNP over the remainder of the pre-modern world. Starting from scratch amidst mass poverty, scarce capital, feeble materials, weak technologies, high information costs, and the risks induced by individuals more given to taking slices of the communal pie than helping to bake it, growth was certain to be slow by modern standards. There does however seem to have been some positive feedback between *intensive* growth once it started and the erosion of the more brutal forms of pie-slicing. It does not do to be fixated on what used to be called man's inhumanity to man. Growth, like truth, will out.

These are very general suggestions, not yet an operational theory but two frameworks which are intended as the agenda for the future. The frameworks may be treated separately but probably ought to be combined. Firstly, we need to look well back and far afield if we are to give a fair account of the history of growth; in particular we need to get away from the belief that growth came about abruptly and only once, and away from the almost exclusive concern in English-language economic history with relatively recent Western cases. Our arena needs to be broader. Above all the economic history of East Asia, ancient and modern, deserves its due. Secondly, we need to construct a new explanation of how growth starts, and here the most fruitful approach seems to be to consider the removal of impediments, not to search for laser-beam miracles.

Growth comes in more than one variety. There are different mixes of the division of labour, trade growth, new techniques, capital-widening and capital-deepening, though all of these were evident in the main successful cases of history. Different aspects of the general propensity for growth, propensities to barter, tendencies to tinker, may have been implicated according to the type of growth. The overall propensity is plastic enough to assume different guises; what need more work are the various shapes of the forces that channelled it in one direction or another, or suppressed one or other form of growth. Perhaps there was too much entropy in the world, or the sources are simply too poor, for all the intricate interactions to be disentangled; maybe each situation was a unique constellation of particular growth forms struggling with particular negative forces, all obscured in the clouds of imperfect historical sources, so that they can never be properly ordered by the generalizations of social science. Luckily the exercise itself is instructive, and the new frameworks may help to bring new relationships and evidence into view.

Even when the past was superficially changeless, there was a detectable long-run trend, with cycles about it. The repeated restoration of an unfortunate equilibrium, a low-level political trap, explains more of the record of non-growth than does an appeal to non-Western inertia and perpetual stagnation. We need to restore history to growth and growth to history. Specific political histories, amplifying or dampening the propensities for growth and for rent-seeking, were responsible for the switching between *extensive* and *intensive* growth. Economic history is a morality play on a vast canvas. No less than good and evil wrestled here throughout the ages. Good, though often thrown, came back for more.

Notes

1: 'A KNOW-ALL'S GUIDE TO THE INDUSTRIAL REVOLUTION'

1. This chapter was first given as a paper to the staff seminar in economic history at the University of Exeter in Jan. 1985. Since then another critique of the industrial revolution concept and the over-extension of the English model has appeared, Rondo Cameron, 'A New View of European Industrialization', *Economic History Review*, 2nd ser. 38 (1985), 1–23.
2. Joel Mokyr, 'Growing-up and the Industrial Revolution in Europe', *Explorations in Economic History*, 13 (1976), 371–96.
3. C. K. Harley, *British Industrialization before 1841: Evidence of Slower Growth during the Industrial Revolution* (Research Report 8120, Department of Economics, University of Western Ontario, 1981), 20.
4. Gerald A. Gunderson, *A New Economic History of America* (New York: McGraw-Hill, 1976), 154–9.
5. The key volume is W. W. Rostow, *The Stages of Economic Growth* (Cambridge: CUP, 1960). It should be noted that the surprising influence of the take-off concept and the stages sequence was what primarily locked economic history into identifying growth with the industrialization of the past 200 years.

   This was a product of 1950s and 1960s 'growthmanship' embodied in parallel concepts such as Simon Kuznets's MEG (Modern Economic Growth), widely touted as a quantifiable phenomenon, although it rests partly on a judgement concerning how far 'modern' science and technology have been adopted.

   The take-off metaphor had a far greater appeal than a study of the literature of the time would now show; much of what is 'in the air' at a given period is never formally written down. The concept was admittedly always more influential among 'consumers' of economic history in economics and neighbouring social-science subjects than in traditional economic history or history departments. Despite professional rebuttal in some quarters virtually from the outset, Rostow's stages sequence continues to be baldly presented in the literature, e.g. in A. G. Kenwood and A. L. Lougheed, *Technological Diffusion and Industrialization Before 1914* (London: Croom Helm, 1982), 20.

Professor Rostow's work is historically more sensitive than the popularized 'take-off' idea would lead one to suppose; see e.g. the first chapter of *How It All Began* (New York: McGraw-Hill, 1975), which considers 'Why Traditional Societies Did Not Generate Self-sustained Growth' with respect to the ancient and oriental worlds. This question may seem an obvious one, indeed it has a tradition stretching back at least to Montesquieu in the early 18th century, yet it is otherwise scarcely addressed in industrial revolution studies.

6. P. B. Medawar, *Advice to a Young Scientist* (London: Pan Books, 1981), 29.

7. Hugo Lemon, 'The Development of Hand Spinning Wheels', *Textile History*, i (1968), 83–91; Marta Hoffman, 'The "Great Wheel" in the Scandinavian Countries', in Geraint Jenkins (ed.), *Studies in Folk Life* (London: Routledge and Kegan Paul, 1969).

8. For the case of cotton see M. F. Mazzaoui, *The Italian Cotton Industry in the later Middle Ages 1100–1600* (Cambridge: CUP, 1981), esp. p. 162.

9. Dolores Greenberg, 'Reassessing the Power Patterns of the Industrial Revolution: An Anglo-American Comparison', *American Historical Review*, 87 (1982), 1237–61.

10. Terry S. Reynolds, 'Medieval Roots of the Industrial Revolution', *Scientific American*, 251 (1984), 115, and *Stronger than a Hundred Men: A History of the Vertical Water Wheel* (Baltimore, Md.: Johns Hopkins University Press, 1983), 67–70, 96, 155.

11. D. G. Watts, 'Water-power and the Industrial Revolution', *Transactions of the Cumberland and Westmorland Antiquarian and Archaeological Society*, NS 67 (1967), 205.

12. A. E. Musson, 'Industrial Motive Power in the United Kingdom 1800–70', *Economic History Review*, 2nd ser. 29 (1976), 413–39.

13. 'Power Patterns', p. 1261.

14. F. T. Evans, 'Wood since the Industrial Revolution: A Strategic Retreat?', *History of Technology*, vii (1982), 37–56. According to data in Oliver Rackham, *Ancient Woodland: Its History, Vegetation and Uses in England* (London: Edward Arnold, 1980), 162–71, the price of oak timber was falling from about 1830, of ash from before 1820, and the number of businesses in eastern England using underwood to make hurdles, rakes, and wooden barrel hoops was actually increasing from the 1840s into the 20th century.

15. Evans, 'Wood', p. 44.

16. W. A. Cole and Phyllis Deane, *British Economic Growth* (Cambridge: CUP, 1962).

17. Malcolm Falkus, 'Modern British Economic Development: The Industrial Revolution in Perspective', *Australian Economic History Review*, 19 (1979), 42–62.
18. E. L. Jones, 'Afterword', in W. N. Parker and E. L. Jones (eds.), *European Peasants and Their Markets* (Princeton, NJ: Princeton University Press, 1975), 330.
19. D. H. Whitehead, 'The English Industrial Revolution as an Example of Growth', in R. M. Hartwell (ed.), *The Industrial Revolution* (Oxford: Basil Blackwell, 1970), 9.
20. Joel Mokyr, 'Disparities, Gaps, and Abysses', *Economic Development and Cultural Change*, 33 (1984), 175.
21. Sidney Pollard, review of P. Mathias, *The First Industrial Nation*, 2nd edn. (1983), in *Business History*, 26 (1984), 89.
22. My assessment of trends in the output of publications is based on the major bibliography in Joel Mokyr (ed.), *The Economics of the Industrial Revolution* (Totowa, NJ: Rowman and Allanheld, 1985); see also Roderick Floud and Donald McCloskey (eds.), *The Economic History of Britain since 1700*, 2 vols. (Cambridge: CUP, 1981); Greenberg, 'Power Patterns'; Harley, 'British Industrialization before 1841: Evidence of Slower Growth during the Industrial Revolution', *Journal of Economic History*, 42 (1982), 267–89; N. F. R. Crafts, 'British Economic Growth, 1700–1831: A Review of the Evidence', *Economic History Review*, 2nd ser. 36 (1983), 177–99; Crafts, 'Industrial Revolution in England and France: Some Thoughts on the Question, "Why was England First?" ', *Economic History Review*, 2nd ser. 30 (1977), 429–41; Richard Roehl, 'French Industrialization: A Reconsideration', *Explorations in Economic History*, 13 (1976), 233–81, and 'British and European Industrialization: Pathfinder Pursued?', *Review* (Fernand Braudel Center), 6 (1983), 455–73; P. K. O'Brien and C. Keyder, *Two Paths to the Twentieth Century: Economic Development in Britain and France from 1718–1914* (London: Allen and Unwin, 1977); and Lennart Schon, 'British Competition and Domestic Change in Textiles in Sweden 1820–1870', *Economy and History*, 23 (1980), 61–76.
23. An especially strong view of the individual nature of English economic history seems to be held among demographic historians; see e.g. Peter Laslett, 'Demographic and Microstructural History in Relation to Human Adaptation: Reflections on Newly Established Evidence', in D. J. Ortner (ed.), *How Humans Adapt* (Washington, DC: Smithsonian Institution Press, 1983). Laslett associates industrialization with English marital behaviour. One commentator correctly pointed out that a lower-power microscope might help one to see a bigger

picture; that local (English) factors cannot explain general phenomena; and if the English industrial revolution were really unique and regionally homogeneous, it could not properly be explained.

24. Rostow, *How It All Began*, p. 222; Jerome Blum, Rondo Cameron, and Thomas Barnes, *The European World: A History*, 2nd edn. (Boston: Little, Brown, 1970), 579–80.

25. Max Barkhausen, 'Government Control and Free Enterprise in Western Germany and the Low Countries in the Eighteenth Century', in Peter Earle (ed.), *Essays in European Economic History 1500–1800* (Oxford: Clarendon Press, 1974), 212–73.

26. Mokyr (ed.), *Economics*, pp. 371–96. See also the remarks by David Landes in 'What Do Bosses Really Do?', *Journal of Economic History*, 46 (1986), 585–623.

27. Peter Burke, 'Some Reflections on the Pre-Industrial City', *Urban History Yearbook* (1975), 13–21.

28. Jan de Vries, *European Urbanization 1500–1800* (Cambridge, Mass.: Harvard University Press, 1984).

29. Ann Kussmaul, 'Agrarian Change in Seventeenth-century England: The Economic Historian as Paleontologist', *Journal of Economic History*, 45 (1985), 1–30.

30. Crafts, 'British Economic Growth', p. 199.

31. D. N. McCloskey, 'The Industrial Revolution 1780–1860: A Survey', in Floud and McCloskey (eds.), *Economic History of Britain*, i. 115.

32. A review which expresses some of the points which follow is Barry J. Eichengreen, 'The Economic History of Britain since 1700', *Journal of European Economic History*, 12 (1983), 437–43.

2: 'ECONOMIC GROWTH AS VIRGIN BIRTH'

1. Phyllis Deane, *The First Industrial Revolution*, 2nd edn. (Cambridge: CUP, 1979), 11.

2. Edward F. Denison, 'Comment', on Douglass North, 'Economic Growth: What Have We Learned From the Past?', in *International Organization, National Policies and Economic Development*, 6 (n.d.), 230.

3. Robert W. Clower, 'Snarks, Quarks and Other Fictions', in Louis P. Cain and Paul J. Uselding (eds.), *Business Enterprise and Economic Change* (Kent State University Press, 1973), 8.

4. Lloyd G. Reynolds, *Economic Growth in the Third World, 1850–1980* (New Haven: Yale University Press, 1985), 7–10.

5. These matters are discussed in E. L. Jones, 'No Stationary State: The World before Industrialisation' (Workshop in Economic History, Department of Economics, University of Chicago, 8283–9, 1982).

6. D. C. North and R. P. Thomas, *The Rise of the Western World* (Cambridge: CUP, 1973). The deficiency of the model was discussed in E. L. Jones, 'Institutional Determinism and the Rise of the Western World', *Economic Inquiry*, 12 (1974), 114–24.

7. R. A. Easterlin, 'Why Isn't the Whole World Developed?', *Journal of Economic History*, 41 (1981), 2.

8. N. F. R. Crafts, 'Industrial Revolution in England and France: Some Thoughts on the Question, "Why Was England First?"' *Economic History Review*, 2nd ser. 30 (1977), 429–41.

9. Susan B. Hanley, 'A High Standard of Living in Nineteenth-century Japan: Fact or Fantasy?', *Journal of Economic History*, 43 (1983), 183–92.

10. R. N. Bellah, *Tokugawa Religion: The Values of Pre-Industrial Japan* (Boston: Beacon Press, 1970), 196.

11. Elizabeth A. R. Brown, 'The Tyranny of a Construct: Feudalism and Historians of Medieval Europe', *American Historical Review*, 79 (1974), 1063–88.

12. These are cited in Angus Maddison, *Phases of Capitalist Development* (OUP, 1982), 7, 255 n. 3.

13. See E. L. Jones, *The European Miracle* (Cambridge: CUP, 1981), ch. 6, 'The States-System'.

14. Marshall G. S. Hodgson, *The Venture of Islam* (Chicago: University of Chicago Press, 1974), iii. 198 and see also iii. 34.

15. Advanced societies are separated from archaic societies by Manuel Gottlieb, *A Theory of Economic Systems* (Orlando, Fla.: Academic Press, 1984), 20. He expands the list of characteristics given by Talcott Parsons to include a cosmological religion, upper-class literacy, a coinage, loyalty to the state as much as to kin, the use of iron and ships, and an agricultural surplus.

16. Michael Mann, 'States, Ancient and Modern', *European Journal of Sociology*, 18 (1977), 286.

17. G. L. S. Shackle, 'Comment', *Journal of Post-Keynesian Economics*, 5 (1982–3), 180.

18. W. M. S. Russell, 'Women as Innovators', *Biology and Human Affairs*, 40 (1974), 21–36.

19. W. H. McNeill, 'Comment' on R. M. Adams, 'Anthropological Perspectives on Ancient Trade', in *Current Anthropology* 15 (1974), 252.

20. e.g. by Maurice Godelier, *Rationality and Irrationality in Economics* (New York: Monthly Review Press, 1972), 15–17.
21. Ibid. 21.
22. Adda B. Bozeman, *The Future of Law in a Multicultural World* (Princeton, NJ: Princeton University Press, 1971).
23. Clifford Geertz, 'Culture and Social Change: The Indonesian Case', *Man*, NS 19 (1984), 511–32.
24. Ibid. 516.
25. These issues are discussed further in Kaushik Basu, Eric Jones, and Ekkehart Schlicht, 'The Growth and Decay of Custom: The Role of the New Institutional Economics in Economic History', *Explorations in Economic History* 24 (1987), 1–21.
26. Alexander Field, 'The Problem with Neoclassical Institutional Economics: A Critique with Special Reference to the North/Thomas Model of pre-1500 Europe', *Explorations in Economic History*, 18 (1981), 174–98. The paper by Basu *et al.*, 'Growth and Decay', is a discussion of Field.
27. Loreto Todd, *Modern Englishes: Pidgins and Creoles* (Oxford and London: Basil Blackwell/André Deutsch, 1984), 30–1.
28. M. McPherson, 'Want Formation, Morality and the Interpretive Dimension of Economic Inquiry', in N. Haan *et al.*, *Social Science as Moral Inquiry* (Berkeley: University of California Press, 1983), 96–124.
29. R. M. Adams, 'Anthropological Perspectives on Ancient Trade', *Current Anthropology*, 15 (1974), 239–58.
30. Lars Sandberg, 'The Case of the Impoverished Sophisticate: Human Capital and Swedish Economic Growth before World War I', *Journal of Economic History*, 39 (1979), 225–41.
31. See D. C. North, 'Markets and Other Allocation Systems in History: The Challenge of Karl Polanyi', *Journal of European Economic History*, 6 (1977), who points out (p. 715) that there is nothing in Polanyi's framework which could explain changes over time in the mix of allocations by reciprocity, redistribution, and the market: Gerald A. Gunderson, 'Economic Behavior in the Ancient World', in Roger L. Ransom *et al.* (eds.), *Explorations in the New Economic History* (New York: Academic Press, 1982), 235–56; and M. W. Frederiksen, 'Theory, Evidence and the Ancient Economy', *Journal of Roman Studies*, 65 (1975), 164–71.
32. Frederiksen, 'Ancient Economy', p. 170.
33. The full passage is quoted by Nathan Rosenberg and L. E. Birdzell, Jr., *How the West Grew Rich* (New York: Basic Books, 1986), 11.

3: 'INTIMATIONS OF ANCIENT GROWTH'

1. C. Keyder, 'Protoindustrialisation and the Periphery: A Conceptual Inquiry' (VIIIᵉ Congrès International d'Histoire Economique, Budapest, 1982), 21.
2. Tapan Raychaudhuri and Irfan Habib (eds.), *The Cambridge Economic History of India*, i: c.*1200*–c.*1750* (Cambridge: CUP, 1982), 291.
3. M. W. Frederiksen, 'Theory, Evidence and the Ancient Economy', *Journal of Roman Studies*, 65 (1975), 171.
4. 'Economic Possibilities for our Grandchildren' (1930), in J. M. Keynes, *Essays in Persuasion* (London: Rupert Hart-Davis, 1951, first published 1931), 360.
5. Cited in John H. Kautsky, *The Politics of Aristocratic Empires* (Chapel Hill: University of North Carolina Press, 1982), 7 n. 7.
6. I. R. Sinai, *The Challenge of Modernisation: The West's Impact on the Non-Western World* (London: Chatto and Windus, 1964), 28. See also p. 45. Note the insistence on the absence of the positive movements of European history.
7. In a review of E. L. Jones, *The European Miracle*, in the *Irish Journal of Agricultural Economics*, 9 (1983), 193–5.
8. Yves Lacoste, *Ibn Khaldun: The Birth of History and the Past of the Third World* (London: Verso Edition, 1984), 4–5.
9. Perry Anderson, *Lineages of the Absolutist State* (London: New Left Books, 1974), 402.
10. C. S. Smith, *A Search for Structure: Selected Essays on Science, Art and History* (Cambridge, Mass.: MIT Press, 1981), 330. See also pp. 325, 347.
11. Robert Raymond, *Out of the Fiery Furnace: The Impact of Metals on the History of Mankind* (South Melbourne: Macmillan, 1984), 21–4.
12. The list is from Gerald A. Gunderson, 'Economic Behavior in the Ancient World', in Roger L. Ransom *et al.* (eds.), *Explorations in the New Economic History* (New York: Academic Press, 1982), 235–56.
13. See Harry W. Pearson, 'The Secular Debate on Economic Primitivism', in Karl Polanyi *et al.* (eds.), *Trade and Market in the Early Empires* (Chicago: Henry Regnery, 1971), 3, 9. For modern studies damaging to the Polanyi view of a marketless society in the pre-modern world, see Philip D. Curtin, *Cross-cultural Trade in World History* (Cambridge: CUP, 1984), *passim*.
14. John P. Oleson, *Greek and Roman Mechanical Water-lifting Devices* (Toronto: Toronto University Press, 1984), 397–408.

15. *Science 86*, no. 7 (1986), 8; Storrs L. Olsen and Helen F. James, 'Fossil birds from the Hawaiian Islands: Evidence for Wholesale Extinction by Man Before Western Contact', *Science*, 217, no. 4560 (13 Aug. 1982), 633–5.
16. R. Wallman in *New Scientist*, 28 Feb. 1985, 45; Oleg D. Sherby and Jeffrey Wadsworth, 'Damascus Steels', *Scientific American*, 252 (Feb. 1985), 94–9.
17. J. E. Gordon, *The New Science of Strong Materials* (Princeton, NJ: Princeton University Press, 1976 edn.), 203.
18. Lynn White Jr., 'Tibet, India and Malaya as Sources of Western Medieval Technology', *American Historical Review*, 61 (1960), 526.
19. Derek V. de Solla Price, 'An Ancient Greek Computer', *Scientific American*, 200 (June 1959), 60–7.
20. Denis Diderot (translated by Jacques Barzun and Ralph H. Bowen), *Rameau's Nephew and Other Works* (Indianapolis: Bobbs-Merrill, 1956), 304–5.
21. Anderson, *Lineages*, 541.
22. D. C. North, *Structure and Change in Economic History* (New York: W. W. Norton, 1981), 23.
23. Thomas J. Figueira, *Aegina: Society and Politics* (New York: Arno Press, 1981).
24. Anderson, *Lineages*, 508.
25. Ibid. 402.
26. Marshall G. S. Hodgson, *The Venture of Islam* (Chicago: University of Chicago Press, 1974), iii. 197. W. H. McNeill argues even more strongly that the commercialization of the world economy was triggered by the Sung economic revolution (*The Pursuit of Power*, Chicago: University of Chicago Press, 1982, 24–5).
27. Thomas F. Glick, *Islamic and Christian Spain in the Early Middle Ages* (Princeton, NJ: Princeton University Press, 1979), 22, 132.
28. Hodgson, *Venture of Islam*, iii. 198.
29. Patrick O'Brien, 'European Economic Development: The Contribution of the Periphery', *Economic History Review*, 2nd ser. 35 (1982), 1–18.
30. Compare the maps in A. W. Crosby, *Ecological Imperialism* (Cambridge: CUP, 1986).
31. A. M. Khazanov, *Nomads and the Outside World* (Cambridge: CUP, 1984), 303.
32. A. C. Graham, 'China, Europe, and the Origins of Modern Science: Needham's The Grand Titration', in Shigeru Nakayama and Nathan Sivin (eds.), *Chinese Science: Exploration of an Ancient Tradition* (Cambridge, Mass.: MIT Press, 1973), 45.
33. Terry S. Reynolds, *Stronger than a Hundred Men: A History of the*

Vertical Water Wheel (Baltimore, Md.: Johns Hopkins University Press, 1983), 116.

34. Folke Dovring, 'Peasants, Land Use and Change', *Comparative Studies in Society and History*, 4 (1961–2), 371.
35. Paul Benoit, 'Technology and Crisis: The Great Depression of the Middle Ages and the Technology of the Renaissance (Fourteenth to Sixteenth Centuries)', *History and Technology* 1 (1984), 319–34.
36. Quoted by Jonathan Raban, *Arabia Through the Looking Glass* (London: Fontana, 1983), 285–6.

4: 'THE CASE OF SUNG CHINA'

1. David S. Landes, *Revolution in Time: Clocks and the Making of the Modern World* (Cambridge, Mass.: The Belknap Press of Harvard University Press, 1983), 23.
2. There is a convenient list in Dennis Bloodworth, *Chinese Looking Glass* (Harmondsworth, Middx.: Penguin Books, 1969), 218–22.
3. John H. Kautsky, *The Politics of Aristocratic Empires* (Chapel Hill: University of North Carolina Press, 1982), 42.
4. Kenneth E. Boulding, 'The Great Laws of Change', in Anthony M. Tang *et al.* (eds.), *Evolution, Welfare, and Time in Economics* (Lexington, Mass: Lexington Books, 1976), 9.
5. W. H. McNeill, *The Pursuit of Power* (Chicago: University of Chicago Press, 1982), ch. 2, 'The Era of Chinese Predominance, 1000–1500'. Other useful sources used here are Peter J. Golas, 'Rural China in the Song', *Journal of Asian Studies*, 39 (1980), 291–325; J. W. Haeger, *Crisis and Prosperity in Sung China* (Tucson: University of Arizona Press, 1975); James T. C. Liu and Peter J. Golas (eds.), *Change in Sung China: Innovation or Renovation?* (Lexington, Mass: D. C. Heath and Co., 1969); Laurence J. C. Ma, *Commercial Development and Urban Change in Sung China* (University of Michigan Geographical Publication no. 6, 1971); and Yoshinobu Shiba (trans. Mark Elvin), *Commerce and Society in Sung China* (University of Michigan Abstracts, no. 2, 1970).
6. See esp. Robert Hartwell, 'Markets, Technology, and the Structure of Enterprise in the Development of the Eleventh-century Chinese Iron and Steel Industries', *Journal of Economic History*, 26 (1966), 29–58, and 'A Revolution in the Chinese Iron and Coal Industries During the Northern Sung, 960–1126 A.D.', *Journal of Asian Studies*, 21 (1962), 153–62.

7. D. C. Twitchett, *Financial Administration under the Tang Dynasty* (Cambridge: CUP, 1963), esp. p. 23.

8. W. H. McNeill, *The Human Condition* (Princeton, NJ: Princeton University Press, 1980), 49. Recently McNeill has attributed the rise to economic primacy under the Sung to cheap internal transport on the irrigation canals which were added to the stock of natural waterways ('Organizing Concepts for World History', *Review*, 10 (1986), 226).

9. Max Weber, *The Religion of China* (trans. and ed. by H. H. Gerth), (New York: The Free Press, 1964 edn.), 61; Ma, *Commercial Development, passim.*

10. Francesca Bray in Joseph Needham, *Science and Civilization in China*, 6: *Biology and Biological Technology,* Pt. II: 'Agriculture' (CUP, 1984), 612.

11. Maxime Rodinson, *Islam and Capitalism* (Austin, Tex.: University of Texas Press, 1978), 77, 103–17; Kautsky, *Politics*, pp. 352–3; and Mark Elvin, 'Why China Failed to Create an Endogenous Industrial Capitalism: A Critique of Max Weber's Explanation', *Theory and Society*, 13 (1984), 379–92.

12. Elvin, 'Why China Failed', p. 383.

13. Hartwell, 'Chinese Iron and Coal Industries', p. 162.

14. W. Eberhard, cited in Kautsky, *Politics*, p. 41.

5: 'THE MILLS OF GOD'

1. Cf. Patrick O'Brien, 'European Economic Development: The Contribution of the Periphery', *Economic History Review*, 2nd ser. 35 (1982), 1–18.

2. World System analysis stems from Immanuel Wallerstein, *The Modern World-System* (New York: Academic Press, 1974); the most notable 'One-Worlder' extension is Eric Wolf, *Europe and the People Without History* (Berkeley: University of California Press, 1982).

3. Jean Schneider, 'Was there a Pre-Capitalist World System?', *Peasant Studies*, 6 (1977), 20–9.

4. Colin McEvedy and Richard Jones, *Atlas of World Population History* (Harmondsworth, Middx.: Penguin Books, 1978).

5. Ibid. 124–5.

6. Peter Munz, 'The Purity of Historical Method: Some Sceptical Reflections on the Current Enthusiasm for the History of Non-European Societies', *New Zealand Journal of History*, 5 (1971), 1–17; Hugh Trevor-Roper, *The Rise of Christian Europe*, 2nd edn. (London: Thames and Hudson, 1966), 9.

7. Yves Lacoste, *Ibn Khaldun: The Birth of History and the Past of the Third World* (London: Verso Edition, 1984), 3–4.

8. Albert O. Hirschman, *A Bias for Hope: Essays on Development and Latin America* (Boulder and London: Westview Encore Edition, 1985), ch. 14, 'Obstacles to Development: A Classification and a Quasi-vanishing Act'.

9. M. N. Srinivas, *The Remembered Village* (Delhi: OUP, 1976), 144.

10. William and Arline McCord, 'Singapore's Success Story', *The New Leader*, 12–26 Aug. 1985, 9.

11. W. W. Rostow, *How It All Began: Origins of the Modern Economy* (New York: McGraw-Hill, 1975), 2.

12. See the authorities cited in E. L. Jones, *The European Miracle* (Cambridge: CUP, 1981), 170–1; Victor B. Lieberman, *Burmese Administrative Cycles: Anarchy and Conquest c.1580–1760* (Princeton, NJ: Princeton University Press, 1984), *passim.*

13. C. S. Venkatachar, in Raghavan Iyer (ed.), *The Glass Curtain between Asia and Europe* (London: OUP, 1965), 38.

14. Vera Micheles Dean, *The Nature of the Non-Western World* (New York: New American Library, 1957), 50.

15. Mancur Olson, *The Rise and Decline of Nations* (New Haven: Yale University Press, 1982), 154–5.

16. Maxime Rodinson, *Islam and Capitalism* (Austin, Tex.: University of Texas Press, 1978), *passim.*

17. Claud R. Sutcliffe, 'Is Islam an Obstacle to Development? Ideal Patterns of Belief versus Actual Patterns of Behavior', *Journal of Developing Areas*, 10 (1975), 77–82.

18. Timur Kuran, 'Behavioral Norms in the Islamic Doctrine of Economics: A Critique', *Journal of Economic Behavior and Organization*, 4 (1983), 353–79.

19. Thomas F. Glick, *Islamic and Christian Spain in the Early Middle Ages* (Princeton, NJ: Princeton University Press, 1979).

20. A. Dasgupta, 'India's Cultural Values and Economic Development', *Economic Development and Cultural Change*, 13 (1964), 102.

21. Kuran, 'Behavioral Norms', and his 'The Economic System in Contemporary Islamic Thought: Interpretation and Assessment', *International Journal of Middle East Studies*, 18 (1986), 135–64, and 'Continuity and Change in Islamic Economic Thought', in S. Todd Lowry (ed.), *Pre-classical Political Economy* (Boston: Kluwer-Nijhoff, forthcoming).

22. Quoted by Kaushik Basu, Eric Jones, and Ekkehart Schlicht, 'The Growth and Decay of Custom', *Explorations in Economic History*, 24 (1987), 5–6.

23. Glick, *Islamic and Christian Spain*, p. 252.
24. Dasgupta, 'India's Cultural Values'; Various, 'India's Cultural Values and Economic Development: A Discussion', *Economic Development and Cultural Change*, 7 (1958), 1–12.
25. G. L. Hicks and S. G. Redding, 'The Story of the East Asian "Economic Miracle" ', Pt. I: 'Economic Theory Be Damned!' and Pt. II: 'The Culture Connection', *Euro–Asia Business Review*, 2 (1983), no. 3, 24–32, and no. 4, 18–22.
26. Ibid., Pt. I, 26.
27. Ibid., Pt. II, 22.
28. Ibid. 21.
29. Clarence Ayres, *The Theory of Economic Progress* (New York: Schocken Books, 1962; first published 1944).
30. H. M. Robertson, *Aspects of the Rise of Economic Individualism: A Criticism of Max Weber and his School* (Clifton, NJ: Augustus M. Kelley Reprint, 1973).
31. René David and John E. C. Brierley, *Major Legal Systems in the World Today* (London: Stevens and Sons), 1968.
32. Ibid. 397.
33. Olson, *Rise and Decline*, p. 149.
34. Shannon R. Brown, 'The Partially Opened Door: Limitations on Economic Change in China in the 1860's', *Modern Asian Studies*, 12 (1978), 177–92.
35. D. F. Pocock (trans. and ed.), *Essays on the Caste System by Célestin Bouglé* (Cambridge: CUP, 1971), 32.
36. Olson, *Rise and Decline*, pp. 154–5.
37. The most succinct account of these commonly supposed economic effects is in Angus Maddison, *Class Structure and Economic Growth: India and Pakistan since the Moghals* (New York: Norton, 1971); see also Olson, *Rise and Decline*. For good general accounts see Srinivas, *Remembered Village*, and his *Caste in Modern India* (Bombay: Asia Publishing House, 1962); J. H. Hutton, *Caste in India: Its Nature, Function, and Origins*, 4th edn. (Bombay: OUP, 1963); and Pocock, *Essays*.
38. In Christoph von Furer-Haimendorf (ed.), *Caste and Kin in Nepal, India and Ceylon: Anthropological Studies in Hindu–Buddhist Contact Zones* (New Delhi: Sterling, 1978), 135; see also pp. 136–7.
39. Quoted by Hutton, *Caste in India*, p. 113.
40. Srinivas, *Remembered Village*, p. 40.
41. Ibid. 195. See also Furer-Haimendorf (ed.), *Caste and Kin*, pp. 68–139, and Hutton, *Caste in India*, p. 90.
42. Raymond Firth, *Essays on Social Organization and Values* (London: The Athlone Press, 1964), 4.

6: 'CONQUESTS'

1. James Boswell, *Life of Johnson*, ed. R. W. Chapman (OUP, 1980), 1156.
2. P. Saran, *The Provincial Government of the Mughals 1526–1658* (London: Asia Publishing House, 1973; first published 1941), p. xxiii. For a one-sided interpretation of the effect of British colonialism on the Indian subcontinent and the insinuation that this financed British industrialization, see the quotation in W. W Murdoch, *The Poverty of Nations* (Baltimore: Johns Hopkins University Press, 1980), 260–1.
3. Deepak Lal, *The Poverty of 'Development Economics'* (London: Institute of Economic Affairs, 1983), 84–7.
4. W. Arthur Lewis (ed.), *Tropical Development 1880–1913: Studies in Economic Progress* (London: George Allen and Unwin, 1970); Lloyd G. Reynolds, *Economic Growth in the Third World, 1850–1980* (New Haven: Yale University Press, 1985).
5. Francesca Bray, in Joseph Needham, *Science and Civilization in China*, 6: *Biology and Biological Technology*, Pt. II: 'Agriculture' (Cambridge: CUP, 1984), 616 n.
6. Charles J. Halperin, *Russia and the Golden Horde: The Mongol Impact* (Bloomington: Indiana University Press, 1985), 86.
7. Luc Kwanten, *Imperial Nomads: A History of Central Asia, 500–1500* (n.p.: University of Pennsylvania Press, 1979), 209.
8. Yves Lacoste, *Ibn Khaldun: The Birth of History and the Past of the Third World* (London: Verso Edition, 1984), 5.
9. Tom Allsen, pers. comm.; I. P. Petrushevsky, 'The Socio-economic Condition of Iran under the Il-Khans', in J. A. Boyle (ed.), *The Cambridge History of Iran: Saljuq and Mongol Periods* (Cambridge: CUP, 1968), v. 497–8; see also Alessandro Bausani, *The Persians from the Earliest Days to the Twentieth Century* (London: Elek Books, 1971; first published 1962); and Kwanten, *Imperial Nomads*.
10. Bausani, *The Persians*, p. 108.
11. I owe this report to Professor Bernard Lewis.
12. Bausani, *The Persians*, p. 215.
13. Kwanten, *Imperial Nomads*, p. 215.
14. Terry S. Reynolds, *Stronger than a Hundred Men: A History of the Vertical Water Wheel* (Baltimore, Md.: Johns Hopkins University Press, 1983), 119.
15. F. E. Moghadam, 'Tribal Invasions and the Development of Private Property in Land: A Case Study of Iran (1000–1800)', (paper presented at the International Conference on Middle

Eastern Studies, University of London, July 1986). I am grateful to Dr Moghadam for a copy of this paper.

16. Ibid., Abstract, p. 1.
17. See the section on 'Inertia' in Kaushik Basu, Eric Jones, and Ekkehart Schlicht, 'The Growth and Decay of Custom', *Explorations in Economic History*, 24, (1987), 1–21.

7: 'DERIVATIVE EFFECTS'

1. Richard Bernstein, *From the Center of the Earth: The Search for the Truth about China* (Boston: Little, Brown, 1982), 61.
2. M. Athar Ali, 'The Passing of Empire: The Mughal Case', *Modern Asian Studies*, 9 (1975), 388.
3. Dietmar Rothermund, *Asian Trade and European Expansion in the Age of Mercantilism* (New Delhi: Manohar, 1981), 73–4.
4. C. G. F. Simkin, *The Traditional Trade of Asia* (OUP: 1968), esp. p. 257.
5. Philip D. Curtin, *Cross-cultural Trade in World History* (Cambridge: CUP, 1984), *passim*.
6. Chris Wickham, 'The Uniqueness of the East', *Journal of Peasant Studies*, 12 (1985), 189.
7. Jan Breman, *Patronage and Exploitation* (Berkeley: University of California Press, 1974), 149; Michael N. Pearson, 'Shivaji and the Decline of the Mughal Empire', *Journal of Asian Studies*, 35 (1976), 221–35.
8. C. A. Bayly, 'State and Economy in India over Seven Hundred Years', *Economic History Review*, 2nd ser. 38 (1985), 587–8; Richard B. Barnett, *North India Between Two Empires* (Berkeley, Calif.: University of California Press, 1980), 241.
9. S. A. M. Adshead, 'The Seventeenth Century General Crisis in China', *Asian Profile*, 1 (1973), 280.
10. Alexander Gerschenkron, *Economic Backwardness in Historical Perspective* (Cambridge, Mass.: The Belknap Press, 1962); Mancur Olson, *The Rise and Decline of Nations* (New Haven: Yale University Press, 1982).
11. Cf. Cyril Black, *The Dynamics of Modernization: A Study in Comparative History* (New York: Harper and Row, 1966).
12. Albert O. Hirschman, *A Bias for Hope: Essays on Development and Latin America* (Boulder and London: Westview Encore Edition, 1985).
13. D. C. North and R. P. Thomas, *The Rise of the Western World* (Cambridge: CUP, 1973). For a criticism of this aspect of their work, see E. L. Jones, 'Institutional Determinism and the Rise of the Western World', *Economic Inquiry*, 12 (1974), 114–24.

14. James M. Buchanan, Robert D. Tollison, and Gordon Tullock (eds.), *Toward a Theory of the Rent-seeking Society* (College Station, Tex.: Texas A. and M. University Press, 1980).
15. Herbert F. Schurmann, *Economic Structure of Yuan Dynasty* (Cambridge, Mass.: Harvard University Press, 1967), 6; Perry Anderson, *Lineages of the Absolutist State* (London: New Left Books, 1974), 517.
16. James Geiss, 'Peking Under the Ming (1368–1644)' (Ph.D. dissertation, Princeton University, 1979), 204.
17. Edward L. Farmer *et al.* (eds.), *Comparative History of Civilizations in Asia* (Reading, Mass.: Addison-Wesley, 1977), 409.
18. D. D. Kosambi, *The Culture and Civilization of Ancient India* (London: Routledge and Kegan Paul, 1965).
19. M. N. Srinivas, in Various, 'India's Cultural Values and Economic Development', *Economic Development and Cultural Change*, 7 (1958), 1–12.
20. See Gabriel Baer, 'Guilds in Middle Eastern History', in M. A. Cook (ed.), *Studies in the Economic History of the Middle East* (OUP, 1970), 11–30, and 'Ottoman Guilds: A Reassessment', in Osman Okyar and Halil Inalcik (eds.), *Social and Economic History of Turkey (1071–1920)* (Ankara: Meteksan, 1980), 95–102; Timothy R. Bradstock, 'Ch'ing Dynasty Craft Guilds and their Monopolies', *Tsing Hua Journal of Chinese Studies*, NS 15 (1983), 1430–53; Shannon R. Brown, 'The Partially Opened Door: Limitations on Economic Change in China in the 1860's', *Modern Asian Studies*, 12 (1978), 177–92; Peter J. Golas, 'Early Ch'ing Guilds', in G. William Skinner (ed.), *The City in Late Imperial China* (Stanford, Cal.: Stanford University Press, 1977), 555–80; D. J. MacGowan, 'Chinese Guilds, or Chambers of Commerce and Trade Unions', *Journal of North-China Branch of the Royal Asiatic Society*, 21 (1886), 133–92; and Hosea B. Morse, *The Guilds of China* (London: Longmans, Green, and Co., 1909).
21. The most useful sources on timing are Gabriel Baer, *Egyptian Guilds in Modern Times* (Jerusalem: The Israel Oriental Society, 1964) and Joseph Fewsmith, 'From Guild to Interest Group: The Transformation of Public and Private in Late Qing China', *Comparative Studies in Society and History*, 25 (1983), 617–40.
22. Some parallels with earlier European history may be seen in E. L. Jones, *The European Miracle* (Cambridge: CUP, 1981), 99–102.
23. Olson, *Rise and Decline*, pp. 148–50.
24. William T. Rowe, *Hankow: Commerce and Society in a Chinese City, 1796–1889* (Stanford, Cal.: Stanford University Press, 1984), 296–7.

25. B. F. Musallam, 'Birth Control and Middle Eastern History', in A. L. Udovitch (ed.), *The Islamic Middle East, 700–1900: Studies in Economic and Social History* (Princeton, NJ: Darwin Press, 1981).
26. J. C. Caldwell, 'The Economic Rationality of High Fertility: An Investigation Illustrated with Nigerian Survey Data', *Population Studies*, 31 (1977), 5–27.
27. Oded Stark, 'On the Asset Demand for Children during Agricultural Modernization', *Population and Development Review*, 7 (1981), 671–5.
28. Ester Boserup, *The Conditions of Agricultural Growth* (London: Allen and Unwin, 1965), and *Population and Technology* (Oxford: Basil Blackwell, 1981); Julian L. Simon, *The Economics of Population Growth* (Princeton, NJ: Princeton University Press, 1977), and 'The Present Value of Population Growth in the Western World', *Population Studies*, 37 (1983), 5–21.
29. Julian L. Simon and Gunter Steinmann, 'The Economic Implications of Learning-by-Doing', *European Economic Review*, 26 (1984), 167–85.

8: 'THE LETHARGIC STATE'

1. Edward L. Farmer *et al.* (eds.), *Comparative History of Civilizations in Asia* (Reading, Mass.: Addison-Wesley, 1977), 429.
2. K. N. Chaudhuri, 'Some Reflections on the Town and Country in Mughal India', *Modern Asian Studies*, 12 (1978), 81; Tapan Raychaudhuri in Tapan Raychaudhuri and Irfan Habib (eds.), *The Cambridge Economic History of India, i: c.1200–c.1750* (Cambridge: CUP, 1982), *passim*; Percival Spear, *India: A Modern History*, 2nd edn. (Ann Arbor, Mich.: University of Michigan Press, 1972), 153 ff.
3. Raychaudhuri, in Raychaudhuri and Habib (eds.), *Economic History of India*, i. 173.
4. Shireen Moosvi, 'Share of the Nobility in the Revenues of Akbar's Empire 1595–96', *Indian Economic and Social History Review*, 17 (1980), 342.
5. Albert Feuerwerker, 'The State and the Economy in Late Imperial China', *Theory and Society*, 13 (1984), 300, table 1.
6. P. Saran, *The Provincial Government of the Mughals 1526–1658* (London: Asia Publishing House, 1973; first published 1941), 397–9.
7. John D. Post, *The Last Great Subsistence Crisis in the Western World* (Baltimore, Md.: Johns Hopkins University Press, 1977) and *Food Shortage, Climatic Variability, and Epidemic Disease in*

Preindustrial Europe: The Mortality Peak in the Early 1740s (Ithaca, NY: Cornell University Press, 1985).

8. James Boswell, *Life of Johnson*, ed. R. W. Chapman (OUP, 1980), 446.
9. Herbert F. Schurmann, *Economic Structure of Yuan Dynasty* (Cambridge, Mass.: Harvard University Press, 1967), 12.
10. James Geiss, 'The Chia-ching reign, 1522–1566', in *The Cambridge History of China, vii: The Ming Dynasty, 1368–1644*, (Cambridge: CUP, forthcoming), 794–5. I am indebted to the author for a copy of his typescript.
11. Louis Dumont (trans. Mark Sainsbury), *Homo Hierarchicus: The Caste System and its Implications* (Chicago: University of Chicago Press, 1970), 313 n. 75b.
12. B. Cohn, 'From Indian Status to British Contract', *Journal of Economic History*, 21 (1961), 615.
13. Richard G. Fox, *Kin Clan Raja and Rule: State–Hinterland Relations in Preindustrial India* (Berkeley, Cal.: University of California Press, 1971), 8.
14. Feuerwerker, 'State and Economy', pp. 318–22, and 'Qing Economic History and World Economic History', Paper to the Symposium on the 60th Anniversary of the Founding of the First Historical Archives of China (Beijing, Oct. 1985), *passim*. I am indebted to Albert Feuerwerker for a copy of this conference paper.
15. Feuerwerker, 'State and Economy', p. 312.
16. Cf. Feuerwerker, 'Qing Economic History', p. 5. Original italics.
17. E. L. Jones, 'Industrial Capital and Landed Investment: The Arkwrights in Herefordshire, 1809–43', in E. L. Jones and G. E. Mingay (eds.), *Land, Labour and Population in the Industrial Revolution* (London: Edward Arnold, 1967), 48–9.
18. K. N. Chaudhuri, *Trade Civilisation in the Indian Ocean: An Economic History from the Rise of Islam to 1750* (Cambridge: CUP, 1985), 209–10, 228.
19. Ibid. 228.
20. Feuerwerker, 'State and Economy', p. 318.
21. Robert Marks, 'The State of the China Field. Or, the China Field and State', *Modern China*, 11 (1985), 461–509.
22. Dietmar Rothermund, *Asian Trade and European Expansion in the Age of Mercantilism* (New Delhi: Manohar, 1981), 132.
23. Perry Anderson, *Lineages of the Absolutist State* (London: New Left Books, 1974), 548–9.
24. Ibid. 548–9.
25. Ibid., *passim*; John H. Kautsky, *The Politics of Aristocratic Empires* (Chapel Hill: University of North Carolina Press, 1982).

26. Rajat Datta, review of V. I. Pavlov, *Historical Premises for India's Transition to Capitalism* (Moscow, 1979), in *Journal of Contemporary Asia*, 12 (1982), 235; see also Rothermund, op. cit.
27. Rothermund, *Asian Trade*, p. 132.
28. Feuerwerker, 'State and Economy', p. 312.
29. Hosea B. Morse, *The Guilds of China* (London: Longmans, Green, and Co., 1909), 20–1.
30. Yoshinobu Shiba, 'Ningpo and its Hinterland', in G. William Skinner (ed.), *The City in Late Imperial China* (Stanford, Cal.: Stanford University Press, 1977), 422.
31. I am indebted to Martin Heijdra for lending me his Princeton graduate essay in which he introduces this term.
32. Feuerwerker, 'Qing Economic History', p. 15. However, demographic restraint was also conspicuously absent from India and other parts of Asia from which no such accommodating Chinese-style political economy is reported.
33. R. Huang, *Taxation and Governmental Finance in Sixteenth Century Ming China* (Cambridge: CUP, 1974), esp. 307–23; S. A. M. Adshead, 'The Seventeenth Century General Crisis in China', *Asian Profile*, 1 (1973), 279–80.
34. Quoted by Mark Elvin, 'Why China Failed to Create an Endogenous Industrial Capitalism: A Critique of Max Weber's Explanation', *Theory and Society*, 13 (1984), 379.
35. Any growth was of the *extensive* variety.
36. E. L. Jones, *The European Miracle* (Cambridge: CUP, 1981), 213–20.
37. Cf. John Passmore, *Man's Responsibility for Nature: Ecological Problems and Western Traditions*, 2nd edn. (London: Duckworth, 1980), 25–7; Conrad Totman, *Japan before Perry: A Short History* (Berkeley: University of California Press, 1981), 218–19; and James C. Riley, *The Eighteenth-century Campaign to Avoid Disease* (London: Macmillan, 1987), *passim*. Totman has admittedly retreated from his strong conclusion that Tokugawa Japan achieved growth with a well-husbanded environment, but I think mistakenly, as I argue in the follow chapter.
38. I do not therefore quite agree with the 'to each its own' conclusion of Lynda Schaffer's interesting 'China, Technology, and Change', *World History Bulletin*, 4 (1986–7), 1, 4–6.

9: 'JAPAN'

1. John H. Kautsky, *The Politics of Aristocratic Empires* (Chapel Hill: University of North Carolina Press, 1982), 352.

2. K. Ohkawa and H. Rosovsky, 'The Role of Agriculture in Modern Japanese Development', in G. M. Meier (ed.), *Leading Issues in Development Economics* (New York: OUP, 1964), 304.
3. H. Rosovsky, 'Japan's Transition to Modern Economic Growth, 1868–1885', in H. Rosovsky (ed.), *Industrialization in Two Systems* (New York: Wiley, 1966), 91.
4. Conrad Totman, *Japan before Perry: A Short History* (Berkeley: University of California Press, 1981), 128.
5. Kozo Yamamura, 'Returns on Unification: Economic Growth in Japan 1550–1650', in John W. Hall *et al.*, *Japan before Tokugawa: Political Consolidation and Economic Growth, 1500 to 1650* (Princeton: Princeton University Press, 1981), 330.
6. Totman, *Japan before Perry*, p. 219. On rural development see also J. I. Nakamura, 'Human Capital Accumulation in Premodern Japan', *Journal of Economic History*, 41 (1981), 263–81.
7. Totman, *Japan before Perry*, 190–1.
8. Ibid. 198.
9. Jan de Vries, *European Urbanization 1500–1800* (Cambridge, Mass.: Harvard University Press, 1984).
10. E. S. Crawcour, 'Changes in Japanese Commerce in the Tokugawa Period', *Journal of Asian Studies*, 22 (1963), 399.
11. Mataji Miyamoto *et al.*, 'Economic Development in Preindustrial Japan, 1859–1894', *Journal of Economic History*, 25 (1965), 542–3, and Rosovsky, 'Japan's Transition', 102.
12. J. G. Williamson, 'Regional Inequality and the Process of National Development: A Description of the Patterns', *Economic Development and Cultural Change*, 13 (1965), 44.
13. Susan B. Hanley, 'A High Standard of Living in Nineteenth-century Japan: Fact or Fantasy?' *Journal of Economic History*, 43 (1983), 183–92, and 'Standard of Living in Nineteenth-century Japan: Reply to Yasuba', *Journal of Economic History*, 46 (1986), 225–6.
14. Totman, *Japan before Perry*, pp. 218–19; and his 'Tokugawa Peasants: Win, Lose or Draw?' *Monumenta Nipponica*, 41 (1986), 459–76. The emphasis in the latter on the cost to what Totman calls 'non-collaborating' organisms underrates their self-renewing capacity and the offsetting changes that tended to occur when agriculture reduced the population of some species. For a summary of these effects in the case of England see P. J. Dillon and E. L. Jones, 'Trevor Falla's Vermin Transcripts for Devon', *The Devon Historian*, 33 (1986), 16.
15. Yasukichi Yasuba, 'Standard of Living in Japan before Industrialization: From What Level Did Japan Begin? A Comment', *Journal of Economic History*, 46 (1986), 217–24.

16. Joseph R. Strayer, 'The Tokugawa Period and Japanese Feudalism', in John W. Hall and Marius B. Jansen (eds.), *Studies in the Institutional History of Early Modern Japan* (Princeton: Princeton University Press, 1968), 23.
17. Harold Bolitho, *Treasures Among Men* (New Haven: Yale University Press, 1974), 55.
18. Totman, *Japan before Perry*, p. 228.
19. Sasaki Gin'ya, 'Sengoku Daimyo Rule and Commerce', in J. W. Hall *et al.*, *Japan Before Tokugawa*, pp. 125–48.
20. Yamamura, in J. W. Hall *et al.*, *Japan before Tokugawa*, p. 368.
21. B. R. Tomlinson, 'Writing History Sideways: Lessons for Indian Economic Historians from Meiji Japan', *Modern Asian Studies*, 19 (1985), 670.
22. P. F. Kornicki, 'The Enmeiin Affair of 1803: The Spread of Information in the Tokugawa Period', *Harvard Journal of Asiatic Studies*, 42 (1982), 532–3.
23. Totman, *Japan before Perry*, p. 193.
24. Bolitho, *Treasures*, p. 251.
25. Ibid. 196–7.
26. Takao Tsuchiya, 'An Economic History of Japan', *Transactions of the Asiatic Society of Japan*, 2nd ser. 15 (1937), 161.
27. Strayer, 'The Tokugawa Period', p. 9.

10: 'EUROPE'

1. R. H. Mottram, *If Stones Could Speak* (London: Museum Press, 1953), 130.
2. Probate inventories are a major source of evidence, see e.g. Jan de Vries, 'Peasant Demand Patterns and Economic Development: Friesland, 1550–1750', in William N. Parker and Eric L. Jones (eds.), *European Peasants and Their Markets* (Princeton: Princeton University Press, 1975).
3. Max Barkhausen, 'Government Control and Free Enterprise in Western Germany and the Low Countries in the Eighteenth Century', in Peter Earle (ed.), *Essays in European Economic History 1500–1800* (Oxford: Clarendon Press, 1974).
4. Terry S. Reynolds, *Stronger than a Hundred Men: A History of the Vertical Water Wheel* (Baltimore, Md: Johns Hopkins University Press, 1983), 116.
5. E. L. Jones, S. Porter, and M. Turner, *A Gazetteer of English Urban Fire Disasters, 1500–1900* (Norwich: Geo Books, 1984).
6. Charles Tilly (ed.), *The Formation of National States in Western Europe* (Princeton: Princeton University Press, 1975), *passim.*

7. John Masters, *The Rock* (London: Transworld Publishers, 1971), 331.
8. The issue is discussed further in the Introduction to the second edition of E. L. Jones, *The European Miracle* (Cambridge: CUP, 1987).
9. See C. H. Wilson, 'The Historical Study of Economic Growth and Decline in Early Modern History', in E. E. Rich and C. H. Wilson (eds.), *The Cambridge Economic History of Europe*, v (Cambridge: CUP, 1977), 39–40.

11: 'SUMMARY AND CONCLUSION'

1. Peter F. Drucker, 'Dramatic Shifts in the Global Economy', *Dialogue*, 75 (1987), 2.
2. Graham Greene and Carol Reed, *The Third Man: A Film* (London: Lorrimer Publishing Ltd., 1969 edn.), 114 n.
3. Anon., 'When Croesus Rules', *The Economist*, 7–13 Mar. 1987, 19–20; Geoffrey Moorhouse, *Calcutta: The City Revealed* (Harmondsworth, Middx.: Penguin Books, 1983 edn.); and W. Arthur Lewis, *The Theory of Economic Growth* (London: George Allen and Unwin, 1955), 420–35.
4. Emlyn Williams, *George: An Early Autobiography* (Harmondsworth, Middx.: Penguin Books, 1976), 277.
5. A choice item from my collection: an expert witness called by an assistant US attorney at a trial in 1976, prosecuting with Presidential instructions or at least approval, testified that sexual freedom and pornography caused the downfall of the Roman Empire and other ancient civilizations. Another expert called by the same attorney at a previous trial stated that ninety civilizations had thus fallen, including Rome, Greece, ancient India, Babylon, Egypt, and the Syrian Empire. Richard Rhodes, *Looking for America: A Writer's Odyssey* (Harmondsworth, Middx.: Penguin Books, 1980), 260.
6. T. R. Gurr, 'Historical Trends in Violent Crime: A Critical Review of Evidence', *Crime and Justice*, 3 (1981), 295–355.
7. Irfan Habib, 'Potentialities of Capitalistic Development in the Economy of Mughal India', *Journal of Economic History*, 29 (1969), 33. Italics supplied.
8. Ibid. 33–4.
9. Stefano Fenoaltea, Review of Joel Mokyr (ed.), *The Economics of the Industrial Revolution*, in the *Journal of Economic History*, 46 (1986), 834.

10. A. C. Graham, 'China, Europe, and the Origins of Modern Science', in Shigeru Nakayama and Nathan Sivin (eds.), *Chinese Science: Exploration of an Ancient Tradition* (Cambridge, Mass.: MIT Press, 1973), 45–69.

11. Marc Bloch, *Feudal Society* (London: Routledge and Kegan Paul, 1965), ii. 452.

12. Suraiya Faroqhi, 'Recent Work in the Social and Economic History of the Ottoman Empire (1450–1800)', *Trends in History*, 2 (1982), 16.

13. See the wise words in Joseph Ben-David, 'Innovations and their Recognition in Social Science', *History of Political Economy*, 7 (1975), 434–55.

14. Quoted in a review by Robert E. Ankli, *Journal of Economic Literature*, 24 (1986), 694.

15. See on this Marshall G. S. Hodgson, *The Venture of Islam* (Chicago: University of Chicago Press, 1974), iii. 181 n. 4.

16. An interesting discussion of the issue of European uniqueness is in John H. Kautsky, *The Politics of Aristocratic Empires* (Chapel Hill: University of North Carolina Press, 1982), 352–3.

17. Hodgson, *Venture of Islam*, i. 38.

Select Bibliographical Guide

THE bibliography in this volume lists all the books and articles mentioned in the text, but since some of these have been cited only for passing purposes of illustration it is likely to be less useful for teaching purposes than for scholarly reference. Because the book is concerned with the way we look at the processes of economic change, rather than describing historical episodes fully, there is in any case no regular body of literature underlying it, merely a scattered range. I have often found hints in unexpected places where another reader might find it hard to spot the same significance. It would not be helpful to suggest reading everything I have read. This is a common problem when seeking readings to recommend to tutorial students on topics without established literatures. What follows are therefore only comments on the major sources that have helped to develop my ideas, arranged by the chapters to which they refer.

Having presented an unusual scheme, I am unwilling to turn round and attach to it the 'label of approval' of established writers. Scholarly writers often do that to justify their research after the event. I do not want to engage in the 'touching base' with their own favourite authors that reviewers seem to demand. The literatures of economic development and world economic history are large and sprawling. The tendency of scholars to flock like starlings, citing mainly their own associates, is perhaps understandable, but a requirement to observe a cult of personalities is less forgivable.

The very real expansion of knowledge has increased the number of specialisms and self-referring groups and widened the gaps between them. This means that even opinions about what constitutes the conventional wisdom are not as widely shared as they used to be. Published sources certainly grew in number between when I was working on *The European Miracle* in 1979 and writing *Growth Recurring* in 1985–6. Furthermore, opinion is drawn as much from remarks scattered in innumerable seminars, pre-prints and reviews, broadcasts, students' answers, and popular works as from standard sources. The usual way out is to address only one's professional subgroup, but the nature of my theme closes off that exit. This book is written from the viewpoint of economic history, a strategically placed subject from which to take a look around, but the text distances itself from the short-run, recent-period, and wholly Western bias of most

English-language writing on the subject. As a result, it has to rely on extremely disparate sources.

Precursors of most people's ideas can be found by casting back in the literature, but new interpretations are necessarily ones that have never been worked out in full before. That is the case here. Part of the central conception was certainly foreshadowed by Marshall Hodgson in *The Venture of Islam* (3 vols., Chicago: University of Chicago Press, 1974), even though I do not quite accept his view that the Old World civilizations advanced in lock-step, or his rather routine explanation of economic growth in Europe. The existence of a pause in the development of the non-Western world was also set out well by Yves Lacoste, *Ibn Khaldun: The Birth of History and the Past of the Third World* (London: Verso Edition, 1984), although again his formulation is not quite mine.

My position was formed more directly in opposition to the mainstream habit of walling-off early modern and non-Western studies as if, before 1700 or 1750, and outside Britain or the West, in the hollow words of the Monty Python record, *'nothing happened'*. In addition to the understandable concern of some scholars to defend a long attachment to the study of Western industrialization, part of their habit stems from thinking that *intensive* growth was intrinsically unlikely and could have occurred only once.

Of course *intensive* growth had to negotiate a strait and narrow passage; it was just not so improbable that it could take place only once and only in the industrial form. Life on Earth may have arisen many times unsuccessfully, until there arose an organism that actively adapted by seeking a better environment, at least so Max Perutz summarizes Sir Karl Popper's views in the *New Scientist* (2 Oct. 1986). Why not, then, more than one start for economic growth? Complicated though it was, it was not as complicated as life; it had a long time in which to emerge; and surely there is nothing to require it to have had only a single start.

The challenge in principle is to the way the process has been conceived. In more historical terms, the challenge is to scholarship which is restricted to Western industrialization as if this were the sole origin of growth. Although no one would dispute their intrinsic interest, the Western parts of the developed world have ceased to form a sufficient arena for students who want either to understand economic change as a process or to obtain a balanced perspective on the history and geography of the world economy as it is now shaping.

A broader approach began to seem possible when Sir John Hicks brought out *A Theory of Economic History* (OUP, 1969). This has been followed ever since by a thin but swelling stream of conceptualizing 'world economic histories'. A list of those published up to the end of

1985 appears in the Supplementary Bibliographical Guide to E. L. Jones, *The European Miracle* (Cambridge: CUP, 1981; 2nd edn. 1987). The data, time-span, and geographical scope inherent in work of this kind present problems that are reflected in the great diversity of models currently offered.

Logically, however, this need not mean that the subject is intractable, though it is certainly harder conceptually and descriptively than the macro-economics of the individual Western nation-states. Economic theory is not well adapted to tackling the *very* long term, but the significance of the problem cannot be defined away on that account. Despite a large and growing literature on the big issues, less than 1 per cent of the volume of work done on the economic history of north-western Europe or the United States can have been done on comparative global topics, whose shape will surely change and areas of dispute narrow when they are given due attention. As Albert Einstein said, one has little patience with scholars who take a board of wood, look for its thinnest part, and drill a great number of holes where drilling is easy.

Since long before my student days the economic history profession has accorded centre stage to the British industrial revolution. But what if history has no single centre? I have been teased that asking this kind of question is unconscious 'parent rejection'. Certainly it is not conscious, and if it were I would rely on Marc Bloch's admonition to keep faith with the parent-figures of the past by extending their work. On the other hand, perhaps I did leave Japan out of my previous book because my subconscious knew that modern research on Tokugawa economic history would not fit a model in which Asia held back while Europe forged ahead. The immediate precipitant of the present volume was certainly a question that made me confront the Japanese anomaly.

1. 'A Know-all's Guide to the Industrial Revolution'

On the strict matter of the industrial revolution, mine is a non-Rostovian manifesto. The subject had already been put in its place—flattened out and drawn out—by remarks in Douglass C. North and Robert Paul Thomas, *The Rise of the Western World* (Cambridge: CUP, 1973), Gerald A. Gunderson, *A New Economic History of America* (New York: McGraw-Hill, 1976), and C. K. Harley, 'British Industrialization before 1841: Evidence of Slower Growth during the Industrial Revolution', *Journal of Economic History*, 42 (1982), 267–89, among others, all of them voices so far crying in the wilderness. Like the weather according to Mark Twain, everyone talks about the inappropriateness of the term, industrial revolution, but no one does anything about it.

The best places to start are T. S. Ashton, *The Industrial Revolution* (London: OUP, 1948), one of the few books on economic history that can be recommended to a lay person to read for pleasure; with the editor's introduction to Joel Mokyr (ed.), *The Economics of the Industrial Revolution* (Totowa, NJ: Rowman and Allanheld, 1985) to be read for profit (and a more analytical kind of pleasure); and with Stefano Fenoaltea's enthusiastic and illuminating review of Mokyr in the *Journal of Economic History* 46 (1986), 831–6. For a list of other recent references, see note 22 of this chapter.

2. *'Economic Growth as Virgin Birth'*

The notion that a propensity for growth was the 'normal condition' does not come directly from the literature. Background papers on analytical assumptions are two by Alexander Field, 'The Problem with Neoclassical Institutional Economics: A Critique with Special Reference to the North/Thomas Model of pre-1500 Europe', *Explorations in Economic History*, 18 (1981), 174–98, and 'Microeconomics, Norms, and Rationality', *Economic Development and Cultural Change*, 32 (1984), 683–711. Kaushik Basu, Eric Jones, and Ekkehart Schlicht, 'The Growth and Decay of Custom: The Role of the New Institutional Economics in Economic History', *Explorations in Economic History*, 24 (1987), 1–21 is a reply.

The case for the primacy of culture over economics, which is rejected here, is most succinctly stated by Clifford Geertz, 'Culture and Social Change: The Indonesian Case', *Man*, NS 19 (1984), 511–32, and Basu *et al.* contains some remarks that may be taken as a reply on that issue too.

3. *'Intimations of Ancient Growth'*

Valuable material about early technical change appears in John P. Oleson, *Greek and Roman Mechanical Water-lifting Devices* (Toronto: Toronto University Press, 1984), and Terry S. Reynolds, *Stronger than a Hundred Men: A History of the Vertical Water Wheel* (Baltimore, Md.: Johns Hopkins University Press, 1983); and valuable suggestions in J. E. Gordon, *The New Science of Strong Materials* (Princeton, NJ: Princeton University Press, 1976 edn.), and Cyril Stanley Smith, *A Search for Structure: Selected Essays on Science, Art, and History* (Cambridge, Mass.: MIT Press, 1981). This is not to endorse a technicist approach which finds invention the key to growth; we should rather be concerned with the conditions for innovation.

A copy of the manuscript of Joel Mokyr's forthcoming *Twenty Five Centuries of Technological Change* unfortunately reached me too late for me to use, but it contains some highly congruent material.

Useful correctives to the orthodox view that market forces played little part in the ancient world are M. W. Frederiksen, 'Theory, Evidence and the Ancient Economy', *Journal of Roman Studies*, 65 (1975), 164–71; Gerald A. Gunderson, 'Economic Behavior in the Ancient World', in Roger L. Ransom *et al.* (eds.), *Explorations in the New Economic History* (New York: Academic Press, 1982); and Douglass C. North, 'Markets and Other Allocation Systems in History: The Challenge of Karl Polanyi', *Journal of European Economic History*, 6 (1977), 703–16.

4. *'The Case of Sung China'*

On the Sung in particular, start with W. H. McNeill, *The Pursuit of Power* (Chicago: University of Chicago Press, 1982), chapter 12, 'The Era of Chinese Predominance, 1000–1500', and the other references cited in note 5 of Chapter 4 of the present book.

On China in general, especially on how to approach the question of what may have happened to the economy after the Sung (under the Ming and Ch'ing or Manchu), see Albert Feuerwerker, 'The State and the Economy in Late Imperial China', *Theory and Society*, 13 (1984), 297–326; Robert Marks, 'The State of the China Field. Or, the China Field and the State', *Modern China*, 11 (1985), 461–509; and William T. Rowe, 'Approaches to Modern Chinese Social History', in Oliver Zunz (ed.), *Reliving the Past: The Worlds of Social History* (Chapel Hill: University of North Carolina Press, 1985).

5. *'The Mills of God'*

The status of social 'obstacles' to growth is discussed and partly evaporated by Albert O. Hirschman, *A Bias for Hope: Essays on Development and Latin America* (Boulder and London: Westview Encore Edition, 1985), as 'Obstacles to Development: A Classification and a Quasi-Vanishing Act'.

The acceptability of negative explanations (like the effect of 'obstacles') is challenged by A. C. Graham, 'China, Europe, and the Origins of Modern Science', in Shigeru Nakayama and Nathan Sivin (eds.), *Chinese Science: Exploration of an Ancient Tradition* (Cambridge, Mass.: MIT Press, 1973), 45–69.

On commonly mentioned 'obstacles', M. N. Srinivas, *Caste in Modern India* (Bombay: Asia Publishing House, 1962), and *The Remembered Village* (Delhi: OUP, 1976), are recommended with respect to the caste system. Srinivas wrote *The Remembered Village* after his notes had been burned in a deliberate fire at Stanford, and his book is so clear and compelling as to suggest that one ought to throw one's notes away! On guilds, a starting-point might be Gabriel Baer,

'Guilds in Middle Eastern History', in M. A. Cook (ed.), *Studies in the Economic History of the Middle East* (London: OUP, 1970).

On the case against explaining history in terms of different value-systems, see Mark Elvin, 'Why China Failed to Create an Endogenous Industrial Capitalism: A Critique of Max Weber's Explanation', *Theory and Society*, 13 (1984), 379–92. On the role of religion in general, see Thomas F. Glick, *Islamic and Christian Spain in the Early Middle Ages* (Princeton, NJ: Princeton University Press, 1979); Maxime Rodinson, *Islam and Capitalism* (Austin, Tex.: University of Texas Press, 1978); and Timur Kuran, 'The Economic System in Contemporary Islamic Thought: Interpretation and Assessment', *International Journal of Middle East Studies*, 18 (1986), 135–64. On Confucian values, see G. L. Hicks and S. G. Redding, 'The Story of the East Asian "Economic Miracle"', Pt. I, 'Economic Theory be Damned!', and Pt. II, 'The Culture Connection', *Euro-Asia Business Review*, 2 (1983), no. 3, 24–32, and no. 4, 18–22.

6. *'Conquests'*

On the Mongols, see Charles J. Halperin, *Russia and the Golden Horde: The Mongol Impact* (Bloomington: Indiana University Press, 1985); Luc Kwanten, *Imperial Nomads: A History of Central Asia, 500–1500* (n.p.: University of Pennsylvania Press, 1979); and I. P. Petruschevsky, 'The Socio-economic Condition of Iran under the Il-khans', in J. A. Boyle (ed.), *The Cambridge History of Iran: Saljuq and Mongol Periods* (Cambridge: CUP, 1968), v. 483–582.

On the great empires in general, see Perry Anderson, *Lineages of the Absolutist State* (London: New Left Books, 1974) and John H. Kautsky, *The Politics of Aristocratic Empires* (Chapel Hill: University of North Carolina, 1982), the two outstanding Marxist students writing in English on the pre-modern world.

7. *'Derivative Effects'*

The discussion again begins with Hirschman (see under Chapter 5).

8. *'The Lethargic State'*

On rent-seeking in general see James M. Buchanan, Robert D. Tollison, and Gordon Tullock (eds.), *Toward a Theory of the Rent-seeking Society* (College Station, Tex.: Texas A. and M. University Press, 1980) and Mancur Olson, *The Rise and Decline of Nations* (New Haven: Yale University Press, 1982). On the economic history of the Ottoman, Mughal, and Manchu empires, see E. L. Jones, *The European Miracle* (Cambridge: CUP, 1981; 2nd edn. 1987).

On the lethargy of these empires with respect to fostering growth, seminal hints are in K. N. Chaudhuri, *Trade Civilisation in the Indian Ocean: An Economic History from the Rise of Islam to 1750* (Cambridge: CUP, 1985), 209–10, and Albert Feuerwerker, reference under Chapter 4, above.

9. *'Japan'*

Modern research is summarized and debated in Susan B. Hanley, 'A High Standard of Living in Nineteenth-century Japan: Fact or Fantasy?' *Journal of Economic History*, 43 (1983), 183–92, Yasukichi Yasuba, 'Standard of Living in Japan before Industrialization: From What Level Did Japan Begin? A Comment', *Journal of Economic History*, 46 (1986), 217–24, and Hanley, 'Reply to Yasuba', *Journal of Economic History*, 46 (1986), 225–6; in Conrad Totman, *Japan before Perry: A Short History* (Berkeley: University of California Press, 1981); and in several papers by Kozo Yamamura, notably 'Toward a Reexamination of the Economic History of Tokugawa Japan, 1600–1867', *Journal of Economic History*, 33 (1973), 509–46, and 'The Agricultural and Commercial Revolution in Japan, 1550–1650', *Research in Economic History*, 5 (1980), 85–107.

10. *'Europe'*

A gradualist approach is laid out in Jones, *The European Miracle* (see under Chapter 8, above) and the references are updated in the Select Bibliographical Guide to the second edition (1987). The economic histories of Russia and the United States may be seen, in their different ways and at different periods, as outgrowths of the European experience—the United States in particular as a giant ballooning of growth paralleling that of Western Europe, under conditions of institutionally weaker constraints and much greater physical resources. The divergent performance of these two offshoot countries is explored in Colin M. White, *Russia and America: The Roots of Economic Divergence* (London: Croom Helm, 1987).

11. *'Summary and Conclusion'*

Because this chapter is a summary, appropriate readings would repeat those of the earlier chapters. In all one's reading I would encourage considering just how far the record of economic history fits a gradualist scheme, as opposed to the standard view of a 'great discontinuity'.

Bibliography

Adams, R. M., 'Anthropological Perspectives on Ancient Trade', *Current Anthropology*, 15 (1974), 239-58.

Adshead, S. A. M., 'The Seventeenth Century General Crisis in China', *Asian Profile*, 1 (1973), 271-80.

Ali, M. Athar, 'The Passing of Empire: The Mughal Case', *Modern Asian Studies*, 9 (1975), 385-96.

Anderson, Perry, *Lineages of the Absolutist State* (London: New Left Books, 1974).

Ankli, Robert E., Review of D. C. M. Platt and Guido di Tella, *Argentina, Australia and Canada*, in *Journal of Economic Literature*, 24 (1986), 693-4.

Anon., 'When Croesus Rules', *The Economist*, 7-13 Mar. 1987, 19-20.

Ashton, T. S., *The Industrial Revolution* (London: OUP, 1948).

Ayres, Clarence, *The Theory of Economic Progress* (New York: Schocken Books, 1962; first published 1944).

Baer, Gabriel, *Egyptian Guilds in Modern Times* (Jerusalem: The Israel Oriental Society, 1964).

—— 'Guilds in Middle Eastern History', in M. A. Cook (ed.), *Studies in the Economic History of the Middle East* (OUP, 1970), 11-30.

—— 'Ottoman Guilds: A Reassessment', in Osman Okyar and Halil Inalcik (eds.), *Social and Economic History of Turkey (1071-1920)* (Ankara: Meteksan, 1980), 95-102.

Barkhausen, Max, 'Government Control and Free Enterprise in Western Germany and the Low Countries in the Eighteenth Century', in Peter Earle (ed.), *Essays in European Economic History 1500-1800* (Oxford: Clarendon Press, 1974), 212-73.

Barnett, Richard B., *North India Between Two Empires* (Berkeley: University of California Press, 1980).

Basu, Kaushik, Jones, Eric, and Schlicht, Ekkekart, 'The Growth and Decay of Custom: The Role of the New Institutional Economics in Economic History', *Explorations in Economic History*, 24 (1987), 1-21.

Bausani, Alessandro, *The Persians from the Earliest Days to the Twentieth Century* (London: Elek Books, 1971; first published 1962).

Bayly, C. A., 'State and Economy in India over Seven Hundred Years', *Economic History Review*, 2nd ser. 38 (1985), 583-96.

Bellah, R. N., *Tokugawa Religion: The Values of Pre-Industrial Japan* (Boston: Beacon Press, 1970).

Ben-David, Joseph, 'Innovations and their Recognition in Social Science', *History of Political Economy*, 7 (1975), 434–55.

Benoit, Paul, 'Technology and Crisis: The Great Depression of the Middle Ages and the Technology of the Renaissance (Fourteenth to Sixteenth Centuries)', *History and Technology*, 1 (1984), 319–34.

Bernstein, Richard, *From the Center of the Earth: The Search for the Truth about China* (Boston: Little, Brown, 1982).

Black, Cyril, *The Dynamics of Modernization: A Study in Comparative History* (New York: Harper and Row, 1966).

Bloch, Marc, *Feudal Society* (London: Routledge and Kegan Paul, 1965).

Bloodworth, Dennis, *Chinese Looking Glass* (Harmondsworth, Middx.: Penguin Books, 1969).

Blum, Jerome, Cameron, Rondo, and Barnes, Thomas, *The European World: A History*, 2nd edn. (Boston: Little, Brown, 1970).

Bolitho, Harold, *Treasures Among Men* (New Haven: Yale University Press, 1974).

Boserup, Ester, *The Conditions of Agricultural Growth* (London: Allen and Unwin, 1965).

—— *Population and Technology* (Oxford: Basil Blackwell, 1981).

Boswell, James, *Life of Johnson*, ed. R. W. Chapman (OUP, 1980).

Boulding, Kenneth E., 'The Great Laws of Change', in Anthony M. Tang *et al.* (eds.), *Evolution, Welfare, and Time in Economics* (Lexington, Mass.: Lexington Books, 1976), 3–14.

Bozeman, Adda B., *The Future of Law in a Multicultural World* (Princeton, NJ: Princeton University Press, 1971).

Bradstock, Timothy R., 'Ch'ing Dynasty Craft Guilds and their Monopolies', *Tsing Hua Journal of Chinese Studies*, NS 15 (1983), 1430–53.

Bray, Francesca, 'Agriculture', in Joseph Needham, *Science and Civilization in China*, 6: *Biology and Biological Technology*, Pt. II (CUP, 1984).

Breman, Jan, *Patronage and Exploitation* (Berkeley: University of California Press, 1974).

Brown, Elizabeth A. R., 'The Tyranny of a Construct: Feudalism and Historians of Medieval Europe', *American Historical Review*, 79 (1974), 1063–88.

Brown, Shannon R., 'The Partially Opened Door: Limitations on Economic Change in China in the 1860's', *Modern Asian Studies*, 12 (1978), 177–92.

Buchanan, James M., Tollison, Robert D., and Tullock, Gordon (eds.), *Toward a Theory of the Rent-seeking Society* (College Station, Tex.: Texas A. and M. University Press, 1980).

Burke, Peter, 'Some Reflections on the Pre-industrial City', *Urban History Yearbook* (1975), 13–21.

Caldwell, J. C., 'The Economic Rationality of High Fertility: An Investigation Illustrated with Nigerian Survey Data', *Population Studies*, 31 (1977), 5–27.

Cameron, Rondo, 'A New View of European Industrialization', *Economic History Review*, 2nd ser. 38 (1985), 1–23.

Chapman, F. H., *Architectura Navalis Mercatoria* and *Tractat om Skepps-Byggeriet* (London: Adlard Coles, 1968).

Chaudhuri, K. N., 'Some Reflections on the Town and Country in Mughal India', *Modern Asian Studies*, 12 (1978), 77–96.

—— *Trade Civilisation in the Indian Ocean: An Economic History from the Rise of Islam to 1750* (Cambridge: CUP, 1985).

Clower, Robert W., 'Snarks, Quarks and Other Fictions', in Louis P. Cain and Paul J. Uselding (eds.), *Business Enterprise and Economic Change* (Kent State University Press, 1973), 3–14.

Cohn, B., 'From Indian Status to British Contract', *Journal of Economic History*, 21 (1961), 613–28.

Cole, W. A., and Deane, Phyllis, *British Economic Growth* (Cambridge: CUP, 1962).

Crafts, N. F. R., 'Industrial Revolution in England and France: Some Thoughts on the Question, "Why Was England First?"', *Economic History Review*, 2nd ser. 30 (1977), 429–41.

—— 'British Economic Growth, 1700–1831: A Review of the Evidence', *Economic History Review*, 2nd ser. 36 (1983), 177–99.

Crawcour, E. S., 'Changes in Japanese Commerce in the Tokugawa Period', *Journal of Asian Studies*, 22, (1963), 387–400.

Crosby, A. W., *Ecological Imperialism* (Cambridge: CUP, 1986).

Crotty, R., Review of E. L. Jones, *The European Miracle*, in the *Irish Journal of Agricultural Economics*, 9 (1983), 193–5.

Curtin, Philip D., *Cross-cultural Trade in World History* (Cambridge: CUP, 1984).

Dasgupta, A., 'India's Cultural Values and Economic Development', *Economic Development and Cultural Change*, 13 (1964), 100–2.

Datta, Rajat, Review of V. I. Pavlov, *Historical Premises for India's Transition to Capitalism* (Moscow, 1979), in *Journal of Contemporary Asia*, 12 (1982), 232–6.

David, René, and Brierley, John E. C., *Major Legal Systems in the World Today* (London: Stevens and Sons, 1968).

Dean, Vera Micheles, *The Nature of the Non-Western World* (New York: New American Library, 1957).

Deane, Phyllis, *The First Industrial Revolution*, 2nd edn. (Cambridge: CUP, 1979).

Denison, Edward F., 'Comment', on Douglass North, 'Economic Growth: What Have We Learned from the Past?', in *International Organization, National Policies and Economic Development*, 6 (n.d.), 229–36.

De Solla Price, Derek V., 'An Ancient Greek Computer', *Scientific American*, 200 (June 1959), 60–7.

De Vries, Jan, 'Peasant Demand Patterns and Economic Development: Friesland, 1550–1750', in William N. Parker and Eric L. Jones (eds.), *European Peasants and Their Markets* (Princeton: Princeton University Press, 1975), 205–66.

—— *European Urbanization 1500–1800* (Cambridge, Mass.: Harvard University Press, 1984).

Diderot, Denis, *Encyclopédie, ou, Dictionnaire raisonné des sciences, des arts et des métiers par une société de gens de lettres/mis en ordre & publié par M. Diderot . . .*, 17 vols. (Paris: Chez Briasson, David, Le Breton, Duran, 1751–65).

—— (trans. Jacques Barzun and Ralph H. Bowen), *Rameau's Nephew and Other Works* (Indianapolis: Bobbs-Merrill, 1956).

Dillon, P. J., and Jones, E. L., 'Trevor Falla's Vermin Transcripts for Devon', *The Devon Historian*, 33 (1986), 15–19.

Dovring, Folke, 'Peasants, Land Use and Change', *Comparative Studies in Society and History*, 4 (1961–2), 364–74.

Drucker, Peter F., 'Dramatic Shifts in the Global Economy', *Dialogue*, 75 (1987), 2–7.

Dumont, Louis (trans. Mark Sainsbury), *Homo Hierarchicus: The Caste System and its Implications* (Chicago: University of Chicago Press, 1970).

Easterlin, R. A., 'Why Isn't the Whole World Developed?', *Journal of Economic History*, 41 (1981), 1–17.

Eichengreen, Barry J., 'The Economic History of Britain since 1700', *Journal of European Economic History*, 12 (1983), 437–43.

Elvin, Mark, 'Why China Failed to Create an Endogenous Industrial Capitalism: A Critique of Max Weber's Explanation', *Theory and Society*, 13 (1984), 379–92.

Evans, F. T., 'Wood since the Industrial Revolution: A Strategic Retreat?', *History of Technology*, vii (1982), 37–56.

Falkus, Malcolm, 'Modern British Economic Development: The Industrial Revolution in Perspective', *Australian Economic History Review*, 19 (1979), 42–62.

Farmer, Edward L., *et al.* (eds.), *Comparative History of Civilizations in Asia* (Reading, Mass.: Addison-Wesley, 1977).

Faroqhi, Suraiya, 'Recent Work in the Social and Economic History of the Ottoman Empire (1450–1800)', *Trends in History*, 2 (1982), 15–33.

Fenoaltea, Stefano, Review of Joel Mokyr (ed.), *The Economics of the Industrial Revolution*, in the *Journal of Economic History*, 46 (1986), 831–6.

Feuerwerker, Albert, 'The State and the Economy in Late Imperial China', *Theory and Society*, 13 (1984), 297–326.

—— 'Qing Economic History and World Economic History', Paper to the Symposium on the 60th Anniversary of the Founding of the First Historical Archives of China (Beijing, Oct. 1985).

Fewsmith, Joseph, 'From Guild to Interest Group: The Transformation of Public and Private in Late Qing China', *Comparative Studies in Society and History*, 25 (1983), 617–40.

Field, Alexander, 'The Problem with Neoclassical Institutional Economics: A Critique with Special Reference to the North/ Thomas Model of pre-1500 Europe', *Explorations in Economic History*, 18 (1981), 174–98.

Figueira, Thomas J., *Aegina: Society and Politics* (New York: Arno Press, 1981).

Finley, M. W., *The Ancient Economy* (Berkeley: University of California Press, 1973).

Firth, Raymond, *Essays on Social Organization and Values* (London: The Athlone Press, 1964).

Floud, Roderick, and McCloskey, Donald (eds.), *The Economic History of Britain since 1700*, 2 vols. (Cambridge: CUP, 1981).

Fox, Richard G., *Kin Clan Raja and Rule: State–Hinterland Relations in Preindustrial India* (Berkeley University of California Press, 1971).

Frederiksen, M. W., 'Theory, Evidence and the Ancient Economy', *Journal of Roman Studies*, 65 (1975), 164–71.

Geertz, Clifford, 'Culture and Social Change: The Indonesian Case', *Man*, NS (1984), 511–32.

Geiss, James, 'Peking Under the Ming (1368–1644)' (Ph.D. dissertation, Princeton University, 1979).

—— 'The Chia-ching reign, 1522–1566', in *The Cambridge History of China*, vii: *The Ming Dynasty, 1368–1644* (Cambridge: CUP, forthcoming), Ch. 8.

Gerschenkron, Alexander, *Economic Backwardness in Historical Perspective* (Cambridge, Mass.: The Belknap Press, 1962).

Gin'ya, Sasaki, 'Sengoku Daimyo Rule and Commerce', in J. W. Hall *et al.*, *Japan Before Tokugawa* (Princeton, NJ: Princeton University Press, 1981), 125–48.

Glick, Thomas F., *Islamic and Christian Spain in the Early Middle Ages* (Princeton, NJ: Princeton University Press, 1979).

Godelier, Maurice, *Rationality and Irrationality in Economics* (New York: Monthly Review Press, 1972).

Golas, Peter J., 'Early Ch'ing Guilds', in G. William Skinner (ed.), *The City in Late Imperial China* (Stanford, Cal.: Stanford University Press, 1977), 555–80.

—— 'Rural China in the Song', *Journal of Asian Studies*, 39 (1980), 291–325.

Gordon, J. E., *The New Science of Strong Materials* (Princeton, NJ: Princeton University Press, 1976 edn.).

Gottlieb, Manuel, *A Theory of Economic Systems* (Orlando, Fla: Academic Press, 1984).

Graham, A. C., 'China, Europe, and the Origins of Modern Science: Needham's The Grand Titration', in Shigeru Nakayama and Nathan Sivin (eds.), *Chinese Science: Exploration of an Ancient Tradition* (Cambridge, Mass.: MIT Press, 1973), 45–69.

Greenberg, Dolores, 'Reassessing the Power Patterns of the Industrial Revolution: An Anglo–American Comparison', *American Historical Review*, 87 (1982), 1237–61.

Greene, Graham, and Reed, Carol, *The Third Man: A Film* (London: Lorrimer Publishing Ltd., 1969 edn.).

Gunderson, Gerald A., *A New Economic History of America* (New York: McGraw-Hill, 1976).

—— 'Economic Behavior in the Ancient World', in Roger L. Ransom *et al.* (eds.), *Explorations in the New Economic History* (New York: Academic Press, 1982), 235–56.

Gurr, T. R., 'Historical Trends in Violent Crime: A Critical Review of Evidence', *Crime and Justice*, 3 (1981), 295–355.

Habib, Irfan, 'Potentialities of Capitalistic Development in the Economy of Mughal India', *Journal of Economic History*, 29 (1969), 32–78.

Haeger, J. W., *Crisis and Prosperity in Sung China* (Tucson: University of Arizona Press, 1975).

Halperin, Charles J., *Russia and the Golden Horde: The Mongol Impact* (Bloomington: Indiana University Press, 1985).

Hanley, Susan B., 'A High Standard of Living in Nineteenth-century Japan: Fact or Fantasy?', *Journal of Economic History*, 43 (1983), 183–92.

—— 'Standard of Living in Nineteenth-century Japan: Reply to Yasuba', *Journal of Economic History*, 46 (1986), 225–6.

Harley, C. K., *British Industrialization before 1841: Evidence of Slower Growth during the Industrial Revolution* (Research Report 8120, Dept. of Economics, University of Western Ontario, 1981).

Harley, C. K., 'British Industrialization before 1841: Evidence of Slower Growth during the Industrial Revolution', *Journal of Economic History*, 42 (1982), 267–89.

Hartwell, Robert, 'A Revolution in the Chinese Iron and Coal Industries During the Northern Sung, 960–1126 A.D.', *Journal of Asian Studies*, 21 (1962), 153–62.

—— 'Markets, Technology, and the Structure of Enterprise in the Development of the Eleventh-century Chinese Iron and Steel Industries', *Journal of Economic History*, 26 (1966), 29–58.

Heijdra, Martin, 'China, Japan, and Braudelian Europe, 1400–1800', Graduate Essay, East Asian Studies (Princeton University, Jan. 1984).

Hicks, G. L. and Redding, S. G., 'The Story of the East Asian "Economic Miracle"', Pt. I, 'Economic Theory Be Damned!', *Euro-Asia Business Review*, 2 (1983), no. 3, 24–32.

—— and —— 'The Story of the East Asian "Economic Miracle"', Pt. II, 'The Culture Connection', *Euro-Asia Business Review*, 2 (1983), no. 4, 18–22.

Hirschman, Albert O., *A Bias for Hope: Essays on Development and Latin America* (Boulder and London: Westview Encore Edition, 1985).

Hodgson, Marshall G. S., *The Venture of Islam* (Chicago: University of Chicago Press, 1974).

Hoffman, Marta, 'The "Great Wheel" in the Scandinavian Countries', in Geraint Jenkins (ed.), *Studies in Folk Life* (London: Routledge and Kegan Paul, 1969), 281–92.

Huang, R., *Taxation and Governmental Finance in Sixteenth Century Ming China* (Cambridge: CUP, 1974).

Hutton, J. H., *Caste in India: Its Nature, Function, and Origins*, 4th edn. (Bombay: OUP, 1963).

Jones, E. L., 'Industrial Capital and Landed Investment: The Arkwrights in Herefordshire, 1809–43', in E. L. Jones and G. E. Mingay (eds.), *Land, Labour and Population in the Industrial Revolution* (London: Edward Arnold, 1967), 48–71.

—— 'Institutional Determinism and the Rise of the Western World', *Economic Inquiry*, 12 (1974), 114–24.

—— 'Afterword', in W. N. Parker and E. L. Jones (eds.), *European Peasants and Their Markets* (Princeton, NJ: Princeton University Press, 1975), 327–60.

—— *The European Miracle* (Cambridge: CUP, 1981; 2nd edn. 1987).

—— 'No Stationary State: The World before Industrialisation' (Workshop in Economic History, Dept. of Economics, University of Chicago, 8283-9, 1982).

—— 'Very Long-term Economic Development as the History Survey', in Josef W. Konvitz (ed.), *What Americans Should Know: Western Civilization or World History?* (East Lansing, Mich.: Michigan State University, 1985), 230–47.

—— Porter, S., and Turner, M., *A Gazetteer of English Urban Fire Disasters, 1500–1900* (Norwich: Geo Books, 1984). *

Kautsky, John H., *The Politics of Aristocratic Empires* (Chapel Hill: University of North Carolina Press, 1982).

Kenwood, A. G., and Lougheed, A. L., *Technological Diffusion and Industrialization before 1914* (London: Croom Helm, 1982).

Keyder, C., 'Protoindustrialisation and the Periphery: A Conceptual Inquiry' (VIIIe Congrès International d'Histoire Economique, Budapest, 1982).

Keynes, J. M., *Essays in Persuasion* (London: Rupert Hart-Davis, 1951, first published 1931).

Khazanov, A. M., *Nomads and the Outside World* (Cambridge: CUP, 1984).

Kornicki, P. F., 'The Enmeiin Affair of 1803: The Spread of Information in the Tokugawa Period', *Harvard Journal of Asiatic Studies*, 42 (1982), 503–33.

Kosambi, D. D., *The Culture and Civilization of Ancient India* (London: Routledge and Kegan Paul, 1965).

Kuran, Timur, 'Behavioral Norms in the Islamic Doctrine of Economics: A Critique', *Journal of Economic Behavior and Organization*, 4 (1983), 353–79.

—— 'The Economic System in Contemporary Islamic Thought: Interpretation and Assessment', *International Journal of Middle East Studies*, 18 (1986), 135–64.

—— 'Continuity and Change in Islamic Economic Thought', in S. Todd Lowry (ed.), *Pre-Classical Political Economy* (Boston: Kluwer-Nijhoff, forthcoming).

Kussmaul, Ann, 'Agrarian Change in Seventeenth-century England: The Economic Historian as Paleontologist', *Journal of Economic History*, 45 (1985), 1–30.

Kwanten, Luc, *Imperial Nomads: A History of Central Asia, 500–1500* (n.p.: University of Pennsylvania Press, 1979).

Lacoste, Yves, *Ibn Khaldun: The Birth of History and the Past of the Third World* (London: Verso Edition, 1984).

Lal, Deepak, *The Poverty of 'Development Economics'* (London: Institute of Economic Affairs, 1983).

Landes, David S., *Revolution in Time: Clocks and the Making of the Modern World* (Cambridge, Mass.: The Belknap Press of Harvard University Press, 1983).

Landes, David S., 'What Do Bosses Really Do?', *Journal of Economic History*, 46 (1986), 585–623.

Laslett, Peter, 'Demographic and Microstructural History in Relation to Human Adaptation: Reflections on Newly Established Evidence', in D. J. Ortner (ed.), *How Humans Adapt* (Washington, DC: Smithsonian Institution Press, 1983), 343–70.

Lemon, Hugo, 'The Development of Hand Spinning Wheels', *Textile History*, 1 (1968), 83–91.

Lewis, W. Arthur, *The Theory of Economic Growth* (London: George Allen and Unwin, 1955).

—— (ed.), *Tropical Development 1880–1913: Studies in Economic Progress* (London: George Allen and Unwin, 1970).

Lieberman, Victor B., *Burmese Administrative Cycles: Anarchy and Conquest c.1580–1760* (Princeton, NJ: Princeton University Press, 1984).

Liu, James T. C., and Golas, Peter J. (eds.), *Change in Sung China: Innovation or Renovation?* (Lexington, Mass.: D. C. Heath and Co., 1969).

Ma, Laurence J. C., *Commercial Development and Urban Change in Sung China* (University of Michigan Geographical Publication no. 6, 1971).

McCloskey, D. N., 'The Industrial Revolution 1780–1860: A Survey', in Floud and McCloskey (eds.), *The Economic History of Britain since 1700*, 2 vols. (Cambridge: CUP, 1981), i. 103–27.

McCord, William, and Arline, 'Singapore's Success Story', *The New Leader*, 12–26 Aug. 1985, 8–12.

McEvedy, Colin, and Jones, Richard, *Atlas of World Population History* (Harmondsworth, Middx: Penguin Books, 1978).

MacGowan, D. J., 'Chinese Guilds, or Chambers of Commerce and Trade Unions', *Journal of North-China Branch of the Royal Asiatic Society*, 21 (1886), 133–92.

McNeill, W. H., 'Comment' on R. M. Adams, 'Anthropological Perspectives on Ancient Trade', in *Current Anthropology*, 15 (1974), 252.

—— *The Human Condition* (Princeton, NJ: Princeton University Press, 1980).

—— *The Pursuit of Power* (Chicago: University of Chicago Press, 1982).

—— 'Organizing Concepts for World History', *Review*, 10 (1986), 211–29.

McPhee, John, *Basin and Range* (New York: Farrar, Straus, Giroux, 1980).

McPherson, M., 'Want Formation, Morality and the Interpretive Dimension of Economic Inquiry', in N. Haan *et al.*, *Social Science as Moral Inquiry* (Berkeley: University of California Press, 1983), 96–124.

Maddison, Angus, *Class Structure and Economic Growth: India and Pakistan since the Moghals* (New York: Norton, 1971).

—— *Phases of Capitalist Development* (OUP, 1982).

Mann, Michael, 'States, Ancient and Modern', *European Journal of Sociology*, 18 (1977), 262–98.

Marks, Robert, 'The State of the China Field. Or, the China Field and the State', *Modern China*, 11 (1985), 461–509.

Masters, John, *The Rock* (London: Transworld Publishers, 1971).

Mazzaoui, M. F., *The Italian Cotton Industry in the later Middle Ages 1100–1600* (Cambridge: CUP, 1981).

Medawar, Peter, *Advice to a Young Scientist* (London: Pan Books, 1981).

Miyamoto, Mataji, *et al.*, 'Economic Development in Preindustrial Japan, 1859–1894', *Journal of Economic History*, 25 (1965), 541–64.

Moghadam, F. E., 'Tribal Invasions and the Development of Private Property in Land: A Case Study of Iran (1000–1800)' (paper presented at the International Conference on Middle Eastern Studies, University of London, July 1986).

Mokyr, Joel, 'Growing-up and the Industrial Revolution in Europe', *Explorations in Economic History*, 13 (1976), 371–96.

—— 'Disparities, Gaps, and Abysses', *Economic Development and Cultural Change*, 33 (1984), 173–7.

—— (ed.), *The Economics of the Industrial Revolution* (Totowa, NJ: Rowman and Allanheld, 1985).

Moore, John, *Portrait of Elmbury* (London: Collins, 1946).

Moorhouse, Geoffrey, *Calcutta: The City Revealed* (Harmondsworth, Middx: Penguin Books, 1983 edn.).

Moosvi, Shireen, 'Share of the Nobility in the Revenues of Akbar's Empire 1595–96', *Indian Economic and Social History Review*, 17 (1980), 329–41.

Morse, Hosea B., *The Guilds of China* (London: Longmans, Green, and Co., 1909).

Mottram, R. H., *If Stones Could Speak* (London: Museum Press, 1953).

Munz, Peter, 'The Purity of Historical Method: Some Sceptical Reflections on the Current Enthusiasm for the History of Non-European Societies', *New Zealand Journal of History*, 5 (1971), 1–17.

Murdoch, W. W., *The Poverty of Nations* (Baltimore: Johns Hopkins University Press, 1980).

Musallam, B. F., 'Birth Control and Middle Eastern History', in A. L. Udovitch (ed.), *The Islamic Middle East, 700–1900: Studies in*

Economic and Social History (Princeton, NJ: Darwin Press, 1981), 429–69.

Musson, A. E., 'Industrial Motive Power in the United Kingdom 1800–70', *Economic History Review*, 2nd ser. 29 (1976), 413–39.

Nakamura, J. I., 'Human Capital Accumulation in Premodern Japan', *Journal of Economic History*, 41 (1981), 263–81.

North, D. C., 'Markets and Other Allocation Systems in History: The Challenge of Karl Polanyi', *Journal of European Economic History*, 6 (1977), 703–16.

—— *Structure and Change in Economic History* (New York: W. W. Norton, 1981).

—— and Thomas, R. P., *The Rise of the Western World* (Cambridge: CUP, 1973).

O'Brien, Patrick, 'European Economic Development: The Contribution of the Periphery', *Economic History Review*, 2nd ser. 35 (1982), 1–18.

—— and Keyder, C., *Two Paths to the Twentieth Century: Economic Development in Britain and France from 1718–1914* (London: Allen and Unwin, 1977).

Ohkawa, K. and Rosovsky, H., 'The Role of Agriculture in Modern Japanese Development', in G. M. Meier (ed.), *Leading Issues in Development Economics* (New York: OUP, 1964), 304–15.

Oleson, John P., *Greek and Roman Mechanical Water-lifting Devices* (Toronto: Toronto University Press, 1984).

Olsen, Storrs L., and James, Helen F., 'Fossil Birds from the Hawaiian Islands: Evidence for Wholesale Extinction by Man before Western Contact', *Science*, 217, no. 4560 (13 Aug. 1982), 633–5.

Olson, Mancur, *The Rise and Decline of Nations* (New Haven: Yale University Press, 1982).

Passmore, John, *Man's Responsibility for Nature: Ecological Problems and Western Traditions*, 2nd edn. (London: Duckworth, 1980).

Pearson, Harry W., 'The Secular Debate on Economic Primitivism', in Karl Polanyi *et al.* (eds.), *Trade and Market in the Early Empires* (Chicago: Henry Regnery, 1971).

Pearson, Michael N., 'Shivaji and the Decline of the Mughal Empire', *Journal of Asian Studies*, 35 (1976), 221–35.

Perutz, M., 'A New View of Darwinism', *New Scientist*, 112, no. 1528 (2 Oct. 1986), 36–7.

Petrushevsky, I. P., 'The Socio-economic Condition of Iran under the Il-Khans', in J. A. Boyle (ed.), *The Cambridge History of Iran: Saljuq and Mongol Periods* (Cambridge: CUP, 1968), 483–582.

Pocock, D. F. (trans. and ed.), *Essays on the Caste System by Célestin Bouglé* (Cambridge: CUP, 1971).

Pollard, Sidney, Review of P. Mathias, *The First Industrial Nation*, 2nd edn. (1983), in *Business History*, 26 (1984), 89.

Post, John D., *The Last Great Subsistence Crisis in the Western World* (Baltimore, Md.: Johns Hopkins University Press, 1977).

—— *Food Shortage, Climatic Variability, and Epidemic Disease in Preindustrial Europe: The Mortality Peak in the Early 1740s* (Ithaca, NY: Cornell University Press, 1985).

Raban, Jonathan, *Arabia Through the Looking Glass* (London: Fontana, 1983).

Rackham, Oliver, *Ancient Woodland: Its History, Vegetation and Uses in England* (London: Edward Arnold, 1980).

Raychaudhuri, Tapan, and Habib, Irfan (eds.), *The Cambridge Economic History of India* i: c.*1200*–c.*1750* (Cambridge: CUP, 1982).

Raymond, Robert, *Out of the Fiery Furnace: The Impact of Metals on the History of Mankind* (South Melbourne: Macmillan, 1984).

Reynolds, Lloyd G., *Economic Growth in the Third World, 1850–1980* (New Haven: Yale University Press, 1985).

Reynolds, Terry S., *Stronger than a Hundred Men: A History of the Vertical Water Wheel* (Baltimore, Md.: Johns Hopkins University Press, 1983).

—— 'Medieval Roots of the Industrial Revolution', *Scientific American*, 251 (1984), 108–16.

Rhodes, Richard, *Looking for America: A Writer's Odyssey* (Harmondsworth, Middx: Penguin Books, 1980).

Riley, James C., *The Eighteenth-century Campaign to Avoid Disease* (London: Macmillan, 1987).

Robertson, H. M., *Aspects of the Rise of Economic Individualism: A Criticism of Max Weber and his School* (Clifton, NJ: Augustus M. Kelley Reprint, 1973).

Rodinson, Maxime, *Islam and Capitalism* (Austin, Tex.: University of Texas Press, 1978).

Roehl, Richard, 'French Industrialization: A Reconsideration', *Explorations in Economic History*, 13 (1976), 233–81.

—— 'British and European Industrialization: Pathfinder Pursued?', *Review* (Fernand Braudel Center), 6 (1983), 455–73.

Rosenberg, Nathan, and Birdzell, L. E., Jr., *How the West Grew Rich* (New York: Basic Books, 1986).

Rosovsky, H., 'Japan's Transition to Modern Economic Growth, 1868–1885', in H. Rosovsky (ed.), *Industrialization in Two Systems* (New York: Wiley, 1966), 91–139.

Rosser, Colin, 'Social Mobility in the Newar Caste System', in Christoph von Furer-Haimendorf (ed.), *Caste and Kin in Nepal, India and Ceylon: Anthropological Studies in Hindu–Buddhist Contact Zones* (New Delhi: Sterling, 1978), 68–139.

Rostow, W. W., *The Stages of Economic Growth* (Cambridge: CUP, 1960).

—— *How It All Began: Origins of the Modern Economy* (New York: McGraw-Hill, 1975).

Rothermund, Dietmar, *Asian Trade and European Expansion in the Age of Mercantilism* (New Delhi: Manohar, 1981).

Rowe, William T., *Hankow: Commerce and Society in a Chinese City, 1796–1889* (Stanford, Cal.: Stanford University Press, 1984).

Russell, W. M. S., 'Women as Innovators', *Biology and Human Affairs*, 40 (1974), 21–36.

Sandberg, Lars, 'The Case of the Impoverished Sophisticate: Human Capital and Swedish Economic Growth before World War I', *Journal of Economic History*, 39 (1979), 225–41.

Saran, P., *The Provincial Government of the Mughals 1526–1658* (London: Asia Publishing House, 1973; first published 1941).

Schaffer, Lynda, 'China, Technology, and Change', *World History Bulletin*, 4 (1986–7), 1, 4–6.

Schneider, Jean, 'Was there a Pre-Capitalist World System?', *Peasant Studies*, 6 (1977), 20–9.

Schon, Lennart, 'British Competition and Domestic Change in Textiles in Sweden 1820–1870', *Economy and History*, 23 (1980), 61–76.

Schurmann, Herbert F., *Economic Structure of Yuan Dynasty* (Cambridge, Mass.: Harvard University Press, 1967).

Severin, Tim, *The Sindbad Voyage* (London: Arena, 1983).

Shackle, G. L. S., 'Comment', *Journal of Post-Keynesian Economics*, 5 (1982–3), 180–1.

Sherby, Oleg D., and Wadsworth, Jeffrey, 'Damascus Steels', *Scientific American*, 252 (Feb. 1985), 94–9.

Shiba, Yoshinobu (trans. Mark Elvin), *Commerce and Society in Sung China* (University of Michigan Abstracts, no. 2, 1970).

—— 'Ningpo and its Hinterland', in G. William Skinner (ed.), *The City in Late Imperial China* (Stanford, Cal.: Stanford University Press, 1977), 391–439.

Simkin, C. G. F., *The Traditional Trade of Asia* (OUP: 1968).

Simon, Julian L., *The Economics of Population Growth* (Princeton, NJ: Princeton University Press, 1977).

—— 'The Present Value of Population Growth in the Western World', *Population Studies*, 37 (1983), 5–21.

—— and Steinmann, Gunter, 'The Economic Implications of Learning-by-Doing', *European Economic Review*, 26 (1984), 167–85.

Sinai, I. R., *The Challenge of Modernisation: The West's Impact on the Non-Western World* (London: Chatto and Windus, 1964).

Smith, C. S., *A Search for Structure: Selected Essays on Science, Art, and History* (Cambridge, Mass.: MIT Press, 1981).

Spear, Percival, *India: A Modern History*, 2nd edn. (Ann Arbor, Mich.: University of Michigan Press, 1972).

Srinivas, M. N., *Caste in Modern India* (Bombay: Asia Publishing House, 1962).

—— *The Remembered Village* (Delhi: OUP, 1976).

Stark, Oded, 'On the Asset Demand for Children during Agricultural Modernization', *Population and Development Review*, 7 (1981), 671–5.

Strayer, Joseph R., 'The Tokugawa Period and Japanese Feudalism', in John W. Hall and Marius B. Jansen (eds.), *Studies in the Institutional History of Early Modern Japan* (Princeton: Princeton University Press, 1968), 3–14.

Sutcliffe, Claud R., 'Is Islam an Obstacle to Development? Ideal Patterns of Belief versus Actual Patterns of Behavior', *Journal of Developing Areas*, 10 (1975), 77–82.

Tilly, Charles (ed.), *The Formation of National States in Western Europe* (Princeton: Princeton University Press, 1975).

Todd, Loreto, *Modern Englishes: Pidgins and Creoles* (Oxford and London: Basil Blackwell/André Deutsch, 1984).

Tomlinson, B. R., 'Writing History Sideways: Lessons for Indian Economic Historians from Meiji Japan', *Modern Asian Studies*, 19 (1985), 669–98.

Totman, Conrad, *Japan before Perry: A Short History* (Berkeley: University of California Press, 1981).

—— 'Tokugawa Peasants: Win, Lose or Draw?', *Monumenta Nipponica*, 41 (1986), 459–76.

Trevor-Roper, Hugh, *The Rise of Christian Europe*, 2nd edn. (London: Thames and Hudson, 1966).

Tsuchiya, Takao, 'An Economic History of Japan', *Transactions of the Asiatic Society of Japan*, 2nd ser. 15 (1937), 1–269.

Twitchett, D. C., *Financial Administration under the Tang Dynasty* (Cambridge: CUP, 1963).

Various, 'India's Cultural Values and Economic Development: A Discussion', *Economic Development and Cultural Change*, 7 (1958), 1–12.

Veliz, Claudio, *The Centralist Tradition of Latin America* (Princeton, NJ: Princeton University Press, 1980).

Venkatachar, C. S., in Raghavan Iyer (ed.), *The Glass Curtain between Asia and Europe* (London: OUP, 1965).

von Furer-Haimendorf, Christoph (ed.), *Caste and Kin in Nepal, India and Ceylon: Anthropological Studies in Hindu–Buddhist Contact Zones* (New Delhi: Sterling, 1978).

Wallerstein, Immanuel, *The Modern World-System* (New York: Academic Press, 1974).

Wallman, R., Letter in the *New Scientist*, 28 Feb. 1985, 45.

Watts, D. G., 'Water-power and the Industrial Revolution', *Transactions of the Cumberland and Westmorland Antiquarian and Archaeological Society*, NS 67 (1967), 199–205.

Weber, Max, *The Religion of China* (trans. and ed. H. H. Gerth), (New York: The Free Press, 1964 edn.).

Wells, H. G., *The Anatomy of Frustration* (New York: Macmillan, 1936).

White, Colin M., *Russia and America: The Roots of Economic Divergence* (London: Croom Helm, 1987).

White, Lynn, JR., 'Tibet, India and Malaya as Sources of Western Medieval Technology', *American Historical Review*, 61 (1960), 526.

Whitehead, D. H., 'The English Industrial Revolution as an Example of Growth', in R. M. Hartwell (ed.), *The Industrial Revolution* (Oxford: Basil Blackwell, 1970), 3–27.

Wickham, Chris, 'The Uniqueness of the East', *Journal of Peasant Studies*, 12 (1985), 166–96.

Williams, Emlyn, *George: An Early Autobiography* (Harmondsworth, Middx. Penguin Books, 1976).

Williamson, J. G., 'Regional Inequality and the Process of National Development: A Description of the Patterns', *Economic Development and Cultural Change*, 13 (1965), 1–84.

Wilson, C. H., 'The Historical Study of Economic Growth and Decline in Early Modern History', in E. E. Rich and C. H. Wilson (eds.), *The Cambridge Economic History of Europe*, v (Cambridge: CUP, 1977), 39–40.

Wittfogel, Karl, *Oriental Despotism: A Comparative Study of Total Power* (New Haven, Conn.: Yale University Press, 1957).

Wolf, Eric, *Europe and the People Without History* (Berkeley: University of California Press, 1982).

Yamagawa K., 'Fires in Tokio, in T. C. Mendenhall, *Report on the Meteorology of Tokio 1879–1880* (Tokio: Tokio University Press, 1880–1), 71–86.

Yamamura, Kozo, 'Toward a Reexamination of the Economic History of Tokugawa, Japan, 1600–1867', *Journal of Economic History*, 33 (1973), 509–46.

—— 'The Agricultural and Commercial Revolution in Japan, 1550–1650', *Research in Economic History*, 5 (1980), 85–107.

—— 'Returns on Unification: Economic Growth in Japan 1550–1650', in John W. Hall *et al.*, *Japan before Tokugawa: Political Consolidation and Economic Growth, 1500 to 1650* (Princeton: Princeton University Press, 1981), 327–72.

Yasuba, Yasukichi, 'Standard of Living in Japan before Industrialization: From What Level Did Japan Begin? A Comment', *Journal of Economic History*, 46 (1986), 217–24.

INDEX

Learning to Look at Modern Art

Learning to Look at Modern Art is an accessible guide to the visual understanding, history and analysis of modern art. It suggests that the best way to understand the art of the modern and postmodern period is to look closely at it and to consider the different elements that make up each art work – composition, space and form, light and colour, and subject-matter.

This engaging and beautifully written book covers key art movements including Expressionism, Constructivism, the Bauhaus, Surrealism, Pop Art, Conceptual Art and Young British Art. Mary Acton considers a range of modern art forms, such as architecture and design, sculpture and installation, and works on canvas. The book is richly illustrated with 112 black-and-white images and 27 colour images by the artists, designers and architects discussed, ranging from Picasso and Matisse to Le Corbusier, Andy Warhol and Rachel Whiteread.

Mary Acton is an Associate Tutor and a Course Director of the Undergraduate Diploma in the History of Art at Oxford University Department for Continuing Education. Her first book for Routledge, *Learning to Look at Paintings* (1997), is a bestseller.